Magic Scissors By the Seashore

Also by Linda S. Day

Grandma's Magic Scissors

There's a Frog on a Log in the Bog
with Robert O. Day

Frogazoom!
with MyLinda Butterworth

Coming Soon!
Grandma's Craft File
Magic Scissors Go West
Magic Scissors for the Holidays
The Last Handcart

Magic Scissors By the Seashore

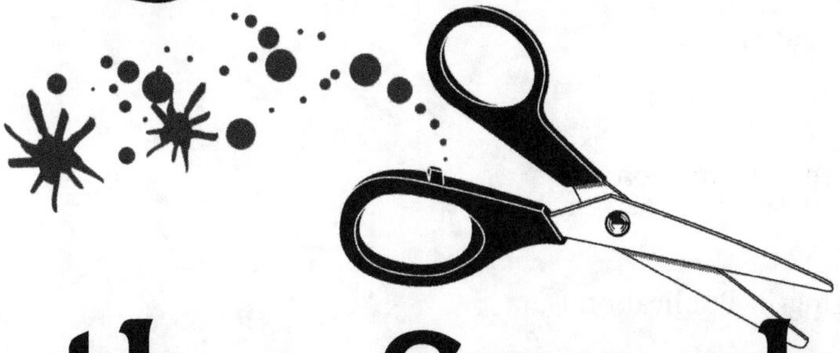

Linda S. Day

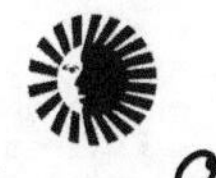

Day to Day Enterprises Oviedo, Florida

Magic Scissors by the Seashore

Cover and Book Design: MyLinda Butterworth
Editor: Cherilyn King

ISBN-13: 978-1-890905-69-9
ISBN-10: 1-890905-69-0

Printed in the United States of America
10 9 8 7 6 5 4 3 2 1

Library of Congress Cataloging-in-Publication Data

Day, Linda S., 1937-
Magic Scissors by the Seashore/Linda S. Day.
p.cm.
ISBN 1-890905-69-0 (softcover; alk.paper)
1, Paper work. I. Title.
TT870.D33 2008
736'.98-dc22

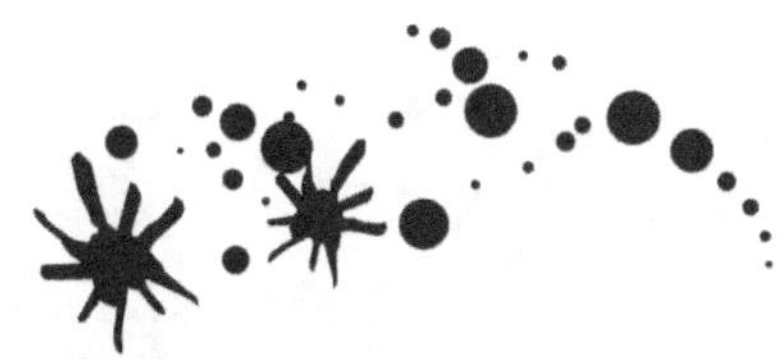

This book is dedicated to a master storyteller
and teacher, the love of my life,
my sweetheart, Robert O. Day
and to our daughter MyLinda Butterworth
whose encouragement, insight, prodding
and unique design talents have made this
book a reality.

Special thanks to Cherilyn King for her wit,
gift of grammar, editing and friendship.

Finally, to all the children whose eyes light
up and whose oohs and aahhs inspire me
every time I pull out my Magic Scissors.

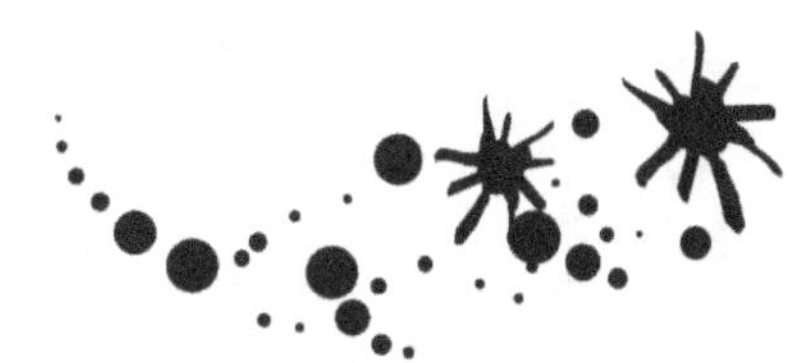

A Note from the Publisher

In the book business we want everything in a hurry and perfect. We often want to take what the artist has created and try to make it perfect, by making sure each line is straight, or each curve is smooth—this time we didn't do that. In putting together this book it has been our intention to show the beauty of each paper cut just the way Grandma cut it. So don't be surprised if you can actually see each snip of the scissors and notice that each additional image is just a little different than the one next to it—each one unique—just like Grandma. We hope you enjoy each creation you make with your own magic scissors as much as we did creating this book for you.

Table of Contents

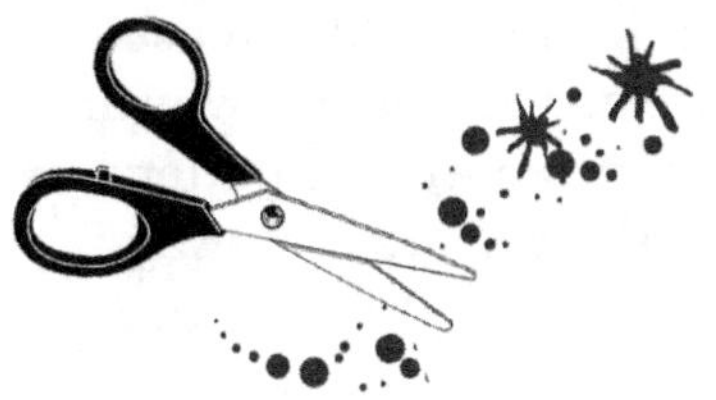

The Magic Begins

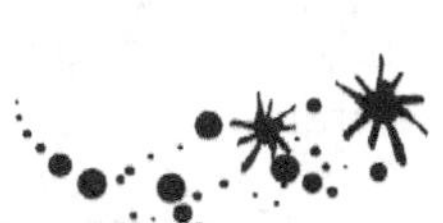

Once upon a time there was a Grandma with ***Magic Scissors*** who amazed the children as she told them stories and cut out paper figures. Hello, my friends! I am Grandma. Are you ready to use your imagination? Let's take an amazing journey together as we discover this ancient folk art of paper cutting. Paper was created in 105 A.D. in China. It has been written on, drawn on, cut into designs and decorations, printed and used in thousands of ways ever since.

You ask if Grandma's scissors are magic? Well, yes, in a way they are! Like any artist who takes a blank piece of paper and draws or paints a beautiful picture, we can use our creativity and imagination to use a blank piece of paper and our ***Magic Scissors*** to make characters and castles for hours of pleasure.

Adults and children (ages 10 and up) will delight in creating the patterns of the seashore and ocean for their projects, displays, reports, dioramas, and just for the sheer fun found in paper cutting. *Magic Scissors By the Seashore* is designed with eco-facts accompanying each pattern. The glossary has references to some books, with page numbers, an index, a books and stories reference, and a bibliography for easy research.

Your school and public library have a wealth of other great titles with intriguing stories of adventure, science, and ecology, with illustrations or actual photographs that may inspire you to read and investigate the subjects of this book even more. We hope that you will become an advocate for the protection and stewardship of our world's natural resources. Whether you are a teacher, parent or child, this book is for you to explore and enjoy the facts and figures as you find fun and pleasure in *Magic Scissors by the Seashore.*

With this fold-and-cut art, we can create:

- ✂ Seashell Chain
- ✂ Top Fold Cards
- ✂ Side Fold Cards
- ✂ Circle Wreaths
- ✂ Mobiles
- ✂ 3-Dimensional Art
- ✂ Stencils
- ✂ Scrapbooking Art
- ✂ Quilting Patterns
- ✂ The possibilities go on!

Imagination is the first key

All eyes are looking at your hands as you take an ordinary piece of paper, fold it, and begin to create images with your ***Magic Scissors*** with no limits on imagination and creativity.

You will understand better the techniques of paper cutting as you fold and cut the patterns that are contained in this book. The same patterns may be used many times by making copies or by tracing onto old laminate scraps, clear acetate, or old transparencies.

Folding the paper is the second key of this art

Follow the directions carefully. Select the pattern you want to use. You may want to reduce or enlarge the pattern at first. Selecting your practice paper should remind you that paper is a gift of nature from the trees. Use recycled paper when you can and begin your practicing with scraps, used copy paper, and newspaper. You should work on a hard flat surface as you begin to fold. Crease the fold carefully with your thumbnail, starting at the top and applying pressure as you come downward. A ruler may also be used to achieve the desired pressure on the fold. Then secure the pattern in place on the folded paper. Remember to let the paper do the turning as your scissors cut away the pattern.

The third key to the art of paper cutting is creativity!

You have the ***Magic Scissors*** in your hands now. So use your imagination and creativity with the fold-and-cut directions and patterns in this book. Your ***Magic Scissors*** will soon snip away new patterns of your own design. The patterns in this book can be useful in oral language arts, reading, storytelling, science, math, as patterns for puppets, 3-dimensional pictures, stencils, and storyboard characters. The size of your design, the folds, shape, color and weight of the paper, along with embellishments such as glitter, glitter glue, sequins and paper punches, all make your design an original work. You are the artist! Create your own designs with all the varieties of paper at your fingertips—the sky is the limit.

Add stories to your Magic!

A story lies behind every pattern, just waiting to be told and unfolded. The art of the storyteller is another book all in itself, but as I finish my stories I always end with my ***Magic Scissors***. Enjoy the oohs and aahs of your audience! The magic of fold-and-cut art is now in your hands with ideas from ***Magic Scissors by the Seashore.*** I love what I'm doing, and I'm doing what I love. There is ***magic*** in my ***scissors***. Your scissors can be magic, too!

Chapter 1

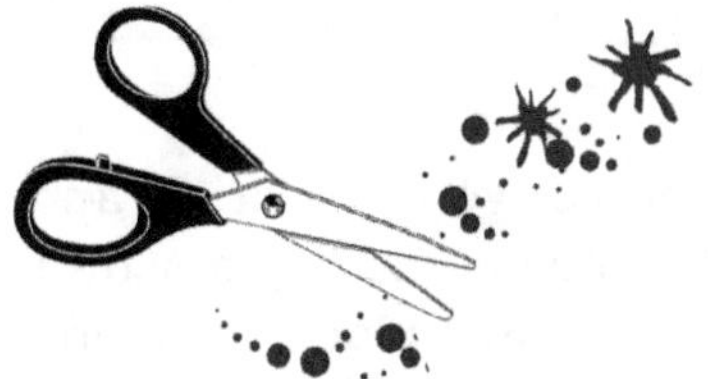

Where to Start

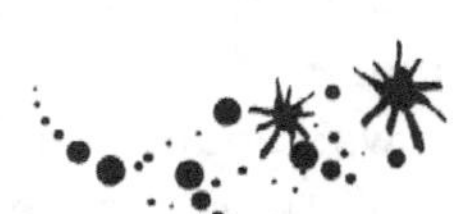

Paper Selection

The various paper colors and styles you choose will add to your stories and give variety to your images. The heavier the weight of the paper, the fewer layers and cuts you will be able to make because of the thickness of the paper. A greeting card, invitation or table display may be more desirable made on card stock. Vibrant neon copy paper colors make the images exciting. Using the rich quality of parchment paper on the 3-dimensional patterns will lend an elegant look to your images. See Papers in Chapter 3: Fold-and-Cut Patterns (page 13).

By sketching, folding, cutting, layering, or embellishing the paper, you can follow my step-by-step instructions to create fun, exciting, and decorative projects. Whether you want a simple animal cutout or ornate lighthouses and flowers, you can do it. Soon you will be able to see the images on your own and patterns will no longer be necessary.

Pattern Preparation

The patterns in this book are listed alphabetically and by classification. Each completed shape is shown along with the actual folded-size pattern.

Copying: Copy the pattern with a copy machine, perhaps reducing or enlarging the image, depending on the size paper you have chosen. The patterns generally are designed for standard 8½ x 11-inch copy paper, using any color. Use transparent tape to secure the pattern to your folded paper in the areas that will be cut away later.

Tracing: You can simply trace an outline of the pattern directly on your folded paper with your stencil of laminate or acetate if you prefer. Just lay the laminate directly over the pattern you wish to cut. Trace it with a black permanent marker, Then cut it out. you have a stencil to use over and over. Store patterns in top loading clear pages in a binder.

Either method works well. As you develop your talent, the need for a pattern will diminish. Some patterns can be adapted to other fold-and-cut styles; that's where your imagination takes over.

Especially for Lefties

If you are left-handed, the instructions will reverse for you. Try it starting from left to right, holding your paper in your right hand, with scissors in your left hand and cutting away the pattern. You need to feel comfortable with this art, so experiment to find the best way for you.

Scissors Selection and Safety

This is a good time to mention safety and order. Scissors are sharp and should be handled and stored carefully. There are many varieties of scissors to choose from and they need to be kept sharp, so they cut well all the way to the point. Standard-size sewing scissors are best for large paper cuttings, small sewing scissors, manicure and embroidery scissors are good for delicate precision cuts. Scissors designed to cut a decorative edge can add to your design. The skill of the person cutting and the pattern chosen will determine which scissors are appropriate. Fine motor skills are enhanced as you work with scissors and paper.

Preparing the Work Area

The work area may be a table or a desk with a hard surface so you can organize your materials and make precision paper folds. It should be covered with news-paper or the cutting should be done over a wastepaper basket. The snips of paper can be very messy at times, so stay in one place when you cut. As you are reading the instructions, stop, fold, and cut. Experiment for a moment. Paper cutting is exciting and fun. With practice you can be a great cut-up!

Getting Started

What you need to begin with is inexpensive. Perhaps some items are already at your fingertips.

- ✂ Yesterday's newspaper (for covering the table of your work area and for practice cutting)
- ✂ Wastebasket
- ✂ 8½ x 11 copy paper (used paper for practice cutting). All colors and sizes can be used.
- ✂ Pencil
- ✂ Compass
- ✂ Transparent tape
- ✂ Paper punches of different hole sizes and shapes for eyes, nose, decoration, windows, etc.
- ✂ Sharp scissors—all the way to the point:
  - Small sewing scissors
  - Manicure scissors
  - Embroidery scissors
  - Sharp sewing scissors for large paper cutting
  - Edging scissors with decorative patterned edges
- ✂ Scissors Sharpener

Lots of patience and practice, practice, practice will help to make your fingers nimble and steady as you learn these papercutting techniques. Imagination and creativity with your scissors will help you develop an eye for new designs. Have a good sense of humor and lots more patience as you master this art of papercutting.

Every pattern is an experiment at first. Don't get discouraged as you exercise this developing talent. Sometimes you might make a cut that separates the figures. It's okay. It is only a piece of paper! Toss the scraps into the trash. Fold a new piece of paper and begin again. Be sure to recycle your paper.

Chapter 2

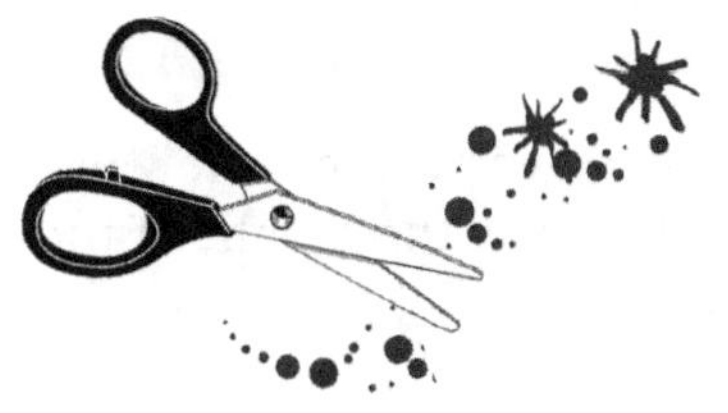

Fold-and-Cut Instructions

ACCORDION FOLD-AND-CUT

Do you remember as a child making a paper fan? The process of folding a piece of paper back and forth at exactly the same interval each time is what I call the accordion fold. You will use this process in several ways as you use this fold-and-cut procedure.

SINGLE FOLD IMAGE

These kinds of patterns can be used for scrapbooking, quilts, and bulletin boards. Enlarged they can be used for placemats or window decorations.

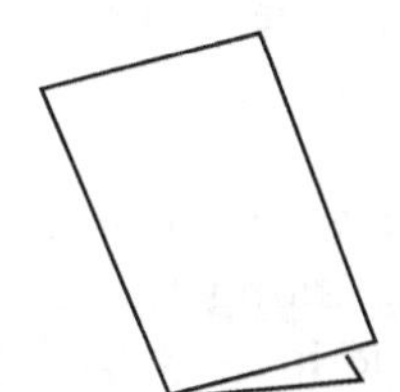

Figure A

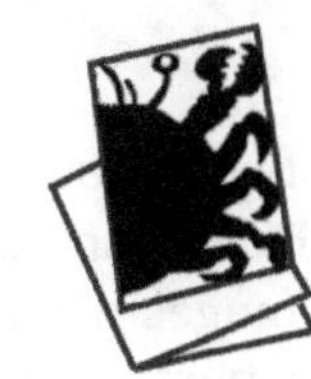

Figure B

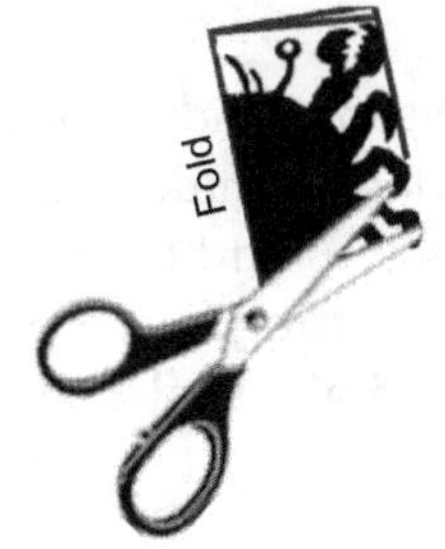

Figure C

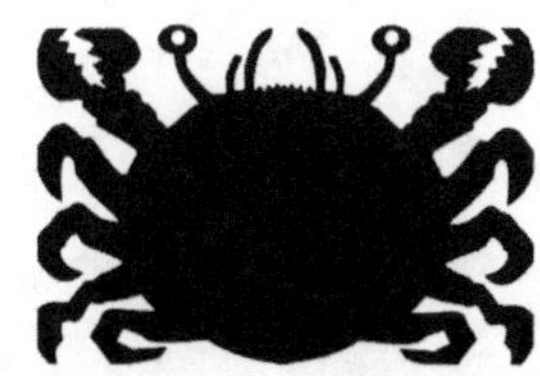

Figure D

1. Select and prepare your pattern.

2. Place your 8½ x 11-inch paper horizontal or vertical on the work area and fold it in half from left to right to cover the height of the pattern you have chosen. This is just one fold (Figure A).

3. Place the cutout pattern over the folded paper and tape the pattern in place along the open edges that you will cut away. I prefer a light pencil outline to follow rather than taping the pattern, but then I have had a little more practice (Figure B).

4. Holding your paper in your left hand, start on the lower right and begin to cut your design. ***Do not cut where the fold holds the image together*** (Figure C).

5. Let your paper do the turning as your scissors follow the pattern. You may need to make a little fold-and-cut to make the eyes of an animal, center of a flower; or use a paper punch.

6. Unfold and use as a decoration, border, wall hanging, mobile, or wreath (Figure D). Paste it to a contrasting color of paper. Sign your picture and display it.

DOUBLE FOLD IMAGE

These patterns are great for borders on bulletin boards or on walls, and notebook covers. Let your imagination and creativity explode.

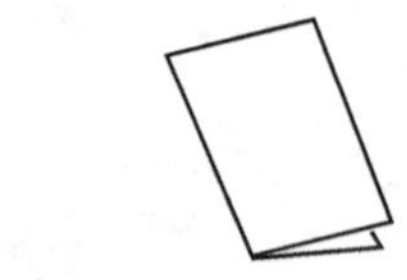

Figure A

1. Select and prepare your pattern.

2. Place your 8½ x 11-inch paper horizontal or vertical on the work area and fold it in half from left to right to cover the height of the pattern you have chosen (Figure A).

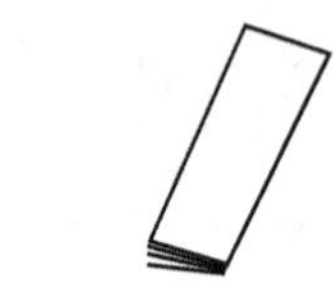

Figure B

3. Fold in half again from left to right. This *accordion fold* can be used for one sheet of paper or for as many as two (Figure B).

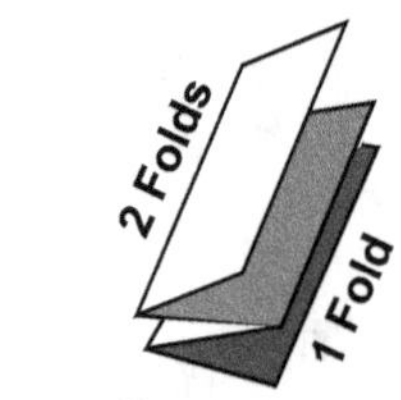

Figure C

4. Now take the accordion fold, which now has two folds, and place the single fold to the right and fold the two left edges back toward your right. As you look at the paper on its side, you now have two folds on the left and one fold in the center of the two edges to the right (Figure C).

5. Place the cutout pattern over the folded paper and make a light pencil tracing or tape the pattern in place along the edges you plan to cut away later. A light pencil outline is easy to follow, as there are less paper layers to cut through. The image is still a silhouette as we cut away the smaller sections of the pattern, unless your pattern is a full image (Figure D).

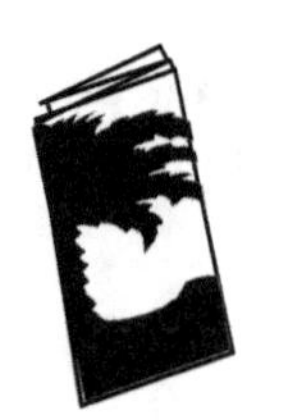

Figure D

6. Holding your paper in your left hand, start on the lower right and begin to cut away the small excess paper. Depending on the pattern you choose, you will have two or four images when your cutting is complete. Be careful in cutting the parts of the pattern out and ***do not cut where the folds are holding the figures together***.

7. Let your paper do the turning as your scissors glide along to follow the pattern. Turn your paper as needed to make the cutting easier. You may decide to use a paper punch to add the eyes, nose or other decoration to the image. After all, cutting is the art of using tools that will enhance the pattern and make it pleasing to the eye of the beholder.

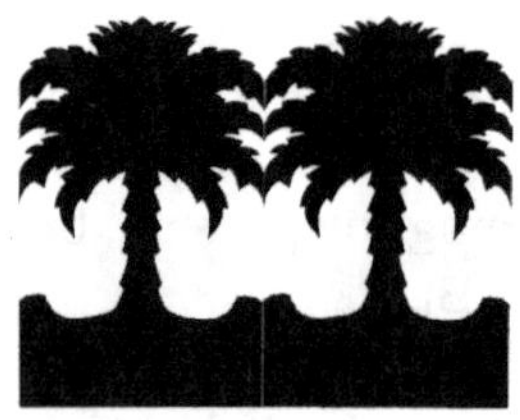

Figure E

8. Snip! Snip! Snap! Voila! Now unfold your paper cutting. It's magic! (Figure E)

MULTI-IMAGE FOLD

Need to decorate for a party, classroom or home decor? These designs make great borders of all kinds. They are also great backgrounds for dioramas.

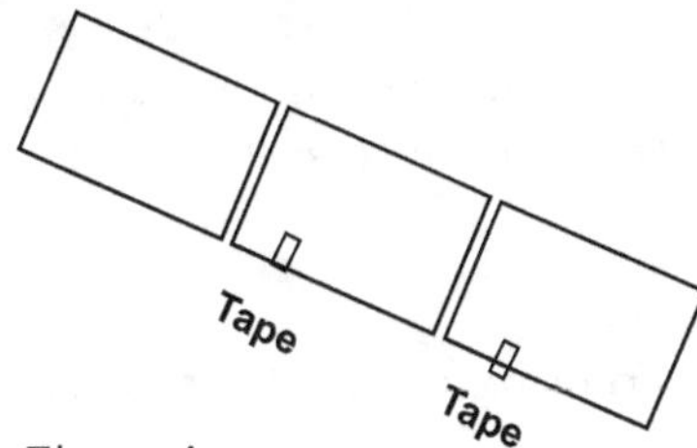

Figure A

1. Select and prepare your pattern.

2. Place two pieces of 8½ x 11-inch paper side by side on the work area and tape the 8½-inch sides together along the inside edges to form a continuous length of 8½ x 33" (Figure A). Some patterns are made for 4¼ x 5½-inch paper and after taping them together you then have a continuous length of paper 4¼ x 16½-inch.

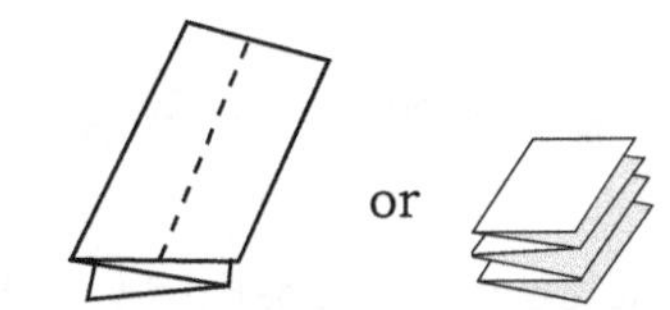

Figure B

3. Placing your paper horizontal on the work area, fold it back and forth at the taped seams into a stack and then fold the stack in half from left to right (Figure B). Some patterns are made to fold vertically or are full size and do not need to be folded again.

4. Fold your papers in half again from left to right. This accordion fold is the same for one sheet of paper or two or three.

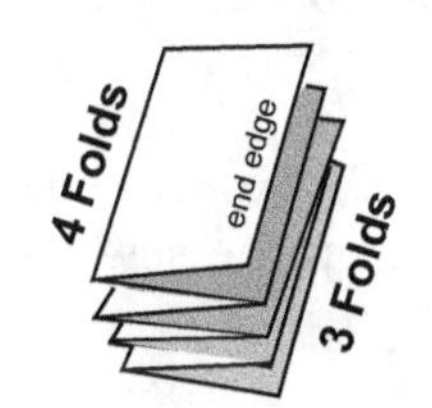

Figure C

5. Now undo all the folds of the paper. Fold to your left then right, back and forth until you have an accordion fold (like a fan) with the end edge on your right. As you look at the paper on its side, you now should have four folds on the left and three on the right (Figure C). The folds on the right are the taped seams from Step 1.

6. Place the cutout pattern over the accordion-folded paper and make a light pencil tracing or tape the pattern in place on the edges of the folded sections you will later cut away. The image is a silhouette as we snip, snip away (Figure D).

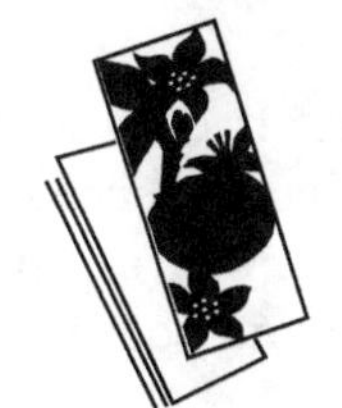
Figure D

7. Starting on the lower right begin to cut. Depending on the pattern you choose, you will have four, six, or eight connecting images when your cutting is complete (Figure E). ***Be careful not to cut where the folds on the left and right hold the figures together***. Use a paper punch for the eyes, noses, windows or other decorations.

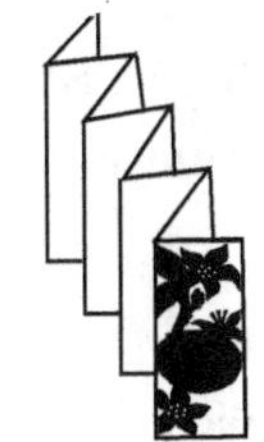
Figure E

8. Let your paper do the turning as your scissors follow the pattern. In some designs you may change the position of your paper to make it easier to complete the cut (Figure F).

Figure F

CARD FOLD-AND-CUT

This simple fold creates two images like a card. The image can be mounted on another piece of folded paper to create a more stable invitation or greeting card.

SIDE FOLD-AND-CUT

The side fold can be used for invitations, greeting cards, little booklets, or unique gift tags.

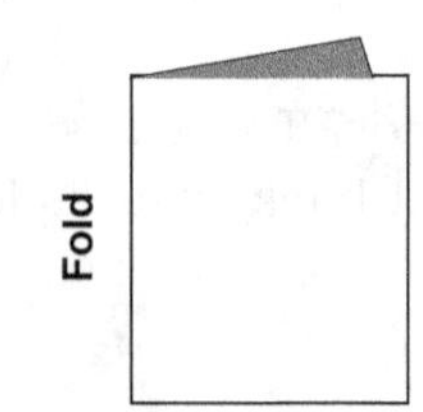

Figure A

1. Select and prepare your pattern.
2. Fold your colored 8½ x 11-inch (or smaller) paper in half with the fold on your left (Figure A).
3. Place the cutout pattern you have chosen on the paper and make a light pencil tracing or tape the pattern in place along the edges you will cut away.

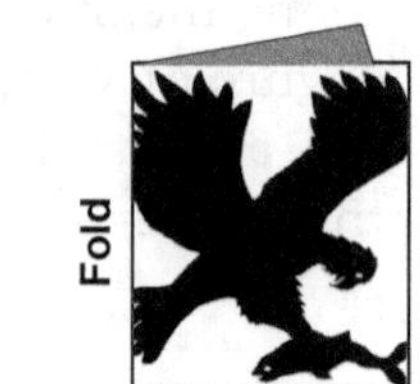

Figure B

4. Begin cutting on the right. ***Be careful not to cut apart the folded area on the left*** (Figure B).
5. Decorate and put a message inside (Figure C). Several sheets of paper can be stapled or stitched in the center on the sewing machine to make a booklet. Simple and easy!
6. Do what is easiest for you. These instructions are similar with slight variations for each image you cut.

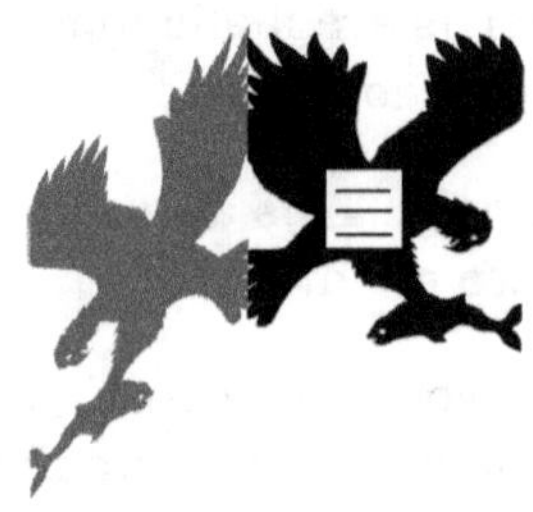
Figure C

TOP FOLD-AND-CUT

The top fold is as easy as the single fold image. It can be used for hanging images on string or fishing line. Make a centerpiece, place cards, a stand-up display, alphabet letters, hearts, bears, pumpkins, leaves, balloons, sun, moon, stars, fish, butterflies and so my list could go on and on.

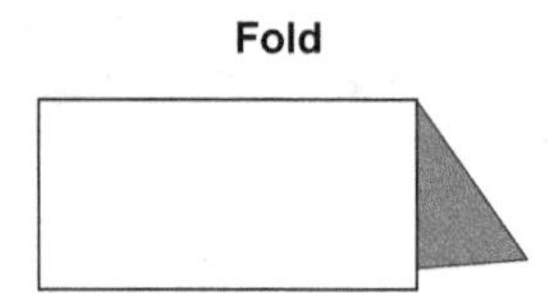

Figure D

1. Select and prepare your pattern.
2. Cut a 8½ x 11-inch paper in half to make a 5½ x 8½-inch piece of paper. Now fold your paper in half with the fold on the top this time (Figure D). It is now 2¾ by 8½.

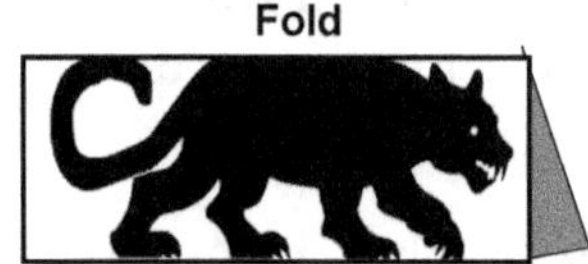

Figure E

3. Place the cutout pattern you have chosen on the paper and make a light pencil tracing or tape the pattern in place on the areas you will cut away.
4. Begin cutting on the right. ***Be careful not to cut apart the folded area on the left*** (Figure E).
5. Unfold your cutting. It will now stand alone. To hang your image, you can place the folded top over string or fishing line (Figure F).

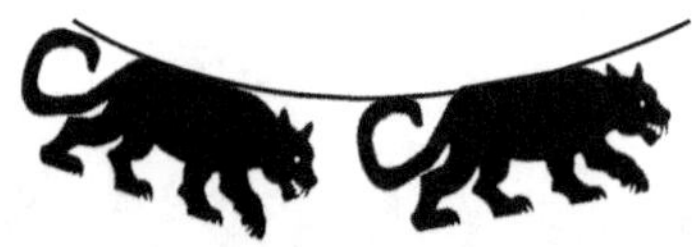
Figure F

3-DIMENSIONAL FOLD-AND-CUT

Use these fabulous creations as stand-up centerpieces or hang them from the ceiling. They make wonderful ornaments for any season and beautiful mobiles to capture the imagination. Enlarge the patterns to any size. Cut from card stock, fade-proof colored paper or parchment paper.

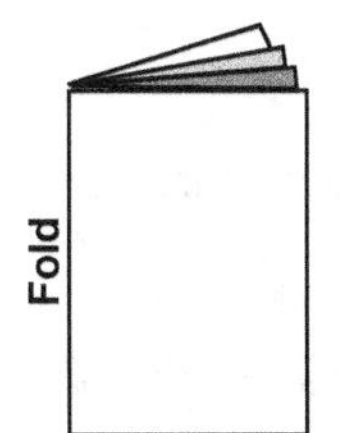

Figure A

1. Select and prepare your pattern.
2. Using the double fold-and-cut technique (page 6), fold two sheets of 8½ x 11-inch size paper in half from left to right (Figure A). Sometimes I put two pieces of paper together and stitch the center together on my sewing machine.
3. Take the two folded pieces apart. Lay them side by side with the folds facing each other. Now tape the folds together, from the top to the bottom (Figure B).

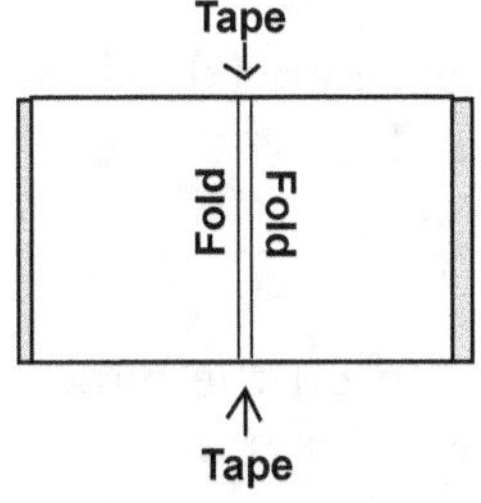

Figure B

4. Lift them up and fold edges to your right, so that one piece is inside the other with a single fold on your left (Figure C), and the edges on your right.
5. Place the cutout pattern over the paper and make a pencil tracing or tape it in place. Be sure the tape is in an area that will be cut away.
6. Start cutting out the smaller portions of the image. Some patterns may require an interior cut (Figure D).

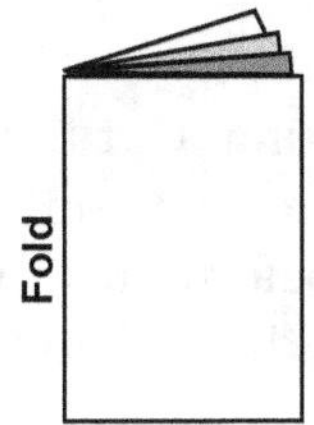

Figure C

7. To make an interior cut, use a paper punch to make the hole and then place your small scissors into the hole to complete the cut. Unfold the four sides (Figure E). There is ***magic*** in your ***scissors***!

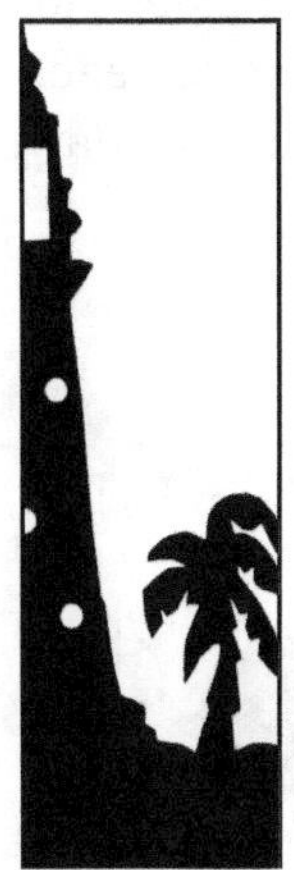

Figure D

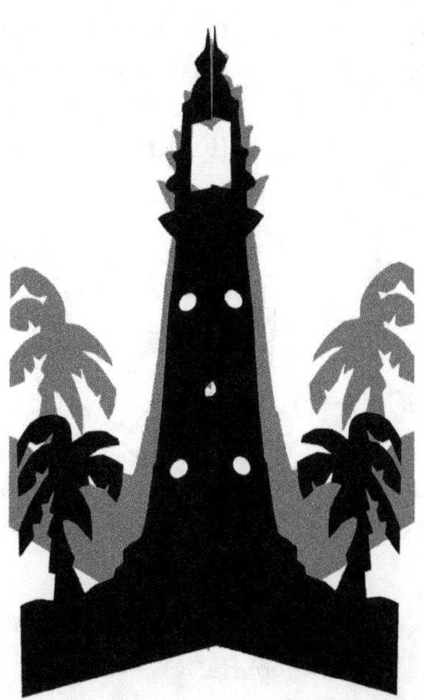

Figure E

TRI FOLD-AND-CUT

This process creates images in the round or in a square.

CIRCLE FOLD-AND-CUT

This cutting is done with three simple folds.

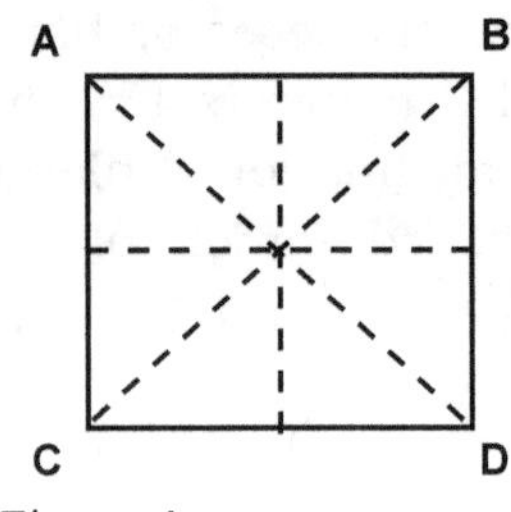

Figure A

1. Select and prepare your pattern.
2. Begin by cutting your paper into a square 8½ x 8½. Make a larger square if you want to cut a larger image (Figure A).
3. Fold the square into a triangle by folding corner A down to meet corner D (Figure B).

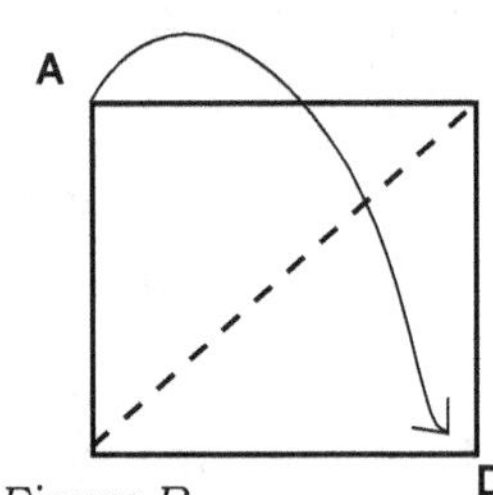

Figure B

4. Fold the triangle again by folding corner B down to corner C (Figure C).
5. Crease the folds firmly and fold your triangle into a third triangle by folding corner C over to meet corner D (Figure D).
6. Keep your folds even and creased firmly.

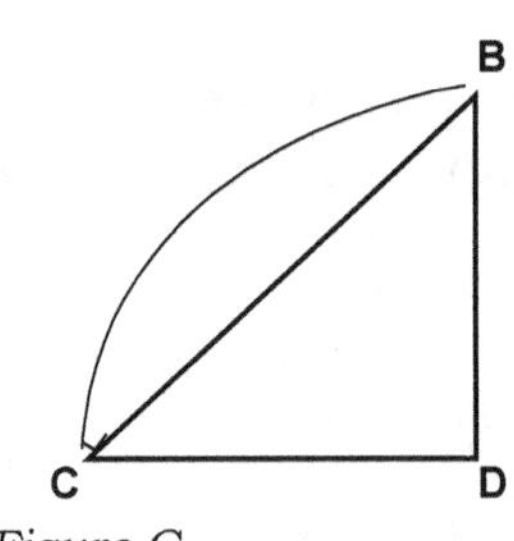

Figure C

7. Place the cutout pattern you have chosen on the paper and tape in place in the areas that will be cut away.
8. The three folds are facing the left and the center point is facing down (Figure E).
9. With the paper in your left hand begin cutting. Cut the features and designs. Use a paper punch for the nose, eyes, windows or decoration. Sometimes I use the paper punch before cutting to conserve time. It is easier to cut the smaller part of the design first. Open up fold once to make it easier to hole punch.

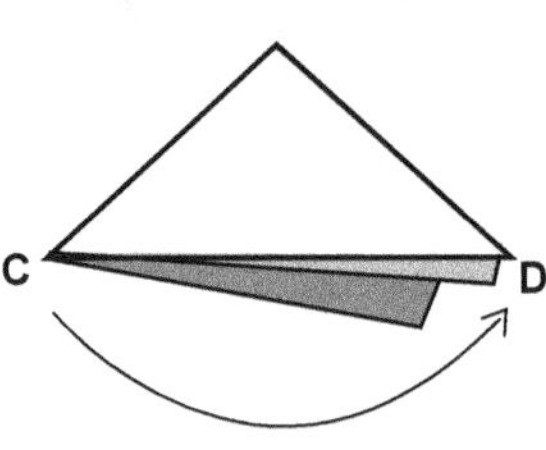

Figure D

10. Let your paper do the turning as your scissors follow the pattern. In some designs you may change the position of your paper to make it easier to complete the cut. Do what is easiest for you. These instructions are similar with slight variations for each image you cut. When you unfold your cutting it will form a circular or square image (Figure F).

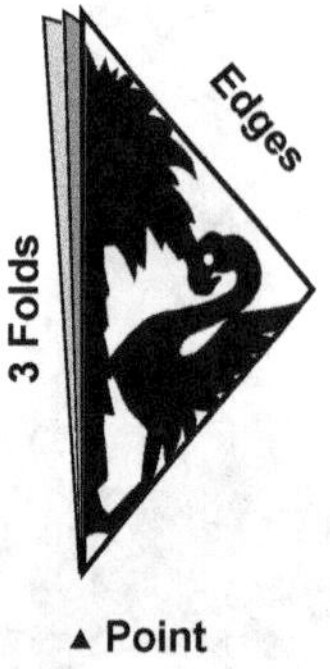

Figure E

Figure F

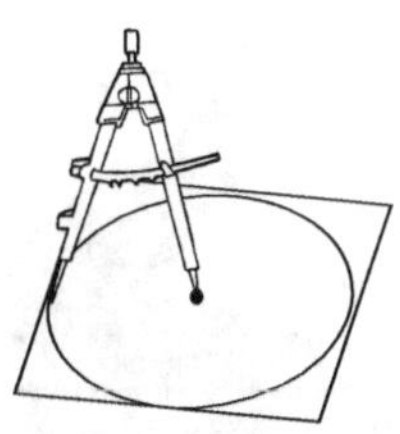
Figure A

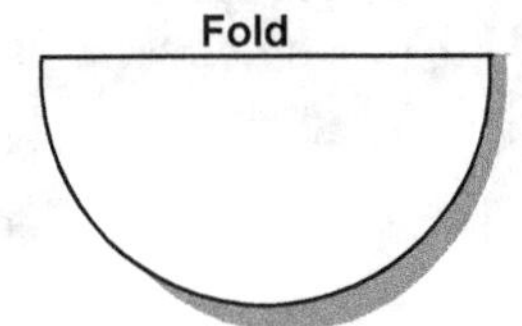

Figure B

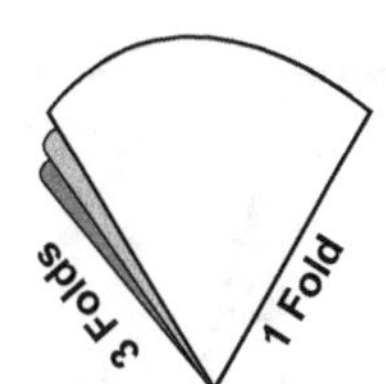

Figure C

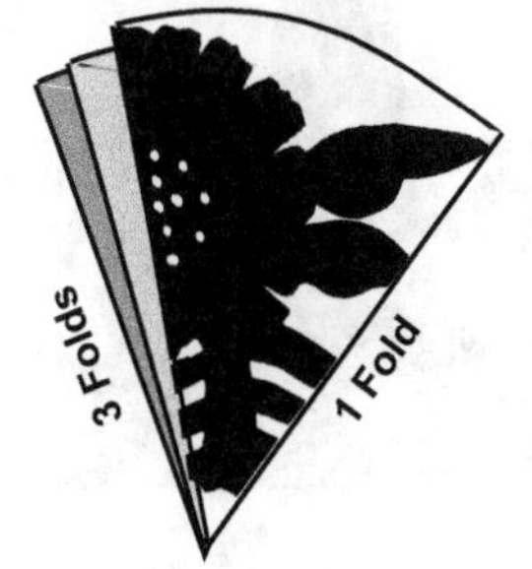

Figure D

Figure E

TRUE CIRCLE FOLD-AND-CUT

This cutting is done by using a compass to make the circle first.

1. Select and prepare your pattern.
2. Place your paper on a piece of heavy paper or cardboard. Using a compass, draw a circle at least 8½-inches in diameter or larger (Figure A).
3. Cut your circle out and fold it in half. You have the option to use the edging scissors with decorative designs. Try free form cutting and see what you can make (Figure B).
4. Fold in half and in half again. That makes three pie shape folds. Crease the folds firmly as you make sure the folds fit closely (Figure C).
5. Place the cutout pattern you have chosen on the folded paper and tape it in place in the areas you will cut away. The three folds are facing to the left and the point is facing down (Figure D).
6. With the paper in your left hand, begin cutting away the smaller portions of the design.
7. Use a paper punch for the nose, eyes, buttons or decoration. Sometimes I use the paper punch before cutting to conserve time. It is easier to cut the smaller parts of the design first.
8. Let your paper do the turning as your scissors follow the pattern. In most designs you will change the position of your paper to make it easier to complete the cut. Do what is easiest for you. These instructions are similar with slight variations for each image you cut. When you unfold your cutting it will form a circular image (Figure E).

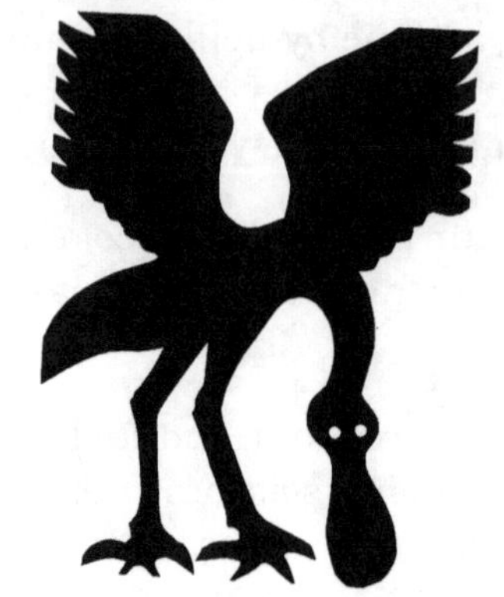
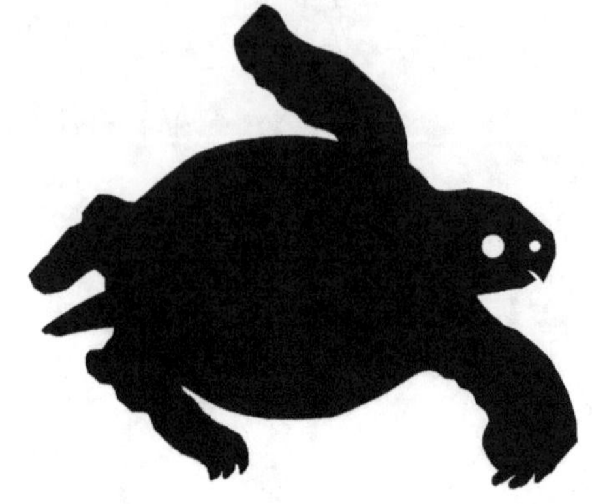

Quick and Easy

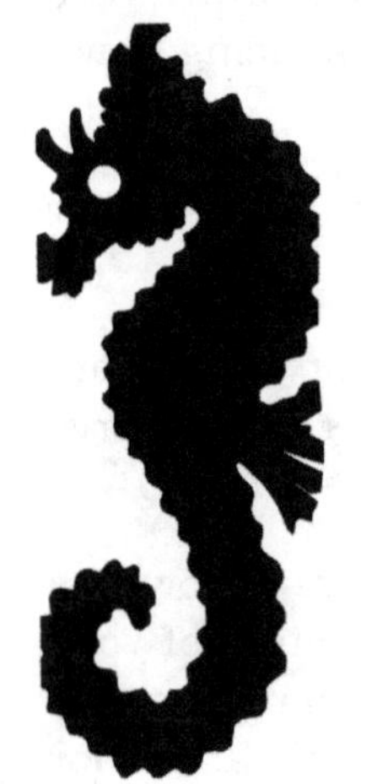
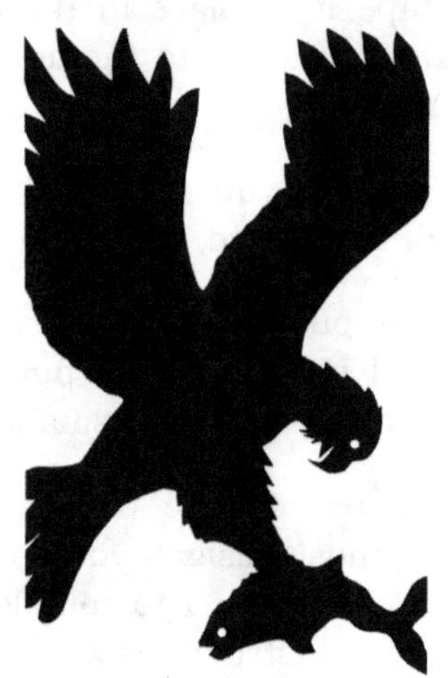
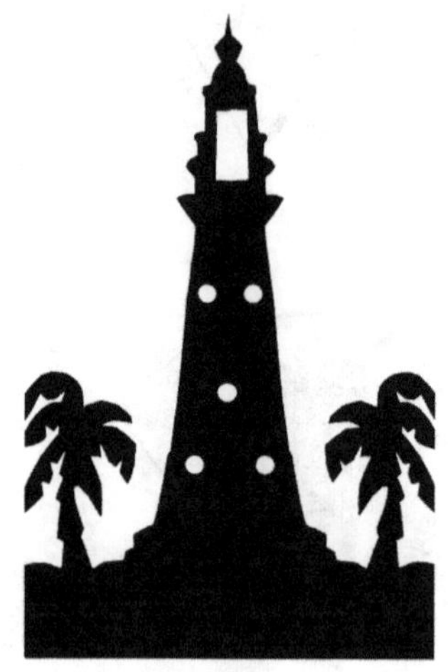

Intermediate

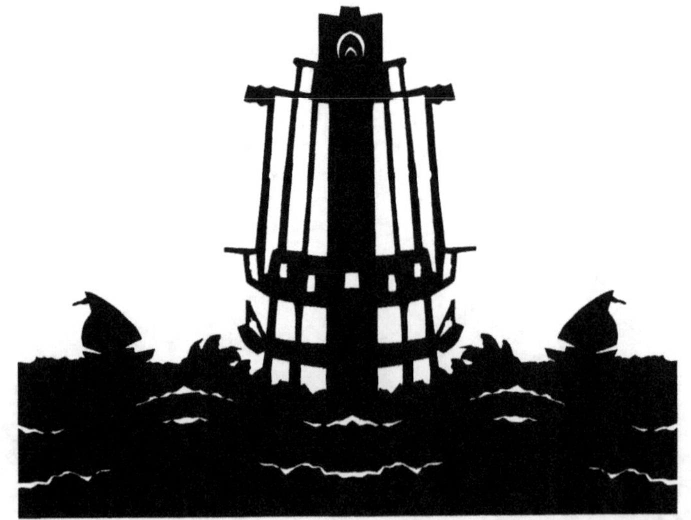
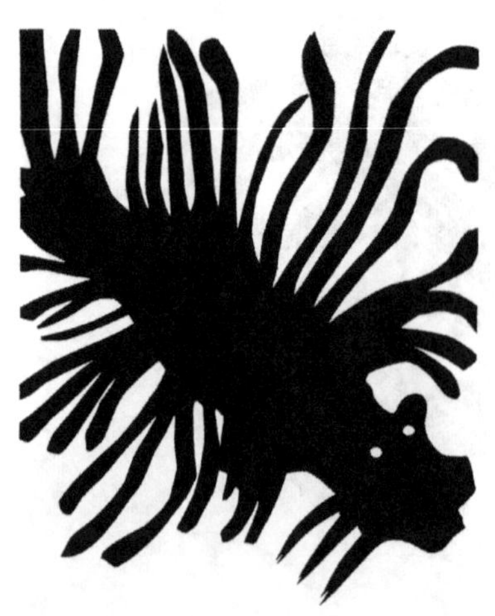

Advanced

Chapter 3

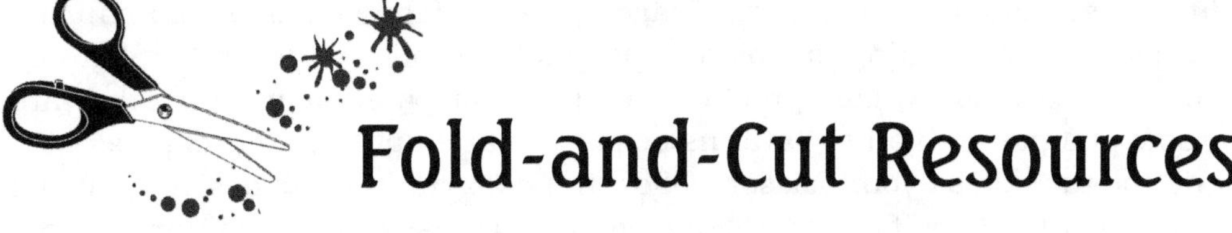

Fold-and-Cut Resources

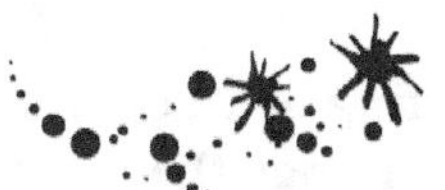

Techniques and Tips

DESIGN PUNCHES

Handheld paper punches offer a variety of large and small shapes and give an added dimension to paper cutting, making the eyes, noses, butterfly spots, and windows. The punch design is easily placed and not clumsy to use like the regular hole punch. I still fold and cut some of the features because the character may need a particular look, such as the squid's eye (page 78).

ENHANCING TECHNIQUES

Enhancing a cutting can add character and profile. Defining the feathers makes the silhouette believable. Details can be tricky, but if you follow the directions and practice you will find it easier and easier. You can attach colored paper additions to embellish the cutting and add to the story. Glitter, watercolors, water markers, markers, well-placed pushpin holes, all these can add individuality and sparkle to your creations. Construction paper is a nice backing for your designs, but the heavy fiber makes it too heavy for a lot of folds and cutting.

PAPERS

Study and understand your project before you choose the paper to cut. What weight paper will work best? Use lightweight and multi-colored paper for *multi-image fold-and-cut* because of the many layers to cut through. Plain 20 lb. white or colored copy paper is inexpensive and simple to work with. Parchment paper is elegant and rich for special events, *3-dimensional fold-and-cut*, and cards.

Does the pattern have intricate curves? You may need to use small manicure scissors for delicate designs and intricate cuts. Those require some practice, yet are simple to work with using all lightweight papers. It will surprise you how quickly you are able to master the techniques.

Card stock for some patterns can work for *top, 3-dimension*, and *side fold* patterns because you are handling only two layers of paper. Colored or white medium card stock (67 lb.) has body and is sturdy enough to stand after cutting. A paper plate, used for a mask or wreath, is really a type of card or index weight paper. The heavier the weight of the paper, the fewer layers and cuts you will be able to make because of the thickness of the paper.

Tissue and wrapping paper can be cut into many layers and have versatile colors and patterns, but are very fragile.

How many folds are required? As you decide on a pattern to use you can choose whether to make it for two images or six. At first you may want to work with fewer folds until you are more skilled with your scissors.

You truly can use almost any paper for fold-and-cut projects. Whether the paper you decide on is colored, parchment, lightweight or card stock paper, or even gift wrap, whether the pattern is large or small—you decide!

3-DIMENSIONAL FIGURES

Three-dimensional cuttings are unique in every way (page 9). These fabulous creations hanging in windows or from the ceiling are fascinating to look at. They make wonderful decorations at any season or for parties. Cut from card stock, fade-proof colored paper or parchment paper, they are amazing. You will need some practice with other patterns before you attempt this style of paper cutting art. Let your paper do the turning as your scissors follow the pattern. In these designs you will change the position of your paper to make it easier to complete the cut. Use transparent tape to hold the papers together. Sometimes I sew the paper together on the sewing machine.

CIRCLE CUTTING

Easy designs are done with just three simple folds (page 10). The images may be ornate or simple. These designs can also be turned into 3-Dimensional mobiles. The *true circle fold-and-cut* is done by using a compass to make the full circle. Make the circle before you apply the pattern (page 11).

SINGLE FOLD

The *side fold* and *top fold* are versatile on any kind of paper, but card stock is often the best for these projects. They can be used as invitations, greeting cards, little booklets, banner type images, or you can make smaller figures as gift tags. The *top fold* is ideal for around the room such as, bears or fish, birds or flowers on string or fishing line (see Figure F on page 8). Make a centerpiece, place cards, little books, alphabet letters, birds, bears, lighthouses, starfish, butterflies and armadillos.

SCISSORS

Scissors are your most important tool, sharp scissors at that! Select your scissors to fit comfortably in your hand. Embroidery, manicure, and small sewing scissors with small blades and sharp points are good for delicate precision cuts. Surgical scissors are by far the best choice because of their sharpness, but they tend to be a bit pricey. For larger cuts, you will need a pair of good sewing scissors to cut through multiple folds and layers. Scissors designed to cut a decorative edge can add a delicate touch to your design, but are limited to the number of layers of paper they will cut through cleanly.

Take care of your scissors and store them safely. As I travel with mine going to book events at schools, book stores, educational conferences, book fairs, festivals, storytelling events, libraries, Book Expo of America, and the American Library and Reading Conference, I keep them in a case so the points are always protected. After all, you have to treat your ***Magic Scissors*** with special care, and keep them sharp at all times.

STORAGE

Store your patterns and fold-and-cut designs in clear page protectors in a binder for easy access. Other options are envelopes or file folders.

Stories with Fold-and-Cut Patterns

Look for words that are in italics they indicate the pattern to use.

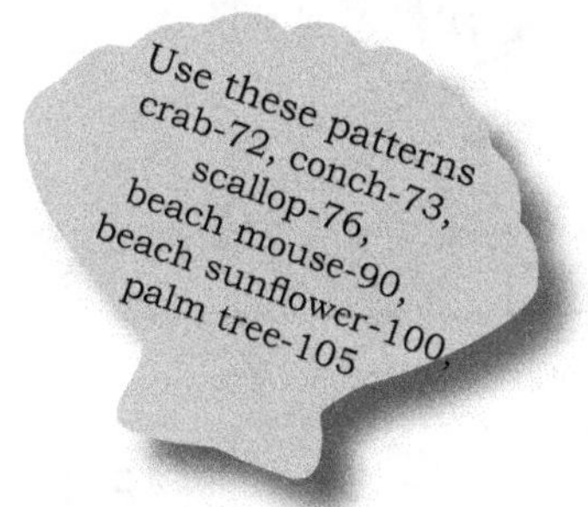

On The Seashore

BY LINDA S. DAY

All:	On the seashore
1:	By the big *palm tree*
2:	*Sunflowers* are dancing-
3:	One
4:	Two
1&2:	Three!
All:	On the seashore
5:	*Mice* playing tricks
3:	Hiding in the sea oats-
2:	Four
6:	Five
3&4:	Six!
All:	On the seashore
4:	Shells to find
6:	The *conch* and the *scallop*-
5:	Seven
1:	Eight
5&6:	Nine!
All:	On the seashore
1&2:	*Crabs* digging again
3&4:	Big ones
5&6:	Little ones
All:	From one to ten!

A group of children with various sizes of palm trees, sunflowers, mice, seashells, crabs, as a choral speaking piece. Could be a puppet presentation for the class, a seashore diorama or fold-and-cut for a mobile or mural. The possibilities are yours....

Use these patterns
Florida Panther - 89,
Sabal Palm - 106

Panther! Panther! On the Prowl

BY LINDA S. DAY

Panther! Panther! On the Prowl.
Oh dear! I think I heard him growl.
Grrrrrrr.

He walks on padded paws.
Closer and closer he draws.
Grrrrrrr.

Tail swaying to and fro.
Which way will he go?
Grrrrrrrr.

I hear a rustling sound.
My hiding place he's found.
Grrrrrrrr.
Grrrrrrrr.

Oh no! His eyes reflect the sun.
Oh me! Oh my! I'm done!
Grrrrrrrrr.
Purrrrrrrr.

Two little cubs! Look! Over there!
She was hunting for the pair.
Purrrrrrrr.
Purrrrrrrr.

GRRRRRRRRRRRRRR!

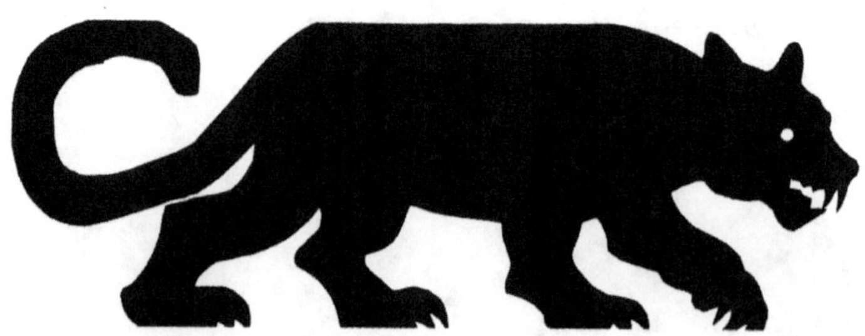

Use these patterns:
Atlantic Cod-54
Atlantic Spadefish-55
Catfish-56, Sailfish-63
Seahorse - 65
Waves - 120

Five Little Fishes

BY LINDA S. DAY

All	Five little *fishes* swimming in the sea
All	The first one said,
1	"Swish your tail, just like me."
All	The second one said,
2	"There's a big fish over there!"
All	The third one said,
3	"Well, we don't care."
All	The fourth one said,
4	"Let's run, run, run."
All	The fifth one said,
5	"Oh, it's just hide and seek fun."
All	"Whoosh," went the *waves* and out went the tide,
All	and five little fishes swam away to hide.

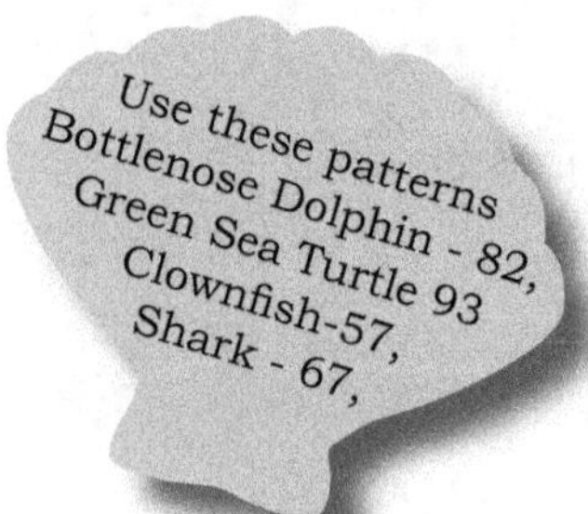

A Tale of Dolphins

BY LINDA S. DAY

Let me tell you a marvelous and magical tale, my friends, a wonderful story of the sea and the strange and amazing creatures that live beneath the waves. Wild things swim deep, others whose bodies glow in the cold, dark depths as they slither and dart among the coral reefs and seaweed, and hide in the sand and rocky caves.

The *dolphins* have been playing all day. Chasing bubbles, playing catch with a piece of kelp and tossing it back and forth, and swimming in circles playing tag. Now it is night and they are hunting as a pod for fish. Swimming and diving with graceful speed they glide through the glistening sea. Suddenly there is a sharp clicking sound and a whistle. The small group comes up and "blows" together, for they are mammals and breathe through the blowhole at the top of the head.

"Whewww! Whewww! Come quickly," says Demetrius, the leader of the pod.

The clicking and whistle sounds echo and bounce back to the pod. For you see my friends, dolphins talk to each other. They understand the bark, click, moan, mew and whistle of each dolphin. They are quick to help each other, to express their feelings, to defend against a shark attack and... but let us continue with our story.

"There! In that shallow ahead is a school of fish for breakfast. We will circle around them," clicks Darcy, swimming past some *anemone* and *clown fish* nestled on the rocks near by. The baby dolphin swims close to her mother. Her rich milk she squirts directly into the mouth of the baby dolphin. The herd moves in quickly. Swish! Splash! Slosh! Plop! Frothy waves appear and disappear. The pod is full, their meal is finished.

Their breakfast over, they swim out to deeper water as the sun pops her brilliant rays out and spreads her pink and purple clouds across the horizon. They spread out as they take off and suddenly there is a savage looking *shark* heading close to one of the groups.

Denny and Darcy are quick to turn and ram their beaks at the side of the shark. "He is looking for a meal, too, but we won't be it," Denny says. Several dolphins swim up to the fierce shark and with their beaks toss him into the air, lifting him clear out of the water. Outnumbered, the shark moves away from the pod, turns and heads north. Exhausted and bruised the dolphins swim to the surface.

"Moan! Mew! Finally, fresh air at last. That was quite an exciting moment. I nearly ran out of air," Deanne says. Denny nudges her and together they take a long deep breath and float slowly, fins and tails gently moving as they rest for awhile.

The dolphins swim by a large *sea turtle* on her way to the shore to lay her eggs. She has traveled over a thousand miles to return to the sandy beach where she was born. She will not stay to swim or play with her young, but will head back to the sea. She smiles at the dolphins as they bark their friendly goodbyes to her. Then, spouting water they leap and dive playfully as they swim out to sea.

This tale of the sea has been full of adventure, my friends, and there are many more marvelous and magical tales to tell. But that is another story for another day.

The Lighthouse

BY LINDA S. DAY

Use these patterns Egmont Key-31, Eagle with Fish-41, Gulls in Flock-45, White Ibis-50, Conch-73, Scallop-76, Manatee-81, Sabal Palm-106

The men and women who kept America's vital shipping lanes safe from 1716 until the early 20th century were courageous in the face of the mighty forces of wind and sea. The *lighthouse* lanterns were fueled with wood, lard, whale oil, tallow, and kerosene. Today, besides electricity and acetylene gas, solar power is also used.

Thousands have lost their lives in the sea. Great ships were sunk on the shoals and reefs in the storms. The keepers of the lights coped with the solitude and the daily tasks that had to be attended to each day. There were banks of fog, storms, and hurricanes, sinking ships, pirates, fierce winds, great crashing waves, catastrophes and the natural world around a lighthouse.

There are the keepers of the lights even yet today. Through the high winds and storms, the balmy breezes and the sunlit days. The memories and stories of the lighthouses live on. Here is such a story to stir your imagination.

The morning was breaking crisp and clear over the lonely lighthouse as the graceful eagle took flight from its lofty nest near the beach. A flock of *gulls* was hovering along the surf in search of breakfast. The *eagle's* strong wings, warmed by the rising sun, eased him above the *sabal palms* and tall pines along the Florida coastline. Riding the currents of the balmy breezes he was an awesome and magnificent sight to behold.

The lighthouse kept its lonely vigil there on the sandy peninsula jutting out into the ocean. Craggy boulders at the base kept the land from eroding away. Yet the unrelenting waves broke against the rocks in a salty spray rising high into the air and the tides teased and pulled at the sand to come with them back to the ocean.

In 1829, workmen had built a masonry tower, with its winding staircase up to the lantern of the lighthouse. The heavy walls of the lighthouse seemed stable, on its rock and sand foundation. But the ever persistent, crashing waves, the whirling winds and the torrents of rain had pounded at the tower now for twenty years.

Johann was the keeper of the lighthouse, with his wife, Rebecca, their son William, twelve, and daughter Katie who was seven. It was the duty of the lighthouse keeper to light the lamp at sunset and put it out at sunrise. During the night, and his eight-hour watch, Johann would have to climb the stairs in the tower two to three times. There were 200 steps up the winding staircase to the top. With his kerosene lamp in one hand and his other hand on the rail, he would check on the lantern and wind the weights. He stopped at the watch room, immediately below the lantern service room, where fuel and other supplies were kept. That is where he and William prepared the lanterns for the night and often stood watch. The clockworks (for rotating lenses) were also located there. The beacon of the lantern sent its lifeline of light 20 miles out across the ocean to warn approaching ships of the reefs and shoals near the coast.

Rebecca kept their cozy little home neat and tidy and schooled the children when they were not helping their father. It was a good life, a happy, but hard and lonely life they had chosen. But they loved the sea. The windows had to be cleaned and all the brass had to shined every day. Yesterday, after the storm, Johann and William had to clean and polish the lens and the lantern room windows and it took the whole day. Keepers were nicknamed "wickie" because one of the chores was the trimming of the burned wick in the lamp. So Katie laughed as she called her brother, Willy "Wickie".

The weeks went by and the day was calm as Johann took the children out onto the lighthouse gallery or balcony, located outside the lantern room. What a magnificent view it was from up so high. The smell of the salt air, the wind whipping round the railing, the glistening sunlight sparkling on the blue ocean below and the great ships, with their sails piled high catching the wind always lifted their imagination. They would pretend to sail with them to the lands beyond the horizon, full of treasures and adventure at every port.

It was a hot summer day that they took the dory out to catch some fish, and then have a picnic on the beach. The sun was warm and the billowing clouds were moving and swirling like soft downy cotton puffs. They ran along the long stretch of the shore and played in the surf.

"Over here Willy. Come over here and see the beautiful white *egret*," called Katie in her loudest, whispered voice. She stood ever so still as the wind blew her long blond hair across her face and the waves wrapped around her feet, letting the sand be pulled out from under her.

William had gathered some *scallops* and *conch* shells that had been beached after the storm. Turning to Katie he said, "See the colors in this shell. What a mystical world it must be under the sea. What kind of animal do you think lived in this shell?" They laughed and played on the beach the rest of the afternoon.

That next day the seas grew heavy with clouds of fog. Eerie yellow lights seemed to flicker out beyond the fierce crashing waves in the black night. High winds began to swirl around the lighthouse and howl at every window trying to break their way through. With each thrashing wave, the old lighthouse would creak and groan. The beacon from the lantern in the lighthouse had burned day and night. The storm was so loud Rebecca couldn't hear Johann as he called from the stairs "It's a bad one! Keep the children close while I check the wick in the lantern. I'm going aloft to see that it's beacon light of warning to the approaching ships is burning."

Suddenly the crashing waves were more than the old lighthouse could stand. The wind whipped and lashed at the bricks and mortar, the windows cracked and the ocean waves came splashing and tumbling into the lighthouse.

Rebecca was huddled under the oak table holding the children tight in her arms when the water engulfed them. Her grasp could not hold them and putting her hand out she called, "Katie, where are you?" The water swirled and the walls crashed about them. The table floated up and broke into pieces as it was dashed against the wall of what was once was their lighthouse home.

"Mama, Mama! I don't know where you are. Help! Help!" Splashing about in the cold darkness Katie cried out again, "Help me Mama! Help me Willie!" as the water swirled about and pulled her down.

Willie was holding on to the staircase now, when his father's arms caught hold of him. "Hang on tight, my boy, we'll make it through this," gulped Johann as he blinked the water back from his eyes. "Where are your mother and Katie?"

Another big wave washed over them and Johann knew that the beacon of the lighthouse was now out. They were cold and shivering in the waves, as they held fast to each other and what was left of the winding stairs of the lighthouse

The day was breaking crisp and clear over what was left of the lighthouse as the graceful eagle took flight from its lofty nest near the beach. A flock of gulls was hovering along the surf in search of breakfast. Debris cluttered the shore with barrels, scraps of wood, a small trunk and an oar from the dory. Lying on the sandy beach, in that gray dawn were four seemingly lifeless forms.

Rolling over in the gentle surf, Willie blinked his eyes, wiped the sand from his face and sat up. "Father! Father! Where are you? Are you all right?" Sputtering and coughing, then rubbing his shoulder, Johann stood up and staggered over to William and hugged him ever so tightly.

Over near the rubble where the lighthouse had been were Rebecca and Katie. Kneeling down he cradled his dear Rebecca in his arms and sobbed. "Oh my sweet, my dear," and her hand trembled and she put it on his cheek.

"We have been saved from the storm, Johann," said Rebecca softly, tears rolling down her cheeks. Together they wept as they hugged each other, William, Rebecca, and Johann.

"But where is our Katie?" Rebecca suddenly cried. All eyes searched the beach around them and there sitting on a fallen palm tree was little Katie, waving out to sea and calling, "Goodbye, dear friends. Thank you. Goodbye. Oh mother, did you see how the mermaids rescued us and brought me to shore? I couldn't find you in the darkness of the water and the awful waves. Then all of a sudden here were the mermaids. Wasn't that wonderful? I hope I get to swim with them again someday."

"Mermaids, you say," Johann smiled as he picked Katie up in his arms. Then, there swimming in the reef, were some *manatees*, with their tails splashing and heads bobbing up and down. Was it the friendly manatees? Or were there really mermaids who rescued the family? Will we ever know? Let us imagine that such things happen in the mysterious sea.

In 1849, the fierce surf and terrible winds of the hurricane had finally stopped. They had toppled the lighthouse into the churning angry sea. Only rubble remains of the once proud lighthouse that had stood there on that sandy peninsula jutting out into the ocean. Sometimes eerie yellow lights seem to flicker over the crashing waves on a stormy black night. And perhaps you will hear a strange voice calling out, the voice of a child, far out in the distance calling, "Help! Mama! Mama! Take my hand."

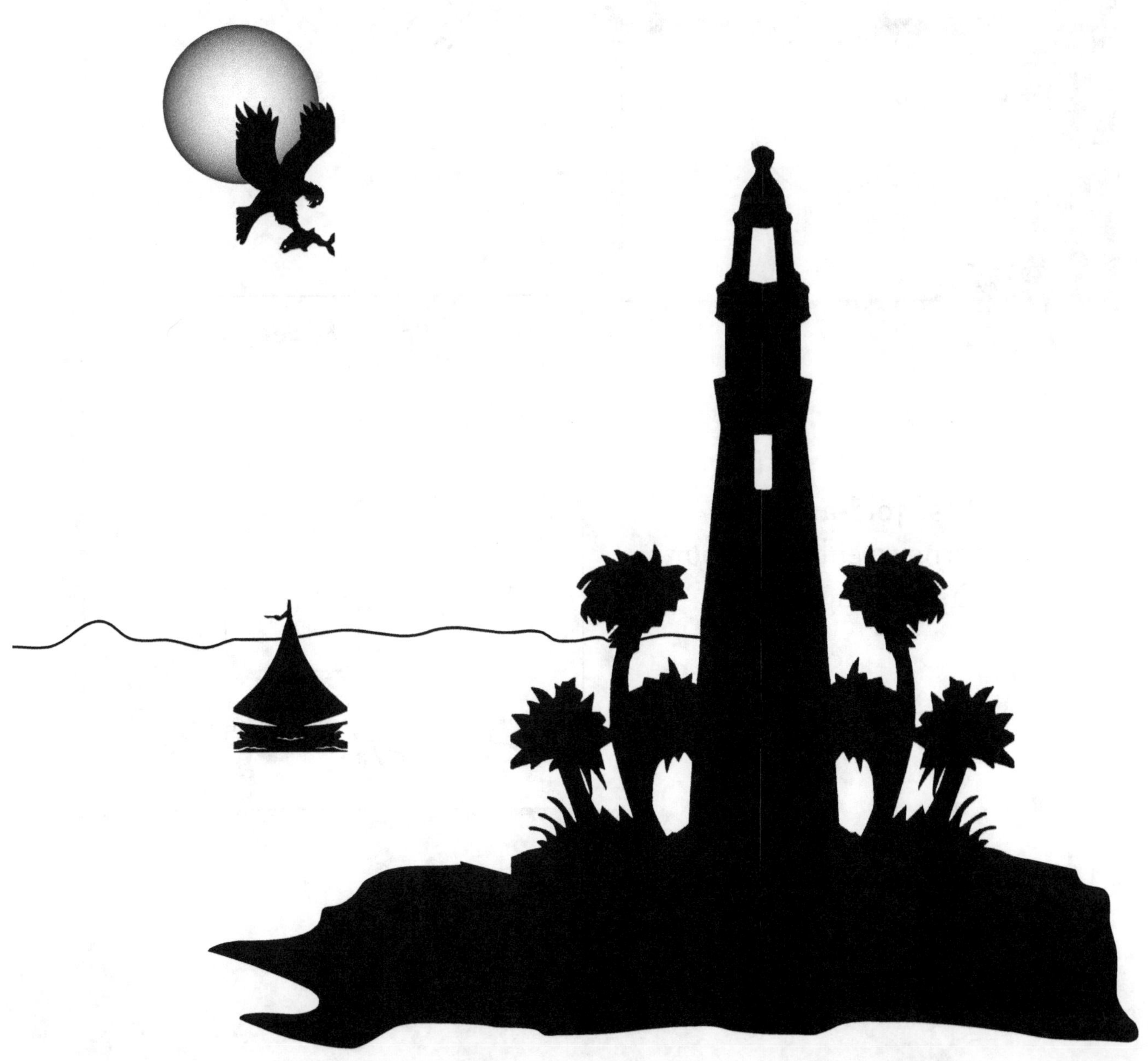

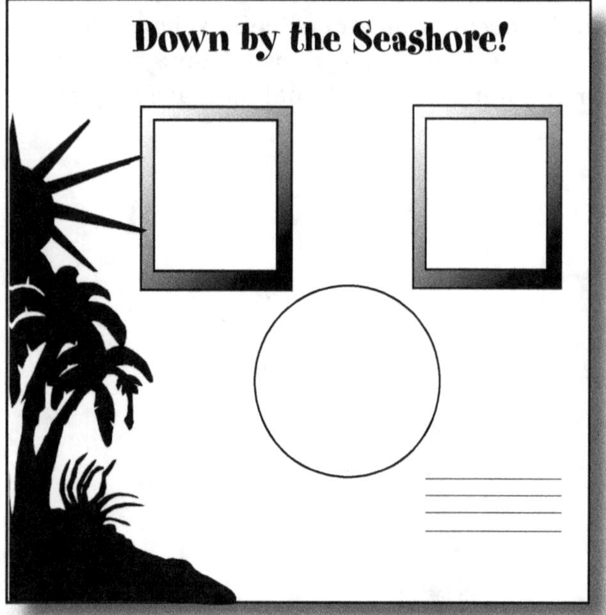

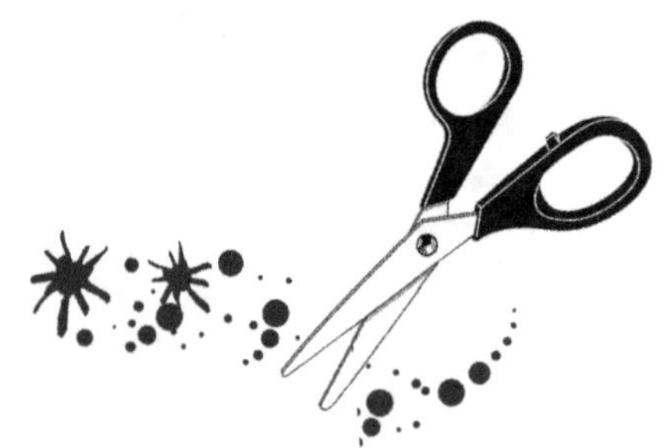

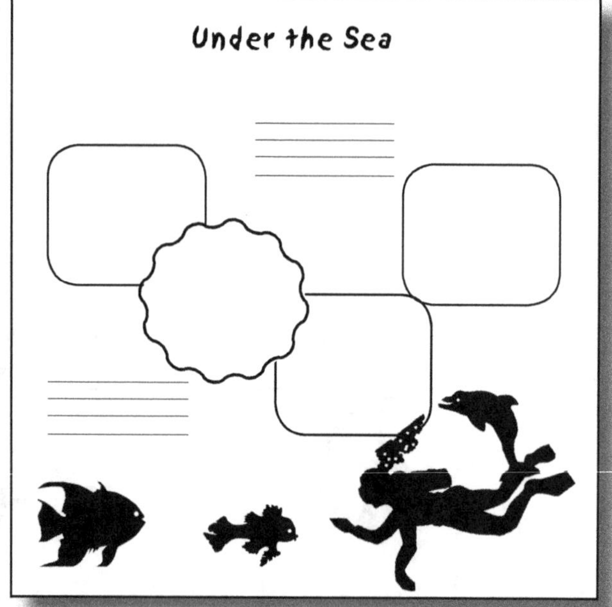

Use fold-and-cut patterns to enhance your scrapbooking pages.

Chapter 4

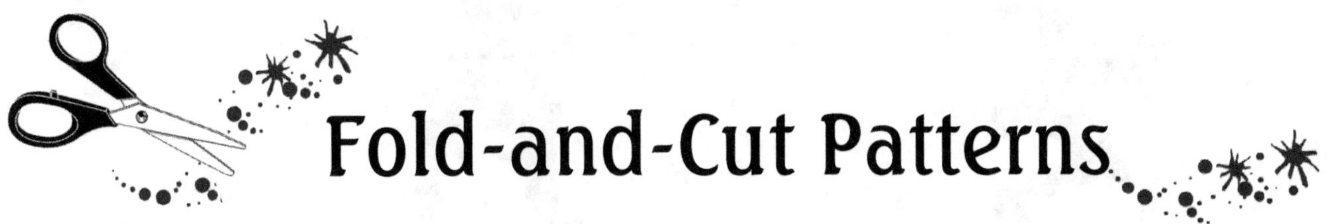

Fold-and-Cut Patterns

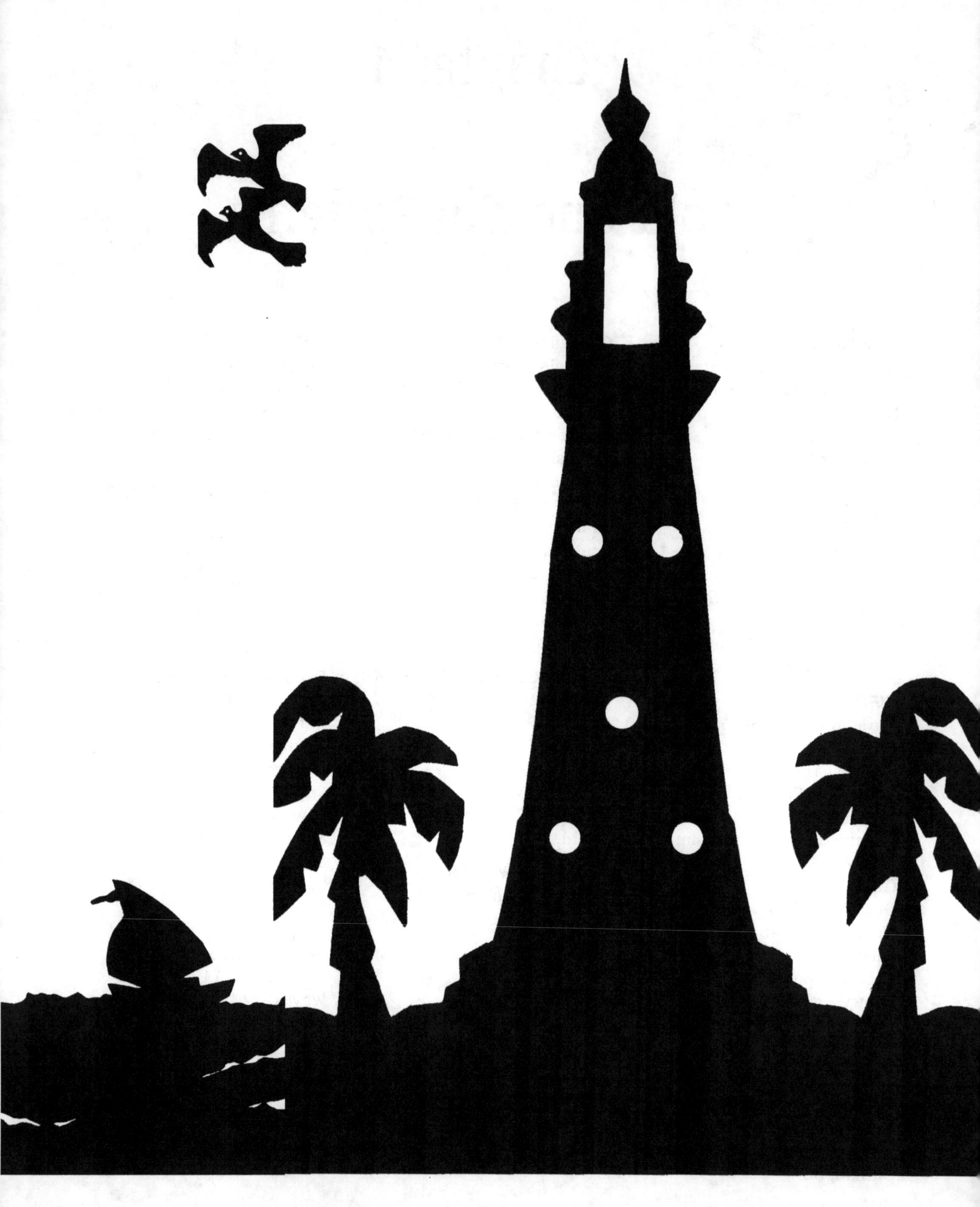

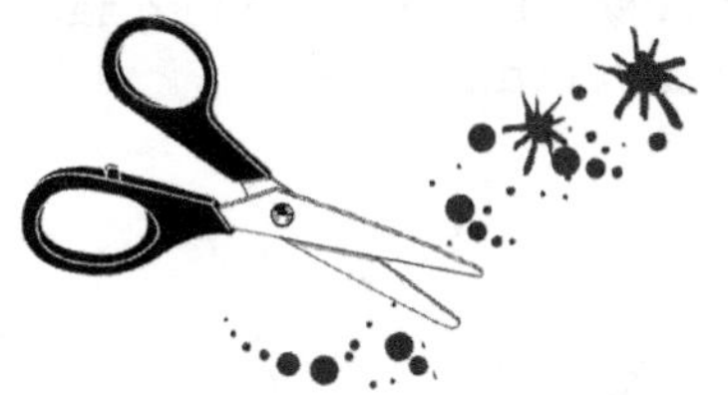

Lighthouses

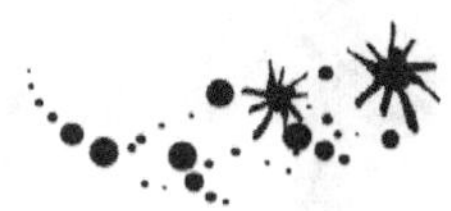

Lighthouses: Sentinels of light on the far horizon to warn the mariners of the treacherous shoals and reefs, of the ominous rocks and waves ahead, or of the safe harbor they had long awaited. Thousands of vessels have been lost to the fathoms of the deep. Countless lives were swept to a watery grave in hurricanes, ice, wind, squalls, shallows, reefs, and pirates. The lighthouse always was and is yet today, a story waiting to be told and a welcome sight to ships at sea.

Want to learn more? See full references in the Bibliography!

FOLD-AND-CUT PATTERNS

Amelia Island Lighthouse
Cape Canaveral Lighthouse
Cape Canaveral Lighthouse Circle
Carysfort Reef Light
East Brother Light
Egmont Key
Lightship Overfalls
Old Port Boca Grande (Gasparilla) Lighthouse
Plymouth Bay Twinlight Beacon
St. Augustine Light
St. Johns Lighthouse

BOOKS AND STORIES

Ancient City Hauntings: More Ghosts of St. Augustine by Dave Lapham
The Ghosts of Black Point High by Penn Millen
Guardians of the Lights: Stories of the U.S. Lighthouse Keepers by Elinor De Wire
The Legend of Gasparilla, A Tale for all Ages by James Kaserman
The Lighthouse Activity Book by Elinor De Wire
The Lighthouse Encyclopedia: The Definitive Reference by Ray Jones
The Lighthouse Family: The Storm by Cynthia Rylant
The Lighthouse Keeper's Daughter by Arielle Olson
Rowing to the Rescue: The Story of Ida Lewis, Famous Lighthouse Heroine by Doris Licameli

Amelia Island Lighthouse

Located on Amelia Island, Florida, a former haven for pirates, smugglers and slave traders in 1839 in this lighthouse. Of classical Victorian architecture, 105 feet above sea level, the beacon can be seen by mariners at sea for up to 23 miles.

Guide to Florida Lighthouses, 19, 20
Southern Lighthouses, 68, 69

- ★ Easy.
- ✂ Double, Multi-image or 3-Dimensional
- ✂ Follow directions on page 6, 7, or 9.
- ✂ Tape the pattern in place or make a light pencil tracing.
- ✂ Use a large hole paper punch to open the area for the window and the spaces near the tree, then finish cutting.

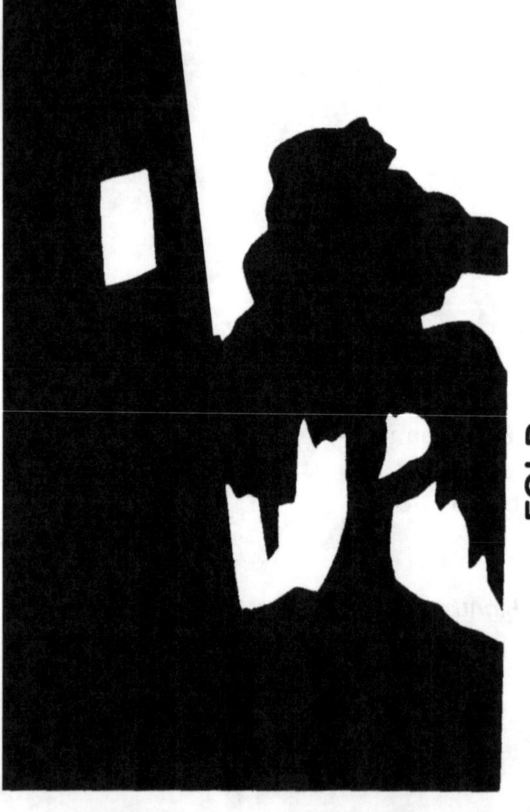

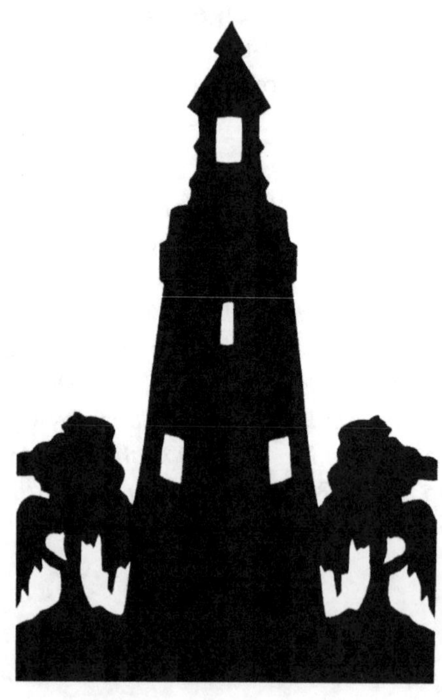

Cape Canaveral Lighthouse

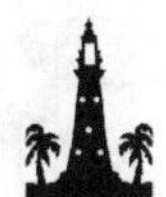

You can tour this sentinel at Cape Canaveral, Florida, on the Kennedy Spaceport bus tour. The first structure was built in 1848. Now the black and white brick tower with iron plates and a concrete base is a relocatable structure that can be dismantled and moved if the shoreline erodes again. It is a beacon to land, sea and air.

Guide to Florida Lighthouses, 35-38
The Lighthouse Encyclopedia: The Definitive Reference, 35-38
Southern Lighthouses, 70, 71

★★ Intermediate.
✂ Double, Multi-image or 3-Dimensional.
✂ Follow directions on page 6, 7, or 9.
✂ Tape the pattern in place or make a light pencil tracing.
✂ Use a large hole paper punch for the windows.

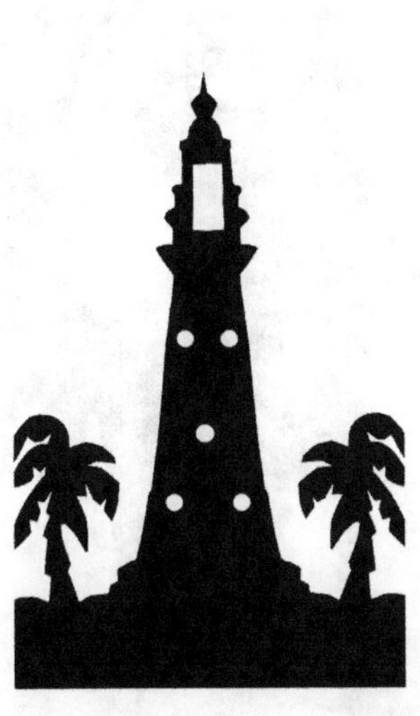

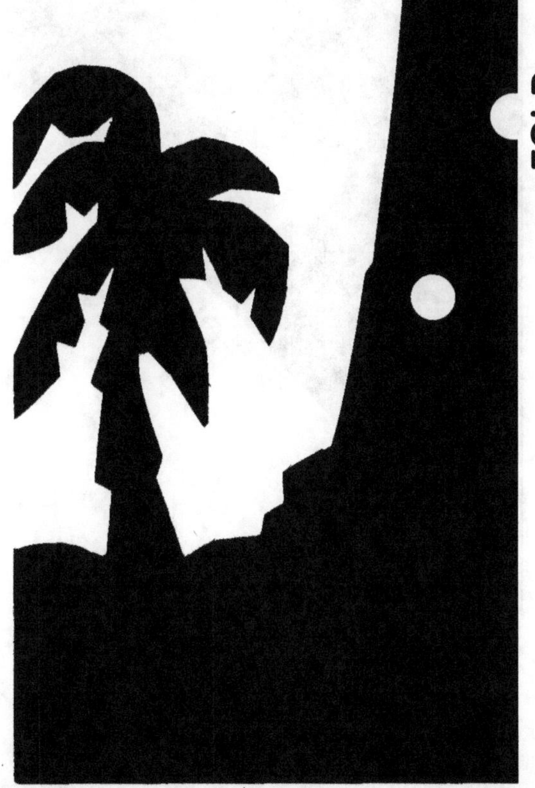

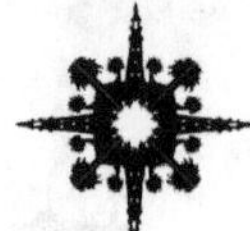

Cape Canaveral Lighthouse Circle

- ★★ Intermediate.
- ✂ Circle fold.
- ✂ Follow directions on page 10.
- ✂ Tape the pattern in place or make a light pencil tracing.
- ✂ Use a small hole paper punch for the windows.
- ☺ Let your paper do the turning.
- ☺ Cut away the smaller areas first. This gives you more paper area to hold as you cut.
- ☺ Unique compass design.

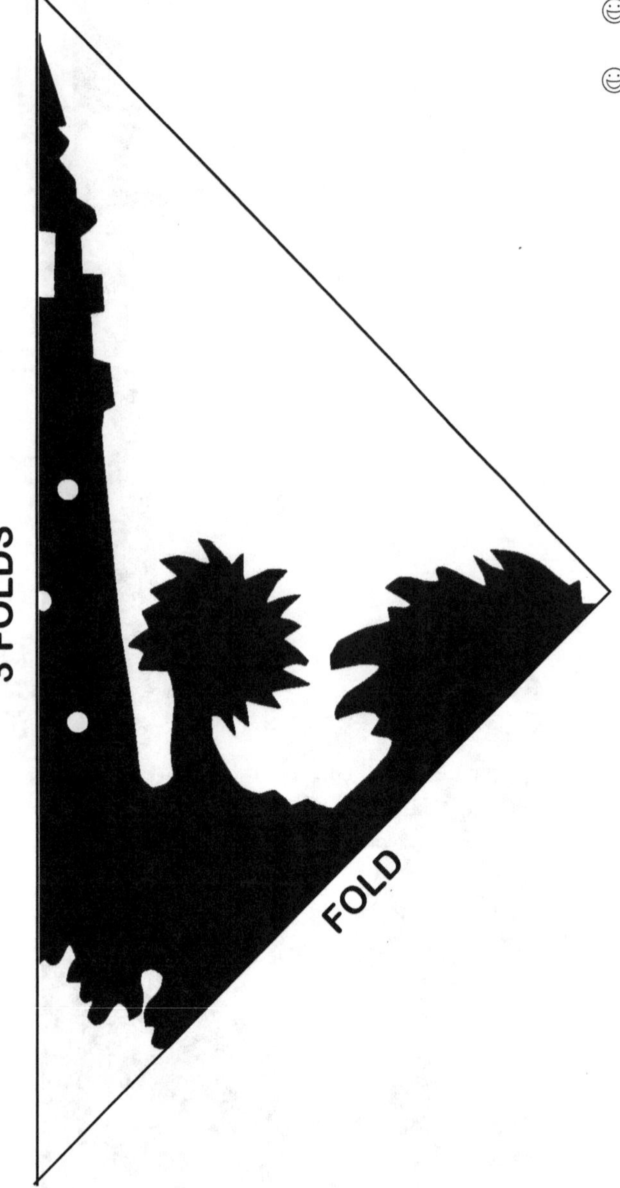

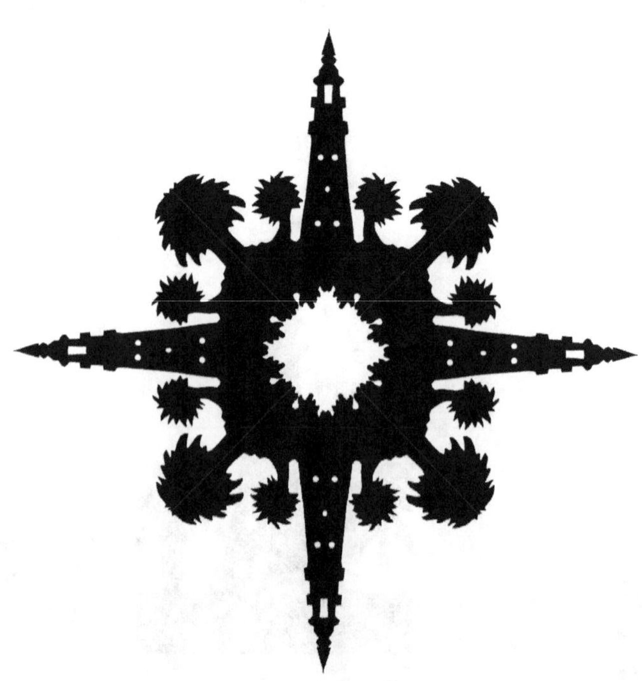

Carysfort Reef Light

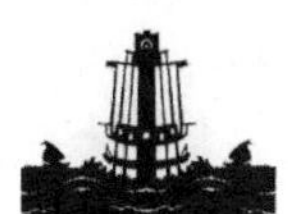

The Atlantic Florida Keys are known as the "Graveyard of the Atlantic" due to treacherous reefs and shoals. The reefs and shoals of the Keys are named for some of the sailing vessels that sank. Carysfort Reef, near Key Largo, Florida, with its steel-skeleton tower, was established in 1852. It is anchored to the coral bottom and sand with screw piles. The tower is 100 feet above the waves and the beacon can be seen for 15 miles.

Learn more! See full references in the Bibliography!

The Lighthouse Encyclopedia: The Definitive Reference, 30, 83, 84, 100, 112, 168-169

⋆⋆⋆ Advanced.
✂ Single image.
✂ Follow directions on page 5.
✂ Tape the pattern in place or make a light pencil tracing.
✂ Cut the outline of the lighthouse first; this gives you solid paper to hold on to until the last.
✂ Use a small hole paper punch for the openings to cut the windows and area where the poles are.
✂ Now use either small scissors or an xacto knife to make the pole cuts.
☺ The waves in the center are cut by folding on the dotted line and then cutting across the line.

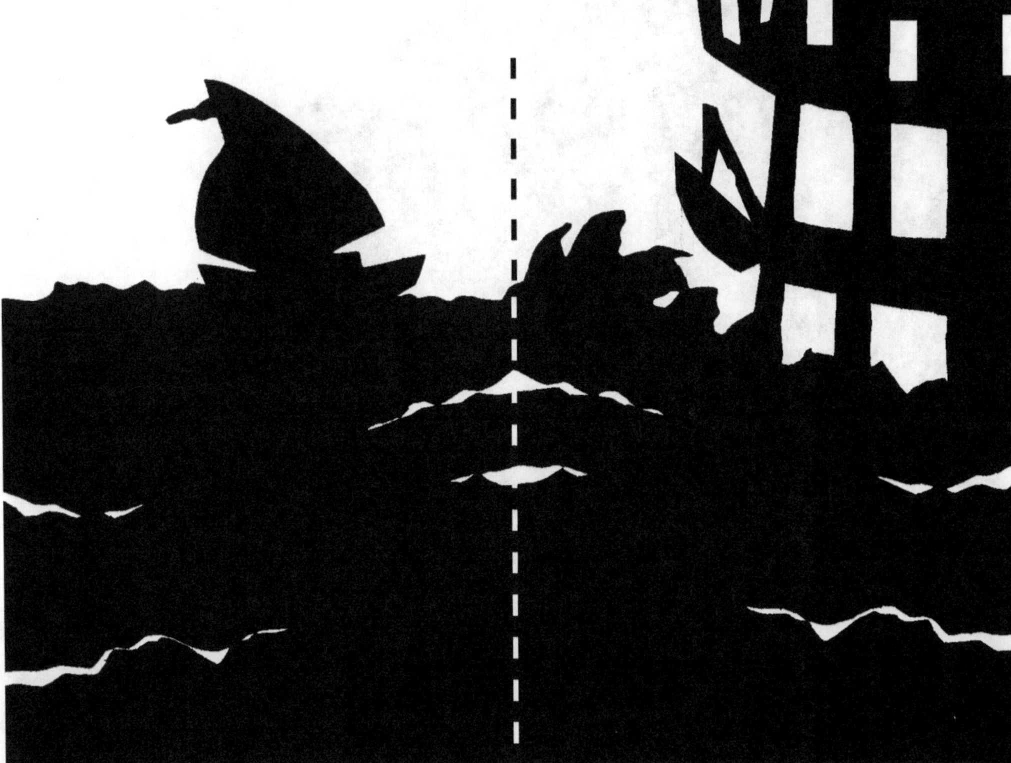

East Brother Light

Located on the Pacific Coast near Richmond, California, this golden beacon guides ships through the San Francisco Bay. Standing like a lonely sentinel to the mariners since 1874, it has a focal elevation of 61 feet.

The Lighthouse Encyclopedia: The Definitive Reference, 35, 112, 113, 178

★★ Intermediate.
✂ Single image.
✂ Follow directions on page 5.
✂ Tape the pattern in place or make a light pencil tracing.
✂ Use a small hole paper punch to open the window so you can finish cutting it.

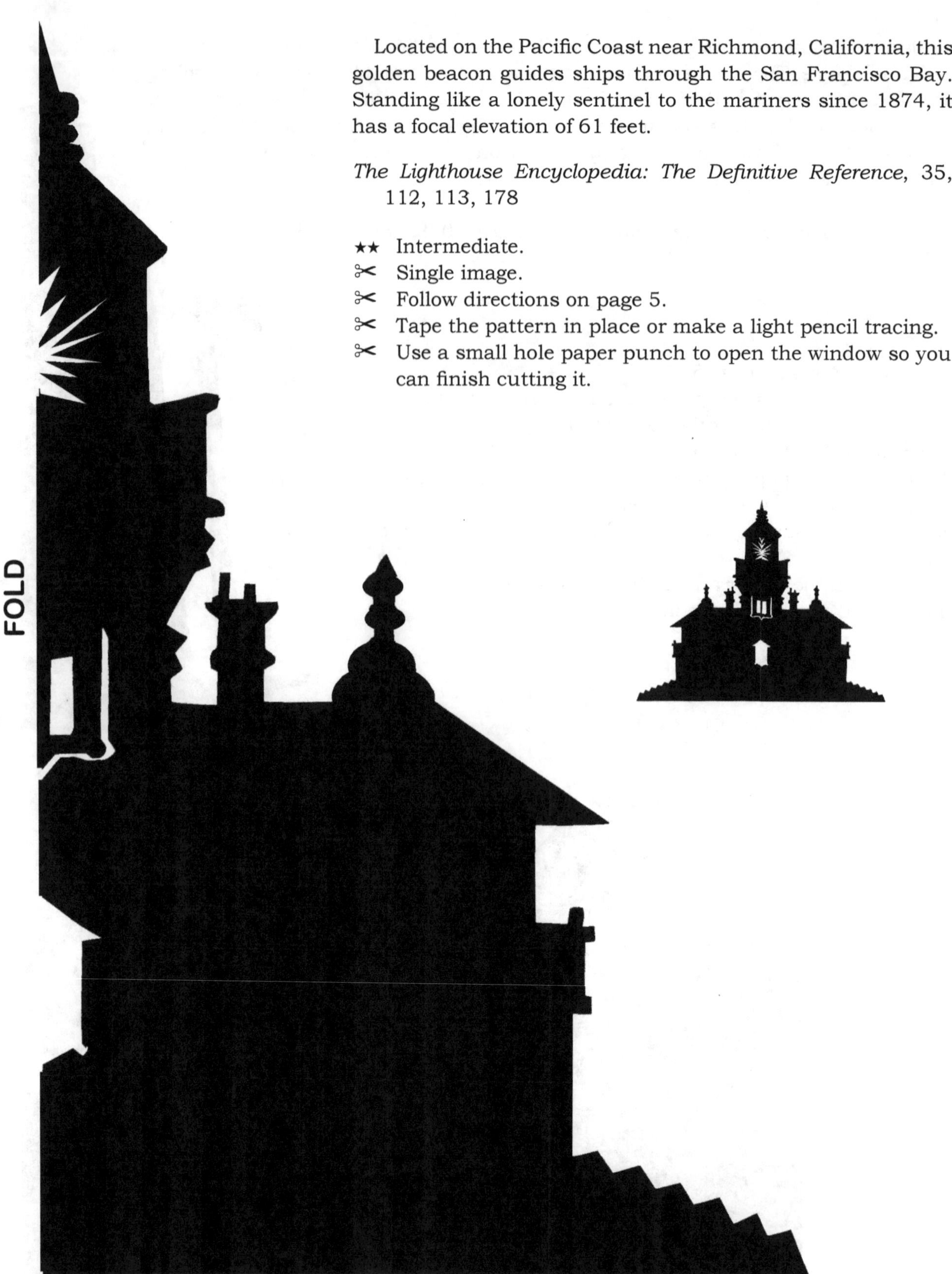

Egmont Key

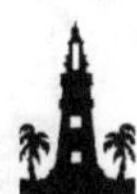

Hernando De Soto anchored in the seas of the Gulf coast of the SW Channel keys in Florida in 1539 and took his voyage from Tampa to the Mississippi. By 1848 a small lighthouse was built. Hurricanes and wars have darkened the light at times, but today with it's 85-foot tower and fog horn, it can send a warning 22 miles out to sea.

Guide to Florida Lighthouses, 76, 77, 78

- ★ Quick and easy.
- ✂ Single fold image or 3-Dimensional.
- ✂ Follow directions on page 5 or 9.
- ✂ Tape the pattern in place or make a light pencil tracing.
- ☺ Stand-up model, border, or in the window, this lighthouse is a striking sight.

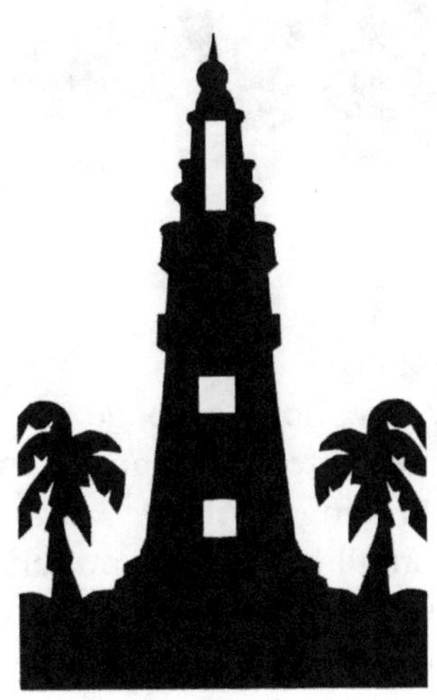

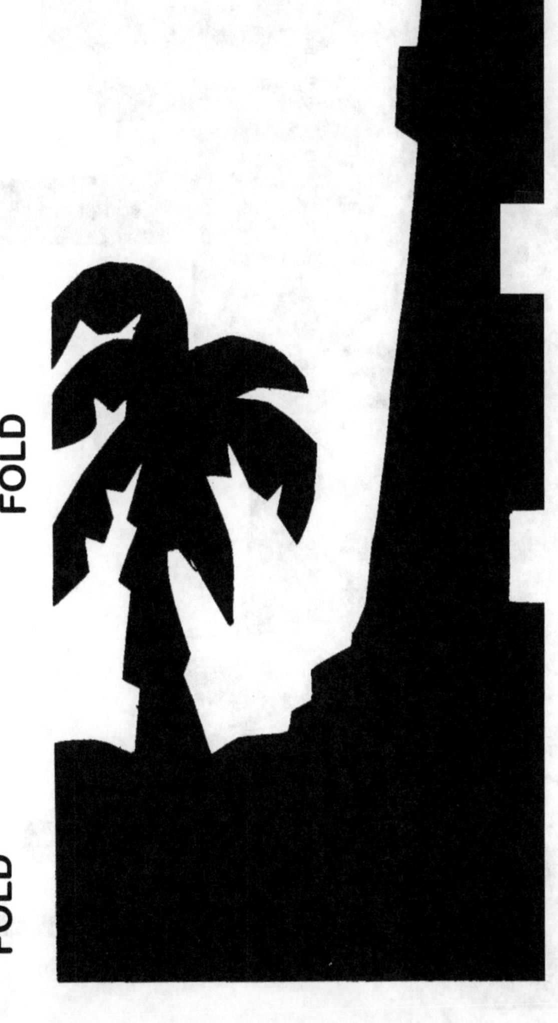

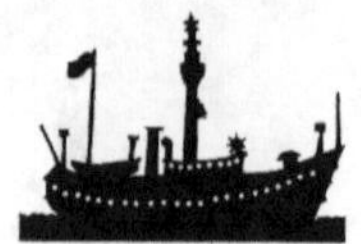

Lightship Overfalls

A lightship like the Overfalls was a floating lighthouse with beacons from the tall central mast that was stationed in Delaware Bay, Delaware. They marked shoals, construction areas, and key navigational points. In 1983 lightships were taken out of service.

The Lighthouse Encyclopedia: The Definitive Reference, 110, 111, 112

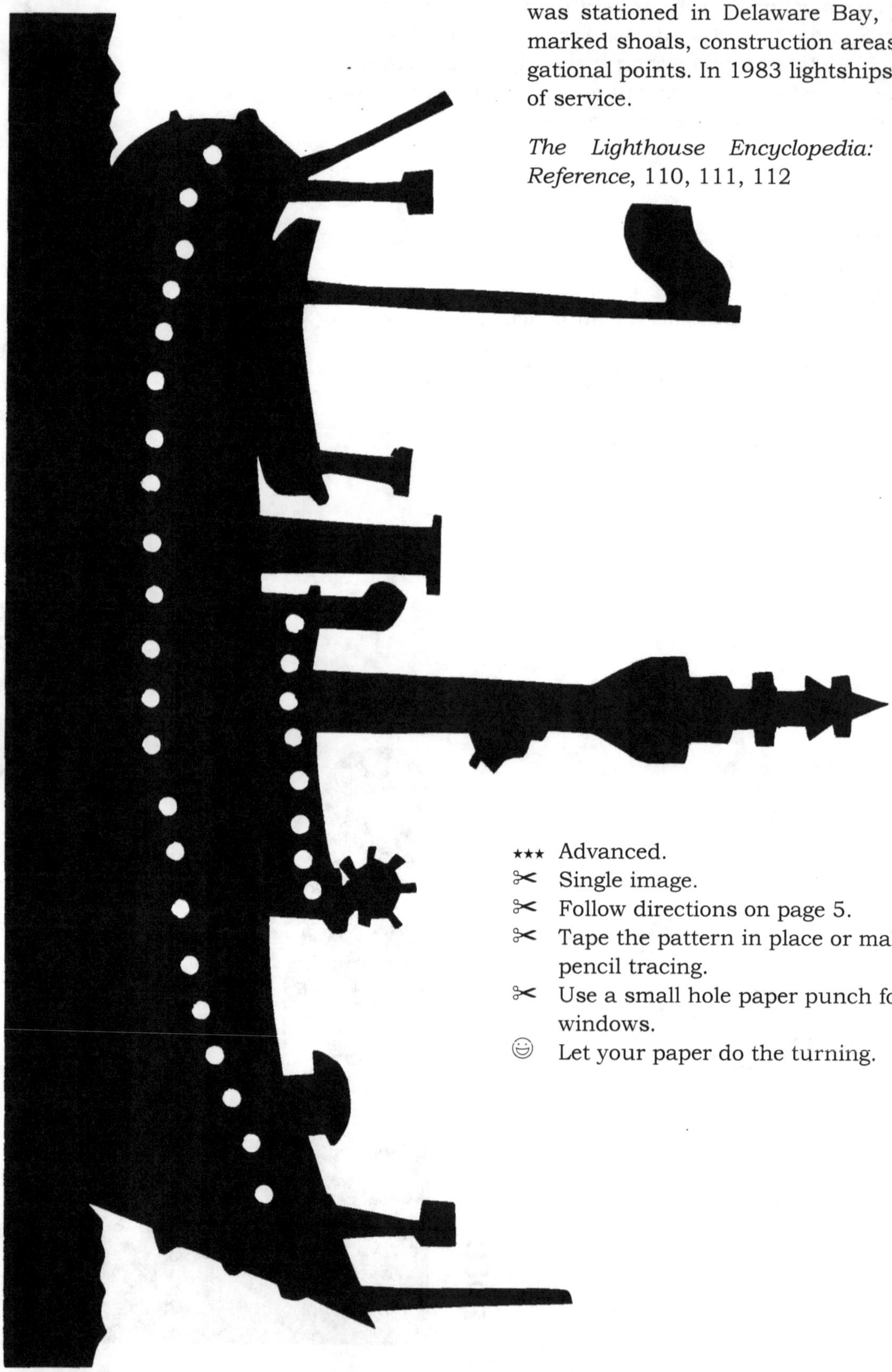

FOLD

- ★★★ Advanced.
- ✂ Single image.
- ✂ Follow directions on page 5.
- ✂ Tape the pattern in place or make a light pencil tracing.
- ✂ Use a small hole paper punch for the windows.
- ☺ Let your paper do the turning.

Old Port Boca Grande (Gasparilla) Lighthouse

Jose Gaspar, a bloodthirsty pirate, looted and pillaged the merchant ships off the Florida coast. A Spanish princess was beheaded by Gaspar in a fit of rage. It is said that her ghost still combs the beach. Gasparilla Island, Florida, is named for him. In 1890, a lighthouse was built on the island. An iron pile Rear Range Lighthouse was built to aid harbor traffic.

Guide to Florida Lighthouses, 70, 71, 73, 74
Southern Lighthouses, 76, 77

★★★ Advanced.
✂ Double or Multi-image.
✂ Follow directions on page 6 or 7.
✂ Tape the pattern in place or make a light pencil tracing.
✂ Use a large hole paper punch to open up the windows and stair section. Then use small scissors to cut out the windows.
✂ Use a rectangular punch for the beam over the door.

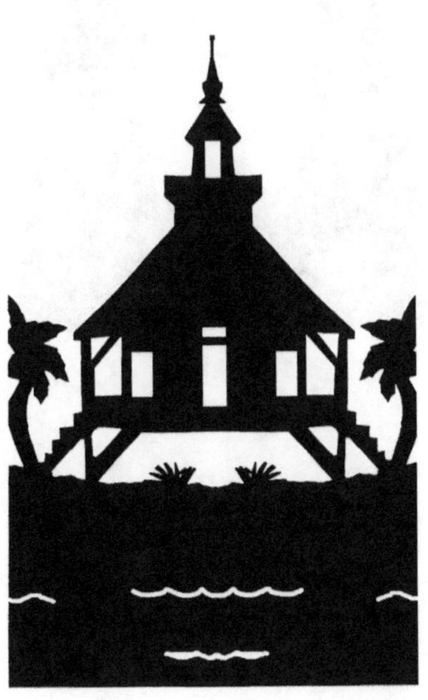

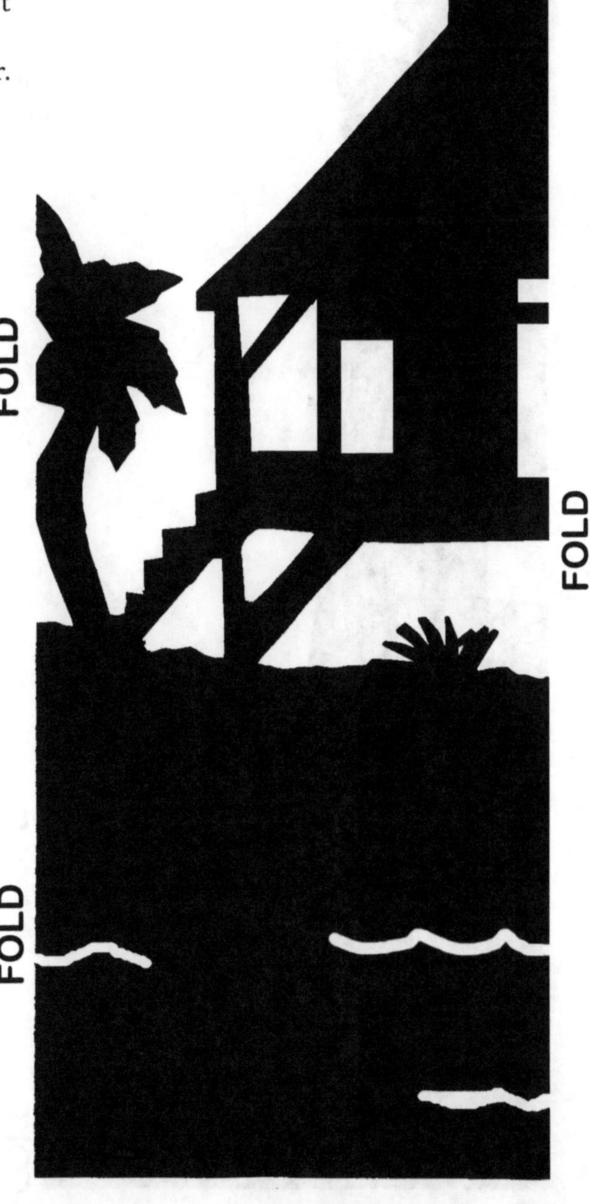

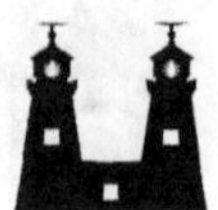

Plymouth Bay Twinlight Beacon

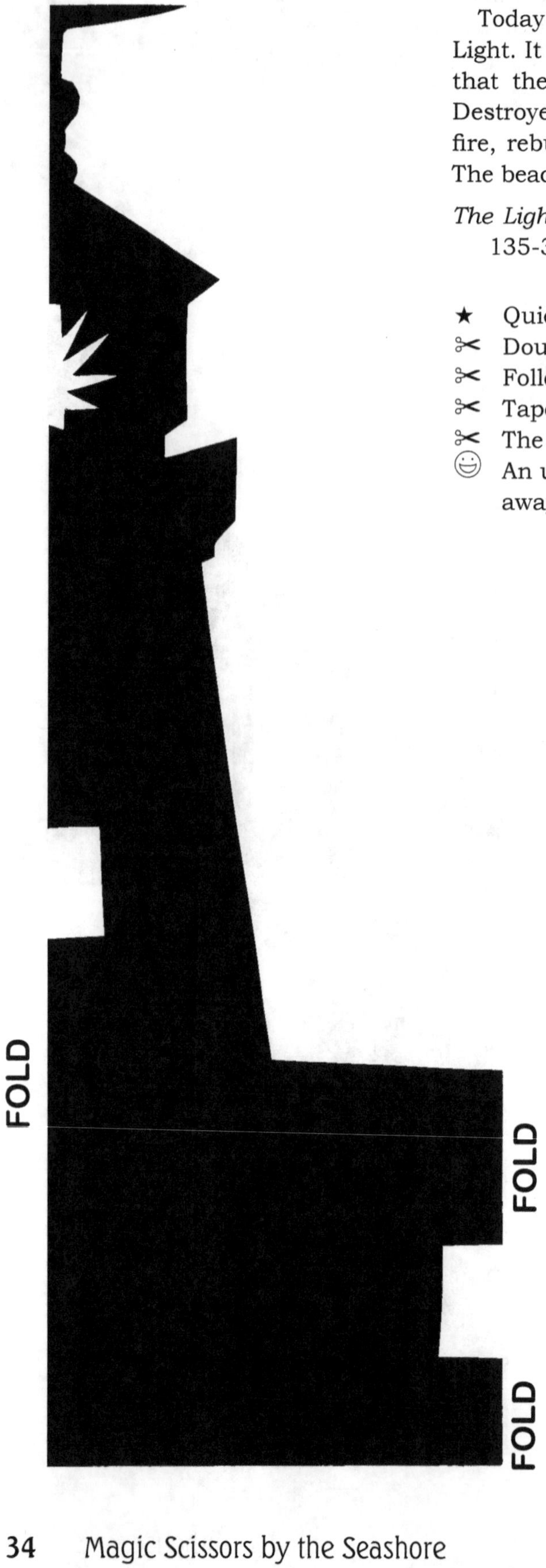

Today in Plymouth Bay, Massachusetts, it is called Gurnet Light. It sits where the pilgrims first settled, and it was in 1769 that the first lighthouse was located as a twinlight beacon. Destroyed in the Revolutionary War, rebuilt and destroyed by fire, rebuilt again in 1924, one of the towers was dismantled. The beacon is now seen for about 16 miles.

The Lighthouse Encyclopedia: The Definitive Reference, 16, 75, 135-36, 223

- ★ Quick and easy.
- ✂ Double or Multi-image.
- ✂ Follow directions on page 6 or 7.
- ✂ Tape the pattern in place or make a light pencil tracing.
- ✂ The center building connects the two lighthouses.
- ☺ An unusual cut, shape the outer tower sides by cutting away the extra building on the right and left.

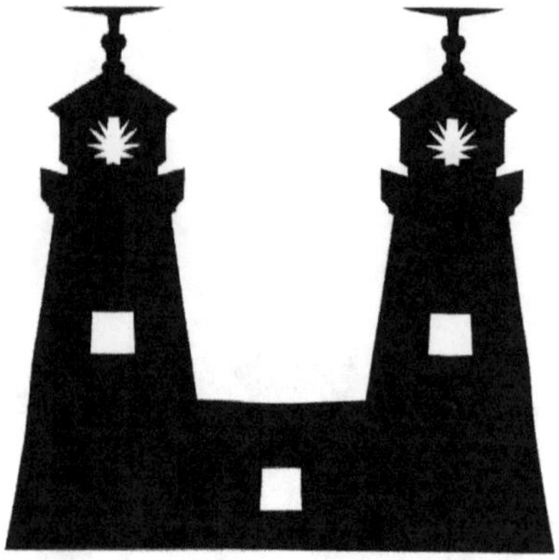

FOLD

FOLD

FOLD

St. Augustine Light

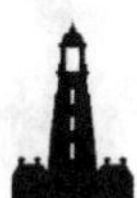

Ponce de Leon first erected a 40 foot stone tower, with flags, to mark the area in 1513. St. Augustine Light was built in 1823. This was Florida's first lighthouse and the tower is 165 feet. The beacon can be seen 19 miles out at sea.

Guide to Florida Lighthouses, 25, 26, 27
The Lighthouse Encyclopedia: The Definitive Reference, 252, 253, 267

★ Quick and easy.
✂ Double, Multi-image or 3-Dimensional.
✂ Follow directions on page 6, 7, or 9.
✂ Tape the pattern in place or make a light pencil tracing.

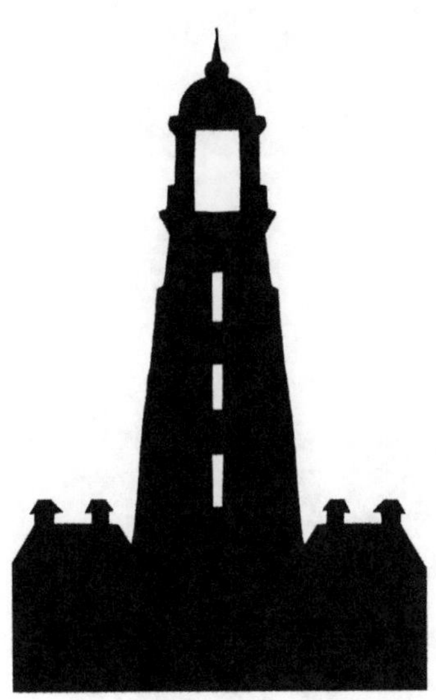

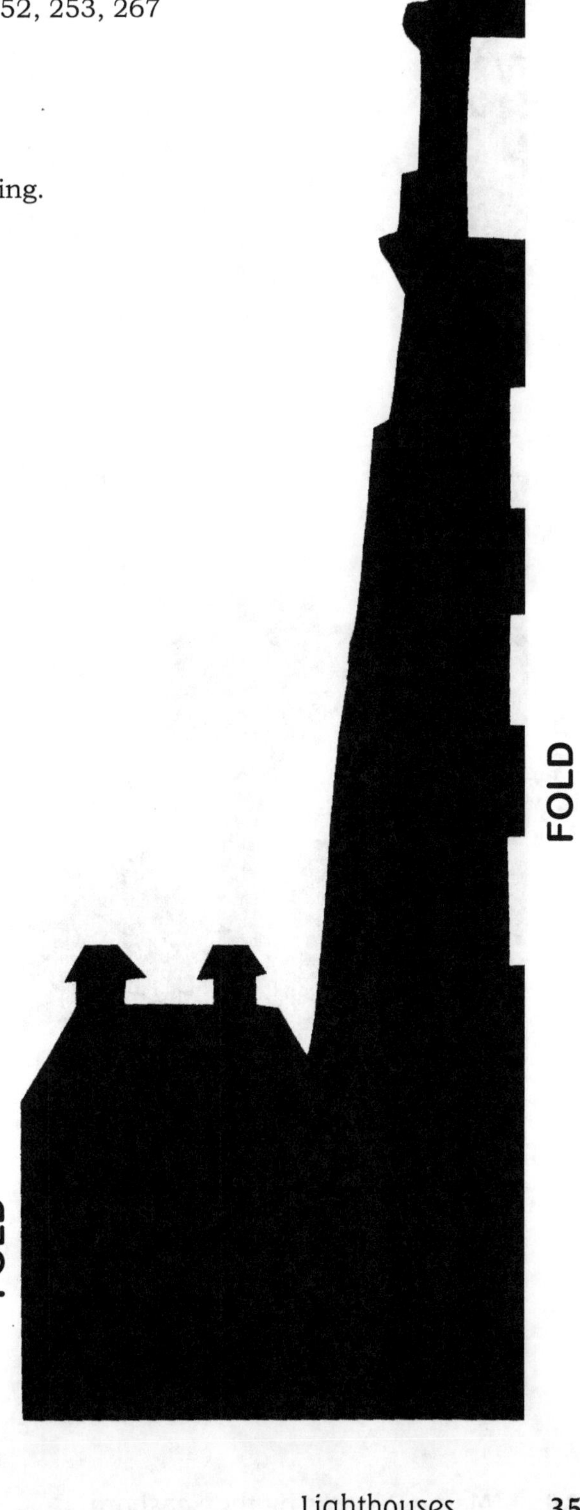

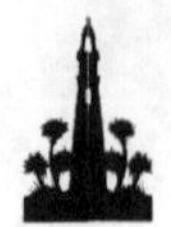

St. Johns Lighthouse

On the St. Johns River and Mayport Naval Station, Florida, we find two lighthouses. The old brick cylinder watched through the fog from 1858 and is no longer in operation. Mayport Lighthouse is a square tower that was illuminated in 1954.

Guide to Florida Lighthouses, 21-24

- ★★ Intermediate.
- ✂ Double, Multi-image or 3-Dimensional.
- ✂ Follow directions on page 6, 7, or 9.
- ✂ Tape the pattern in place or make a light pencil tracing.
- ✂ Use a large hole paper punch in the areas between the palm tree and lighthouse.
- ✂ Use small scissors to cut away remaining paper in tight areas.

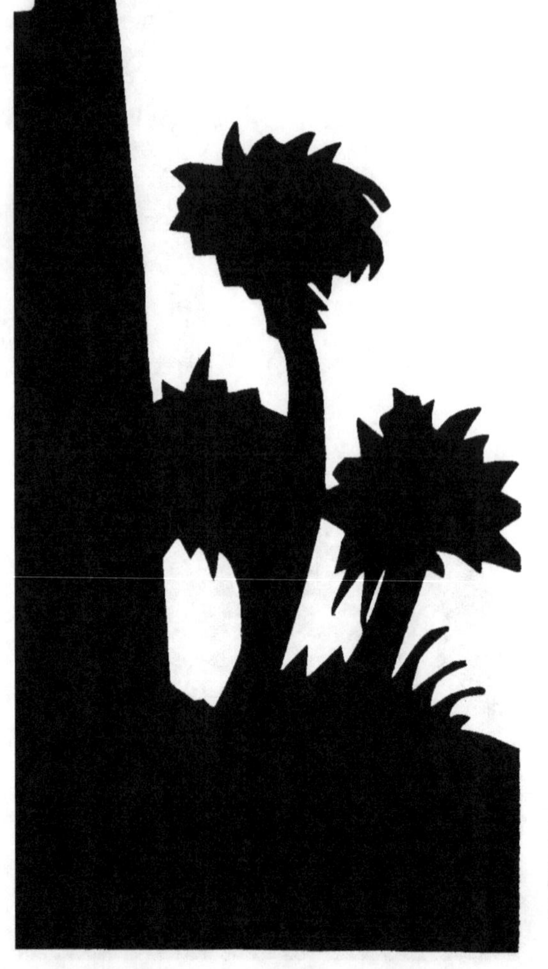

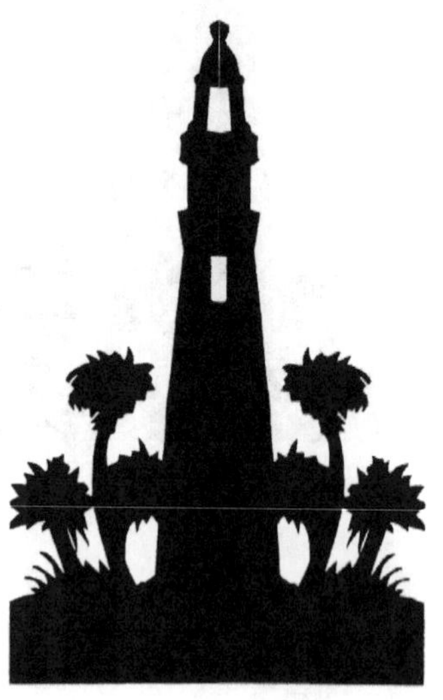

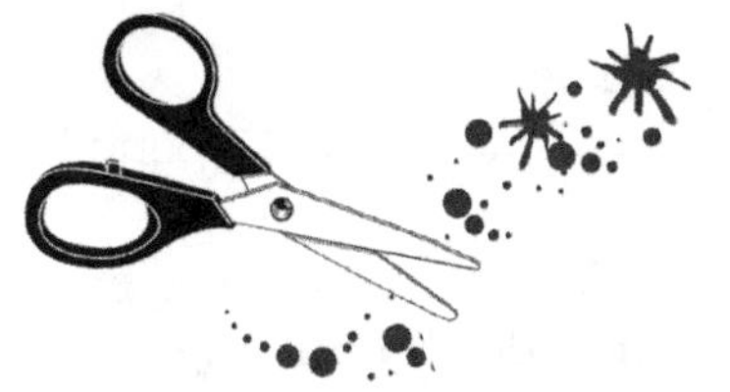

Birds

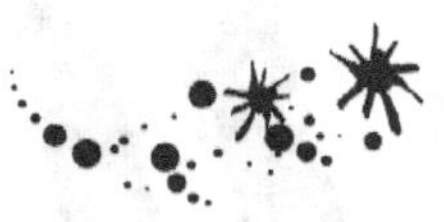

Birds: The habitat of a bird varies by the 967 different species and their location in the world. They are classified into families. Large wading birds have long legs, a flexible neck and feed on a large variety of prey, such as mice, crabs, shorebirds and frogs, as well as fish. Some birds feed on invertebrates, insects and other aquatic life, which they probe from the mud. They all nest in some form and lay eggs. The forelimbs are modified to form wings. Bird life in America has declined with the destruction of their habitat, expanded human population, hunting and other hazards. Many species are protected or endangered.

Want to learn more? See full references in the Bibliography

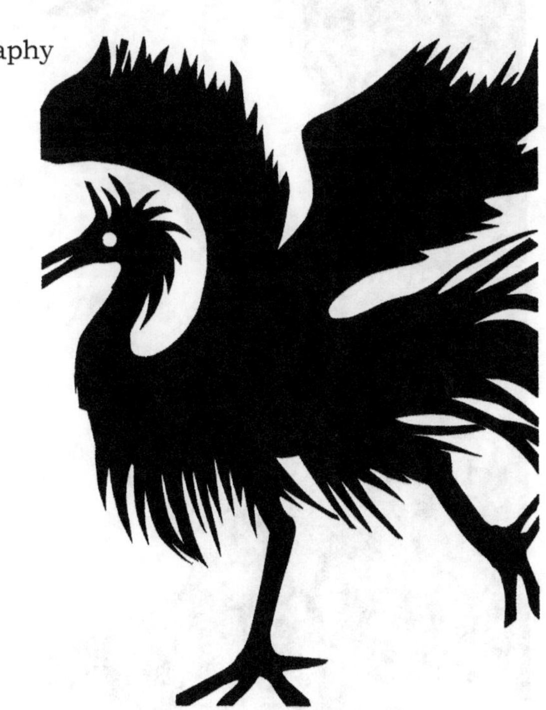

FOLD-AND-CUT PATTERNS

Birds in a Nest
Black Vulture
Double Crested Cormorant
Eagle with Fish
Flamingo
Flamingo Circle with Palm Trees
Gull
Gulls in a Flock
Mockingbird
Pelican
Roseate Spoonbill
Snowy Egret
White Ibis
White Ibis Circle
Wood Stork

BOOKS AND STORIES

The Adventures of Pelican Pete: Annie the River Otter #4 by Frances Keiser & Hugh Keiser
The Adventures of Pelican Pete: A Bird is Born #1 by Frances Keiser & Hugh Keiser
The Adventures of Pelican Pete: First Discoveries #3 by Frances Keiser & Hugh Keiser
The Adventures of Pelican Pete: Preening for Flight #2 by Frances Keiser & Hugh Keiser
The Adventures of Pelican Pete: Un Ave Nace (Spanish #1) by Frances Keiser & Hugh Keiser
Bird Woman: Sacajawea's Own Story (Lewis and Clark Expedition) by James Willard Schultz
Birds of America: Stories by Lorrie Moore
The Boy Who Drew Birds: A Story of John James Audubon by Jacqueline Davies
The Burgess Bird Book for Children by Thornton W. Burgess
Night Bird: A Story of the Seminole Indians (Once Upon America) by Kathleen V. Kudenski
The Story of the Seagull and the Cat Who Taught Her to Fly by Luis Sepulvada
When Birds Could Talk and Bats Could Sing by Virginia Hamilton and Barry Moser

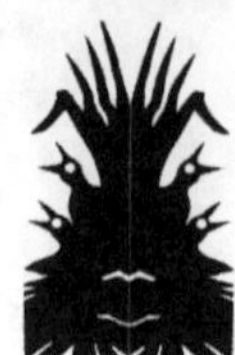

Birds in a Nest

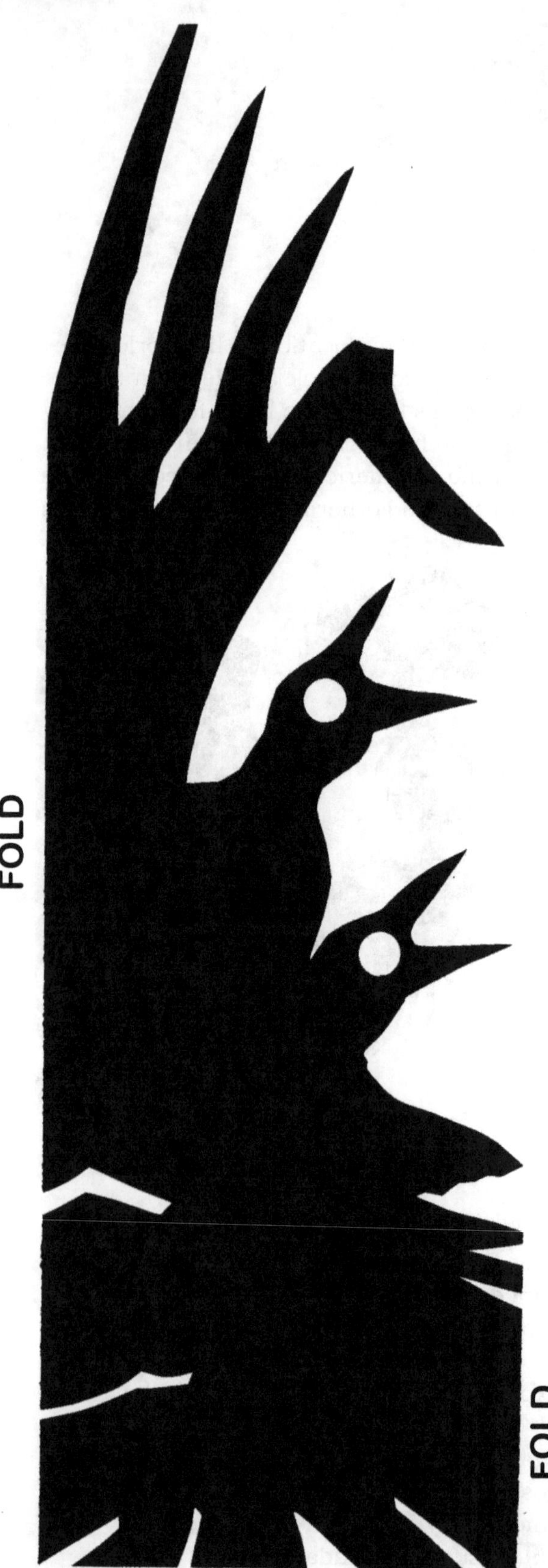

- ★ Quick and easy.
- ✂ Multi-image.
- ✂ Follow the directions on page 7.
- ✂ Tape the pattern in place or make a light pencil tracing.
- ✂ Use a large hole paper punch to make the eyes.
- ☺ Remember to let your paper do the turning.

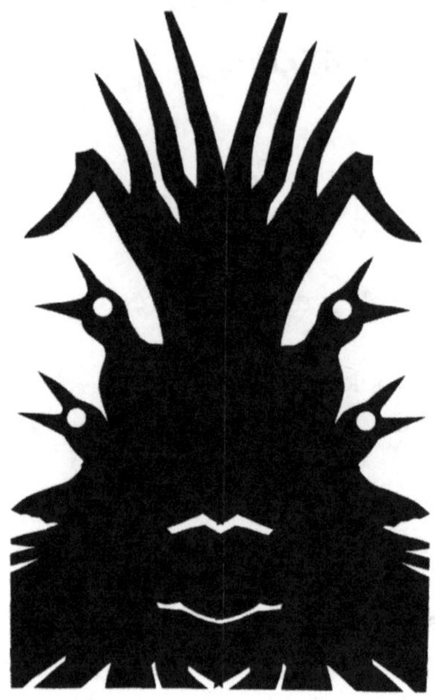

Black Vulture

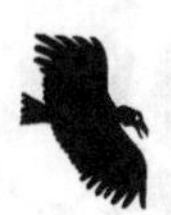

The head of the vulture is black skin and has no feathers while the body has black feathers. The sharp hooked beak is for tearing apart the carrion (dead animals) that it feeds on. They have excellent eyesight and smell. In flight it can be distinguished by the white "windows" (feathers) at the base of the wingspan. Their wingspan is 54 inches. The tail is short and stubby. They are often seen alongside the road hunting for roadkill. The vulture is quite common in Florida. There are 7 species of New World vultures.

Birds of Southern Florida, 28
Eagle and Birds of Prey, 8-13, 15, 17, 18, 24, 25, 28-31, 34-35
Florida's Fabulous Birds: Land Birds: Their Stories, 86, 87, 88
Smithsonian Handbooks of Birds of Florida, 80, 81
Vultures, 6-48

- ★ Quick and easy.
- ✂ Double or Multi-image.
- ✂ Follow directions on page 6 or 7.
- ✂ Tape the pattern in place or make a light pencil tracing.
- ✂ Use a small hole paper punch for the eyes.

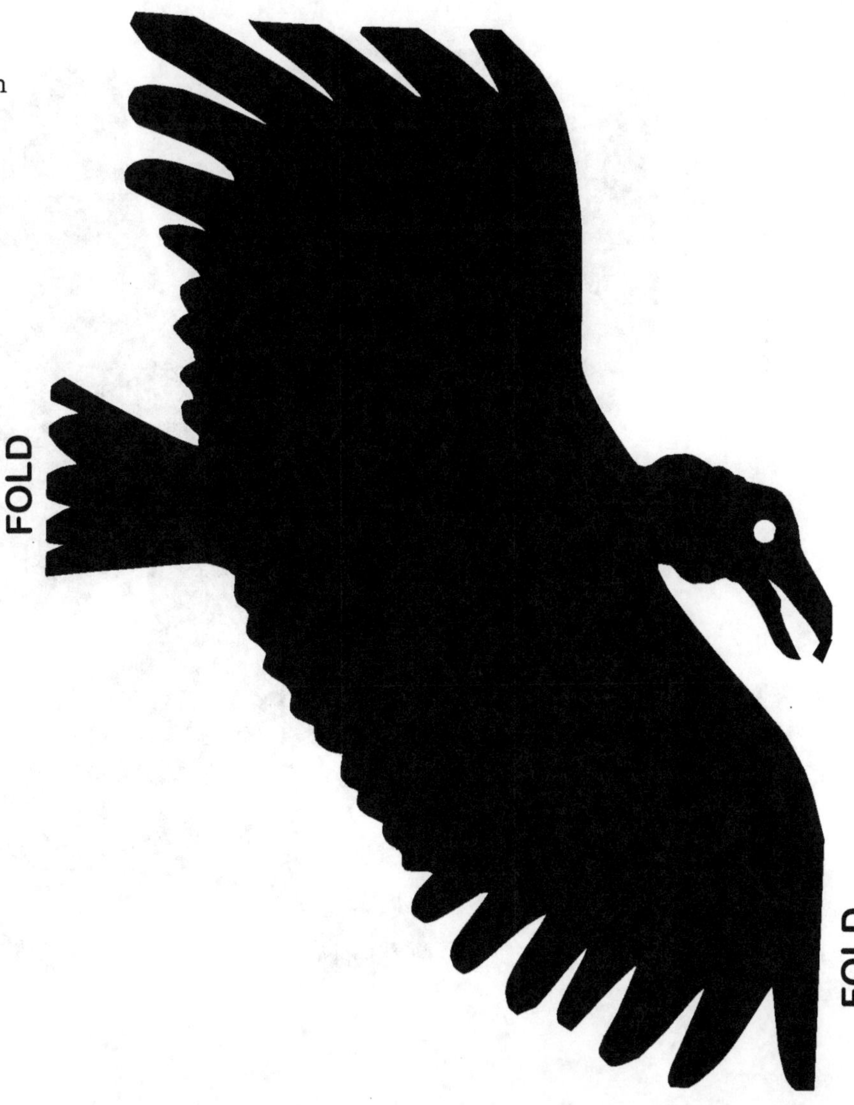

Double Crested Cormorant

This bird is unusual in that it must dry its feathers in the wind. The feathers are not waterproof and it doesn't have oil glands that are well developed. Their feathers are black to dark brown and they have a wing span of about four feet.

Birds of Southern Florida, 19
Florida's Fabulous Waterbirds: Their Stories, 5
Smithsonian Handbooks of Birds of Florida, 60

- ★ Quick and Easy.
- ✂ Multi-image.
- ✂ Follow directions on page 7.
- ✂ Tape the pattern in place or make a light pencil tracing.
- ☺ Looks difficult but is so simple to cut.
- ✂ Use a small hole paper punch for the eye.

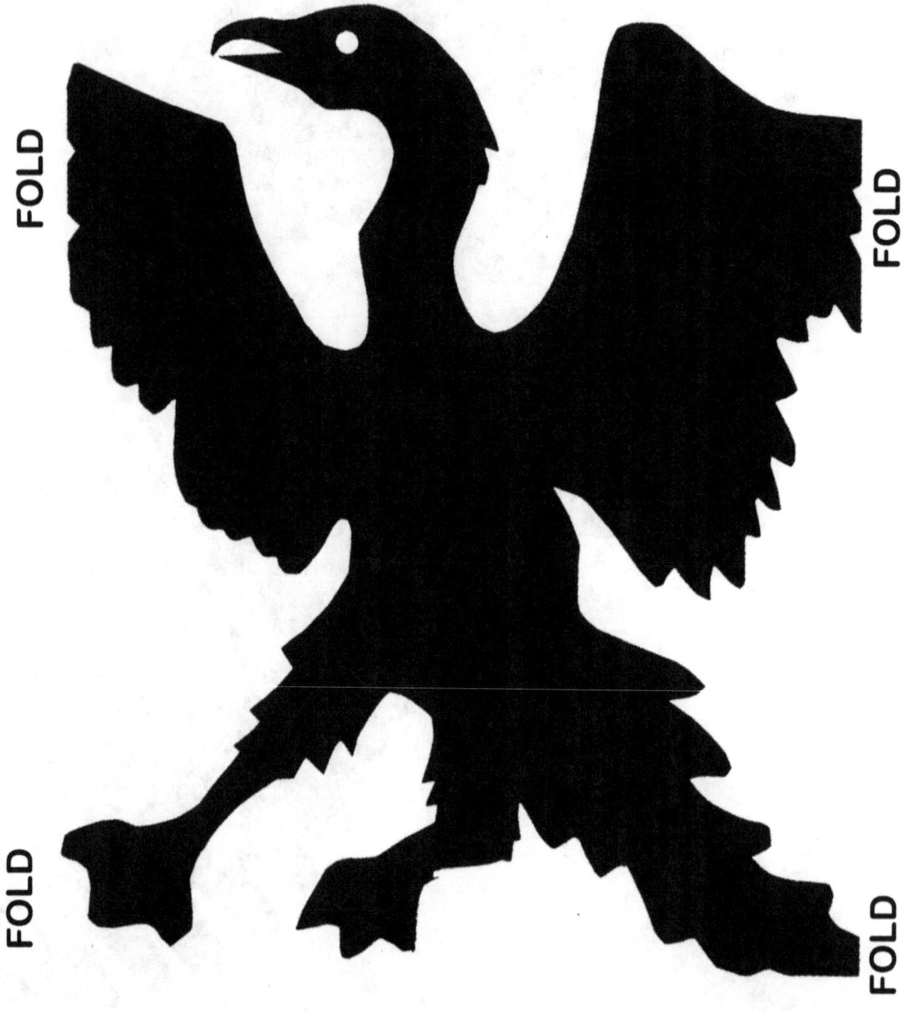

Eagle with Fish

Our national bird, the bald eagle is a raptor or bird of prey. A mature bird has a feathered white head and tail, with brown body and wings. The talons are long and strong for snatching prey. The bill is large and curved. Florida has the largest population of bald eagles of any state in the country, except Alaska. (*The Bald Eagle is an endangered species.)

Birds of Southern Florida, 40
Eagle and Birds of Prey, 9, 11-15, 22-27, 29-34, 36, 42, 48, 51, 53, 56, 57, 58
Florida's Fabulous Birds: Land Birds: Their Stories, 71, 72, 73

- ★ Quick and easy.
- ✂ Single or Double image.
- ✂ Follow directions on page 5 or 6.
- ✂ Tape the pattern in place or make a light pencil tracing.
- ✂ Use a small hole paper punch for the eyes.

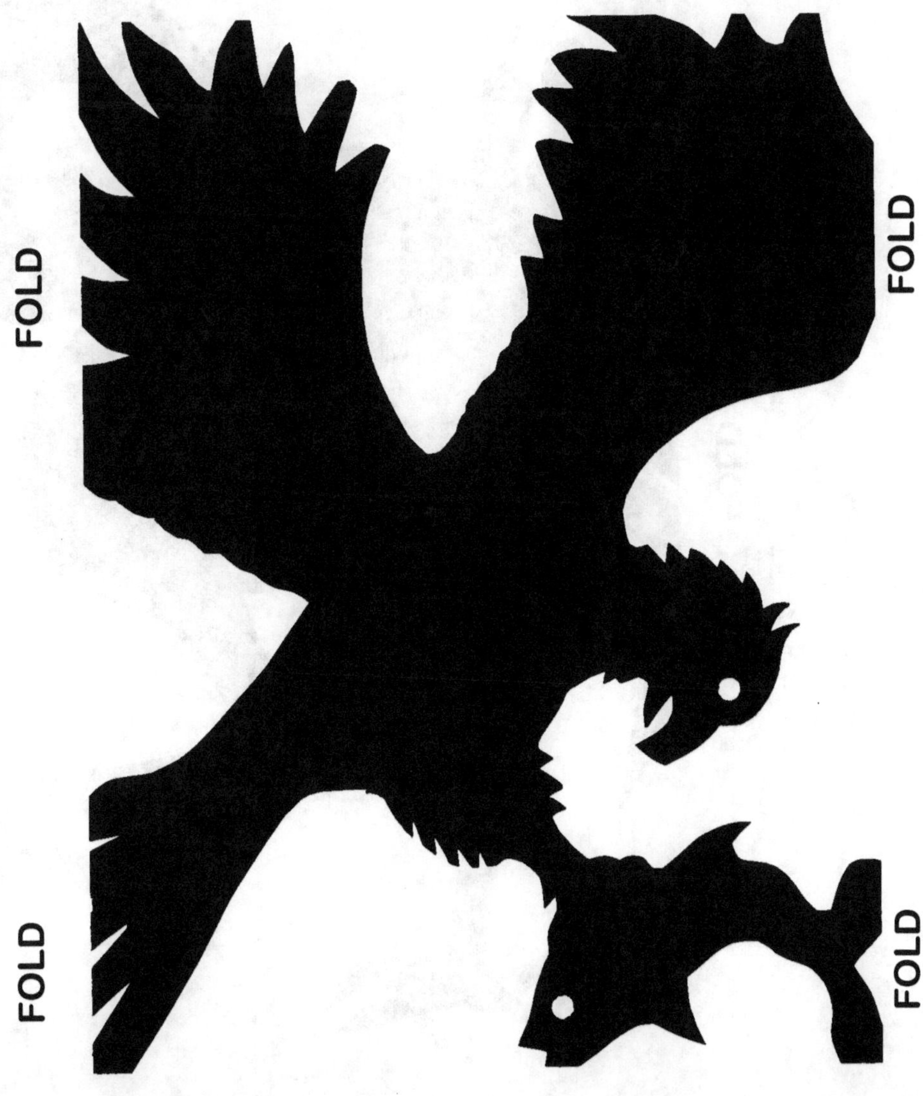

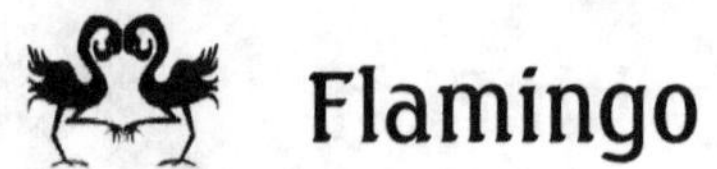

Flamingo

Large pink birds with webbed feet and long pink legs, flamingos have orange and black tipped beaks, bent at an angle that allows them to scoop up and strain small creatures from the water while standing. They even have pink eyes!

Birds of Southern Florida, 29
Florida's Fabulous Waterbirds: Their Stories, 13, 14

★★ Intermediate.
✂ Single or Double image.
✂ Follow directions on page 5 or 6.
✂ Tape the pattern in place or make a light pencil tracing.
✂ Use a small hole paper punch for the eye.
☺ Use hot pink paper for this image.
☺ It is a stunning fold-and-cut enlarged.

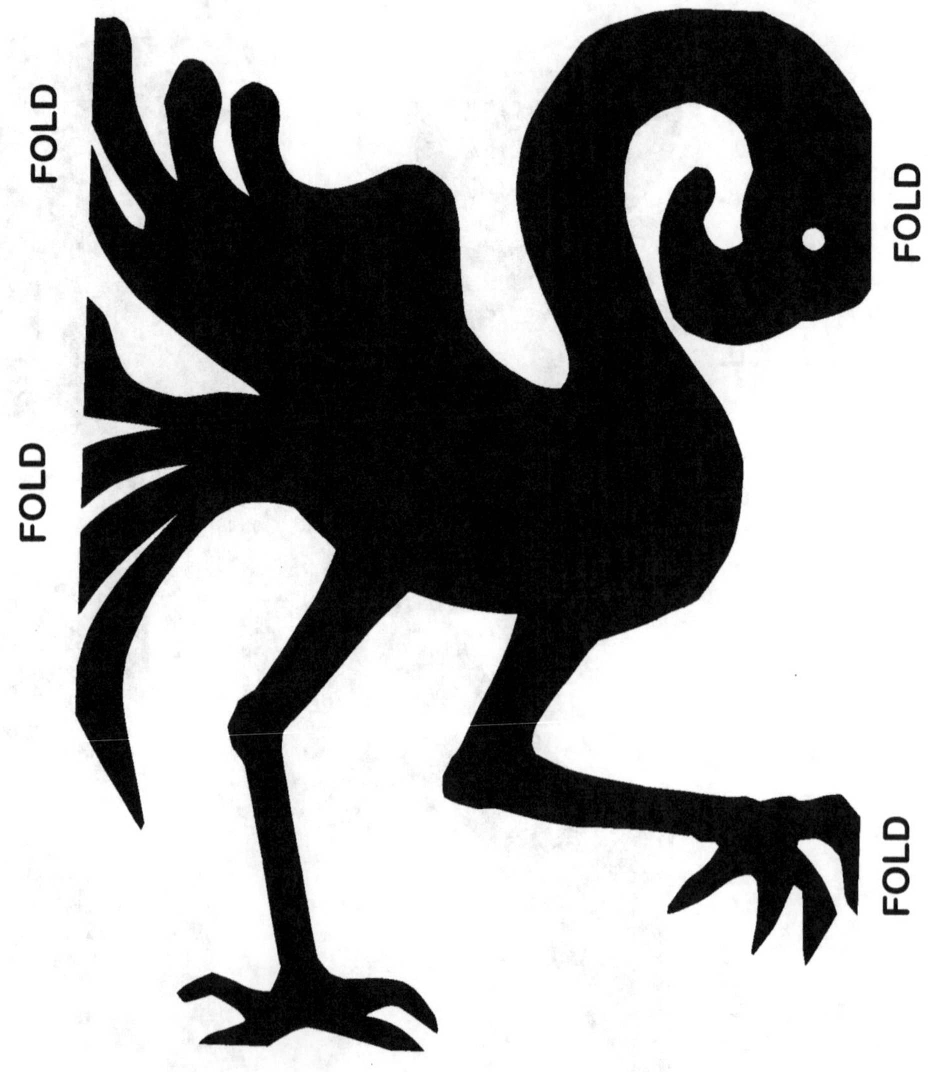

Flamingo Circle with Palm Trees

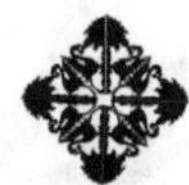

- ★★★ Advanced.
- ✂ Circle fold-and-cut.
- ✂ Follow directions on page 10.
- ✂ Tape the pattern in place or make a light pencil tracing.
- ✂ Use a small hole paper punch for the eyes.
- ✂ Use a large hole paper punch to open up the pattern area between flamingo and palm tree
- ✂ Use your small scissors for the delicate cuts.
- ☺ Let your paper do the turning.
- ☺ Cut away the smaller areas first. This gives you more paper area to hold as you cut.

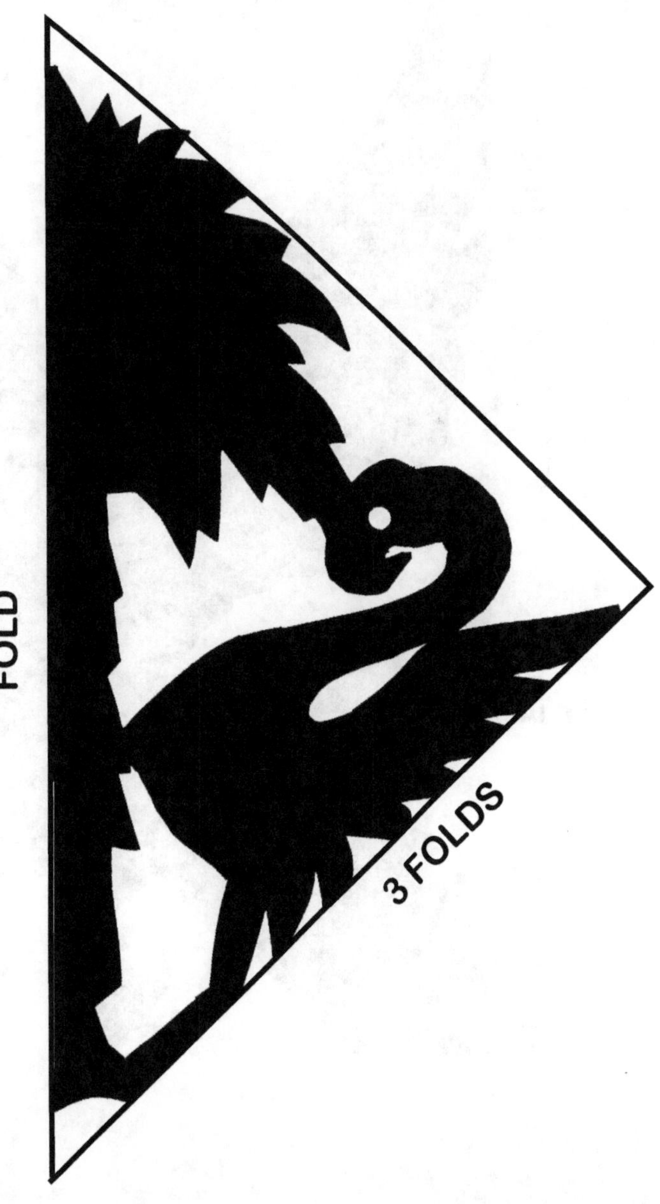

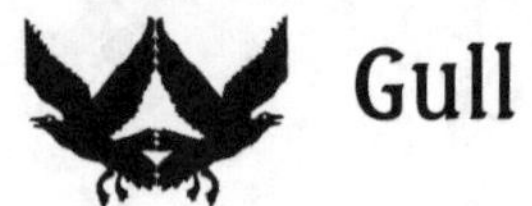

Gull

There is no species known as seagulls, but you'll find many different species and sizes of gulls by the sea. The body is white with black tipped wings and tail. Some have black legs and feet. Gulls gather in flocks.

Birds of Southern Florida, 18, 19, 20
Florida's Fabulous Waterbirds: Their Stories, 18, 19, 20

- ★ Quick and easy.
- ✂ Multi-image or 3-Dimensional.
- ✂ Follow the directions on page 7 or 9.
- ✂ Tape the pattern in place or make a light pencil tracing.
- ✂ Use a small hole paper punch for the eyes.

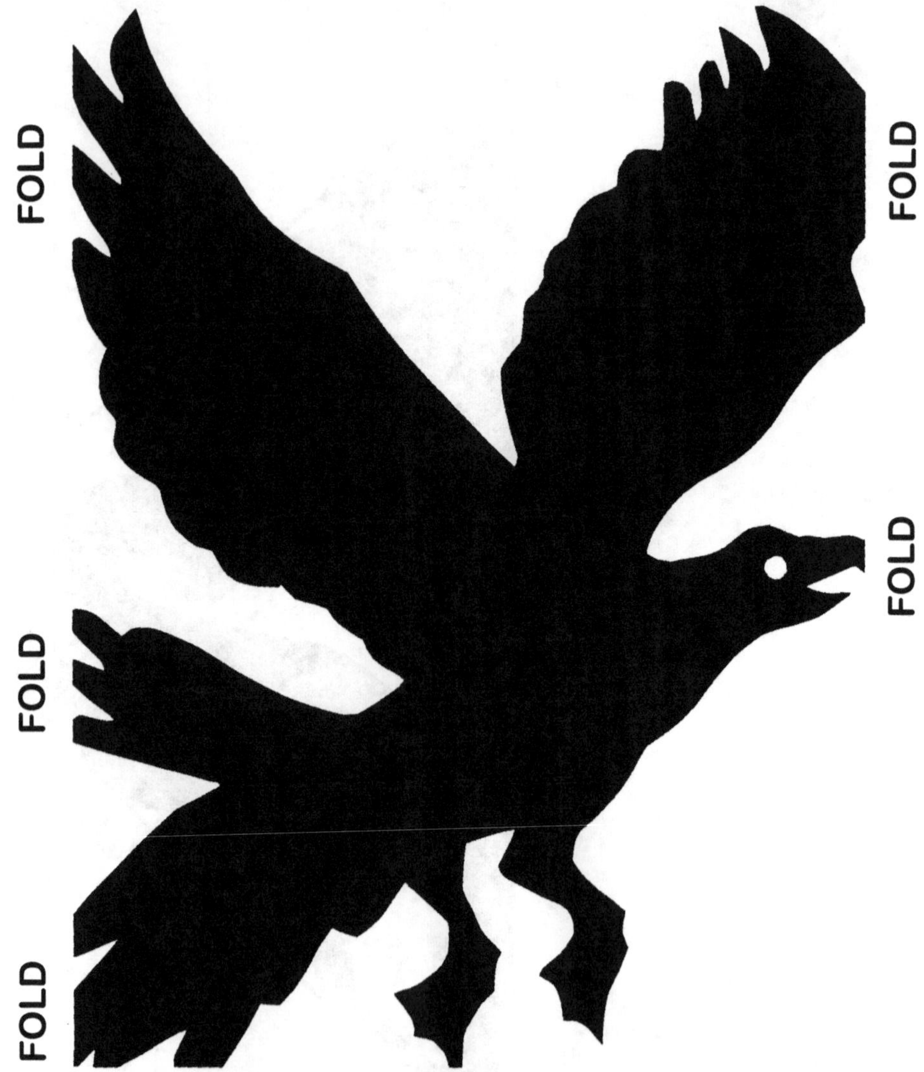

Gulls in a Flock

- ★ Quick and easy.
- ✂ Multi-image or 3-Dimensional.
- ✂ Follow the directions on page 7 or 9.
- ✂ Tape the pattern in place or make a light pencil tracing.
- ✂ Use a small hole paper punch for the eyes.
- ☺ For 3-Dimensional designs have birds flying out of the center.

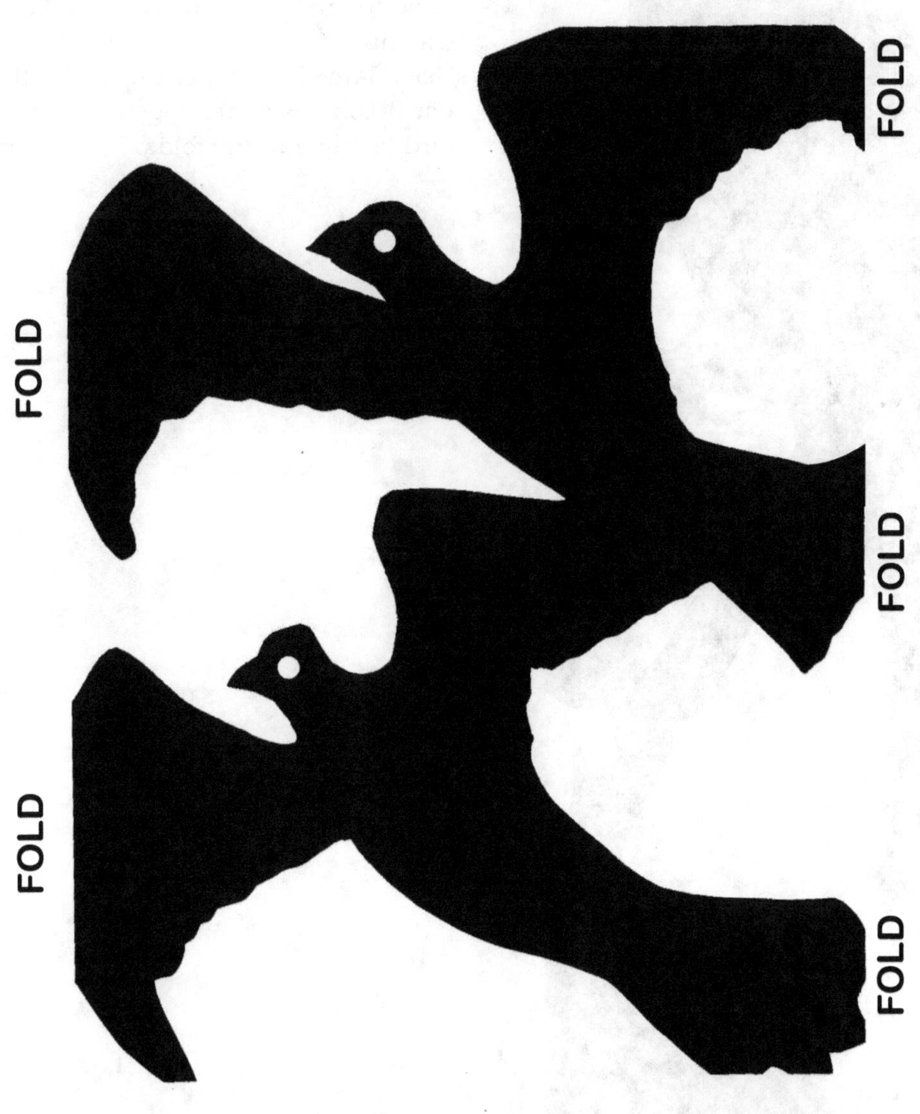

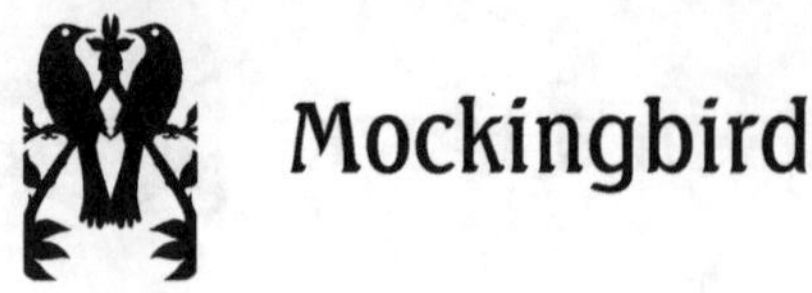

Mockingbird

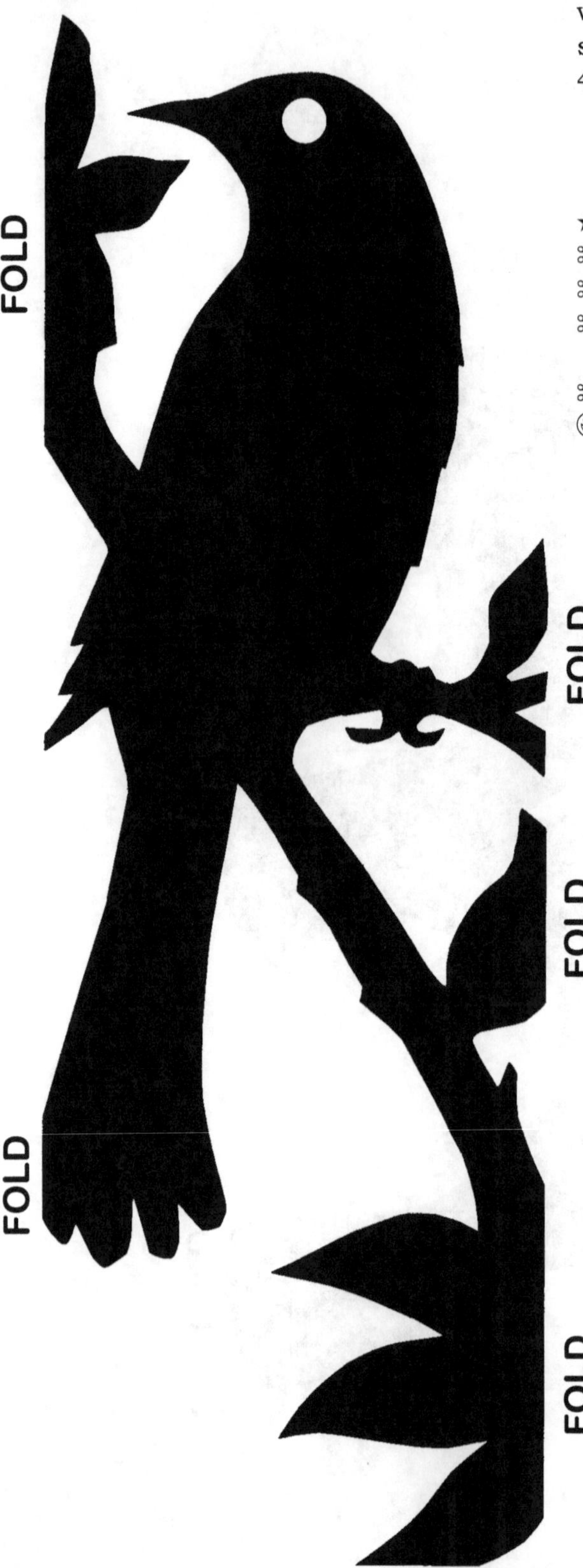

The Florida state bird is the mockingbird. The name means "mimic of many tongues." It is a member of the thrush family. It is a gray, medium size plain songbird with yellow eyes. The mockingbird can mimic other bird songs or calls, even musical instruments, and has over 400 different song types.

Birds of Florida, 278
Florida's Fabulous Bird: Land Birds, 36, 37

- ★ Easy.
- ✂ Double or Multi-image.
- ✂ Follow directions on page 6 or 7.
- ✂ Tape the pattern in place or make a light pencil tracing.
- ✂ Use a large hole paper punch for the eye.
- ☺ For 3-Dimensional image make the center with the bird facing into the folds.

Pelican

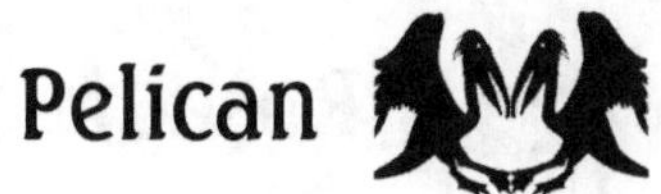

The brown pelican has keen eyesight and will fly high over the ocean, then dive steeply, seeing a school of fish. The lower beak can stretch out to the shape of a basketball hoop and he uses his pouch like a fishnet to catch his fish. The pelican has feet with toes that are webbed. They are called seashore entertainers and jesters. (*Endangered Species)

Birds of Southern Florida, 18
Florida's Fabulous Waterbirds: Their Stories, 42-52

- ★ Easy.
- ✂ Double or Multi-image.
- ✂ Follow directions on page 6 or 7.
- ✂ Tape the pattern in place or make a light pencil tracing.
- ✂ Use a small hole paper punch for the eye.

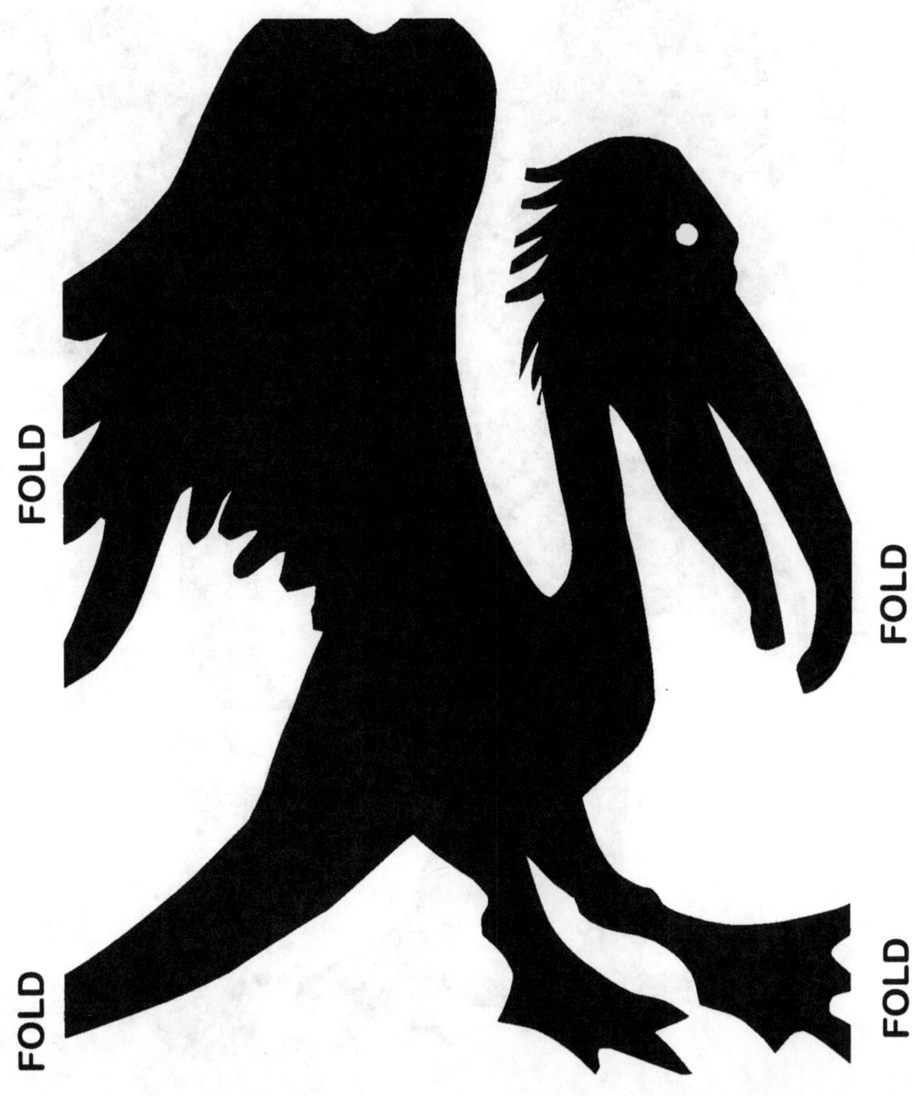

Roseate Spoonbill

The spoonbill is a unique species, with its bare greenish head, a spatulate bill, red legs and feet and pale pink plumage.

Birds of Southern Florida, 27
Florida's Fabulous Waterbirds: Their Stories, 42, 43-52
Smithsonian Handbooks of Birds of Florida, 78

- ★ Quick and easy.
- ✂ Double or Multi-image.
- ✂ Follow directions on page 6 or 7.
- ✂ Tape the pattern in place or make a light pencil tracing.
- ✂ Use a small hole paper punch for the eyes.

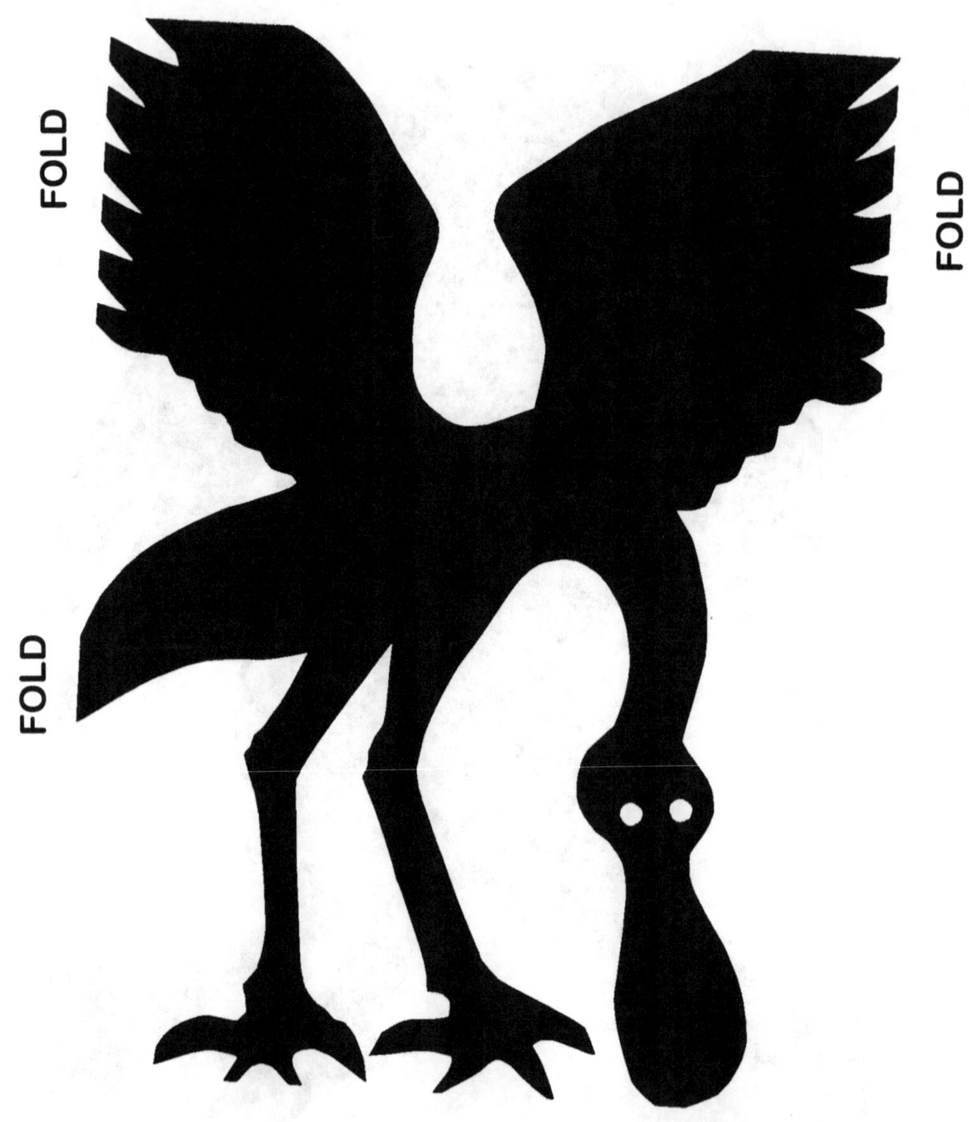

Snowy Egret

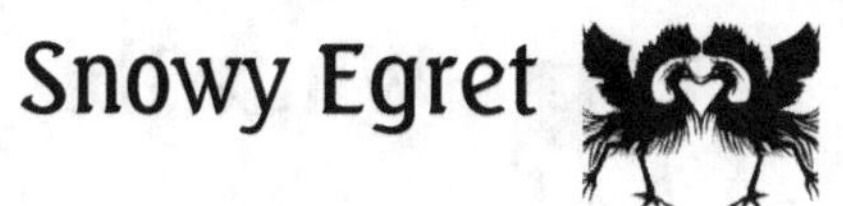

The egret is a common species of bird found throughout the world. The snowy egret has brilliant white plumage, with a long black beak and black legs with bright yellow feet. Its dainty, feathery plumage makes it highly noticeable.

Birds of Southern Florida, 22
Florida's Fabulous Waterbirds: Their Stories, 7-12
Smithsonian Handbooks of Birds of Florida, 68

- ★★★ Advanced.
- ✂ Single or Double image.
- ✂ Follow directions on page 5 or 6.
- ✂ Tape the pattern in place or make a light pencil tracing.
- ✂ Use a small paper punch for the eye.
- ☺ It is a beautiful image enlarged and embellished with additional feathers glued on.

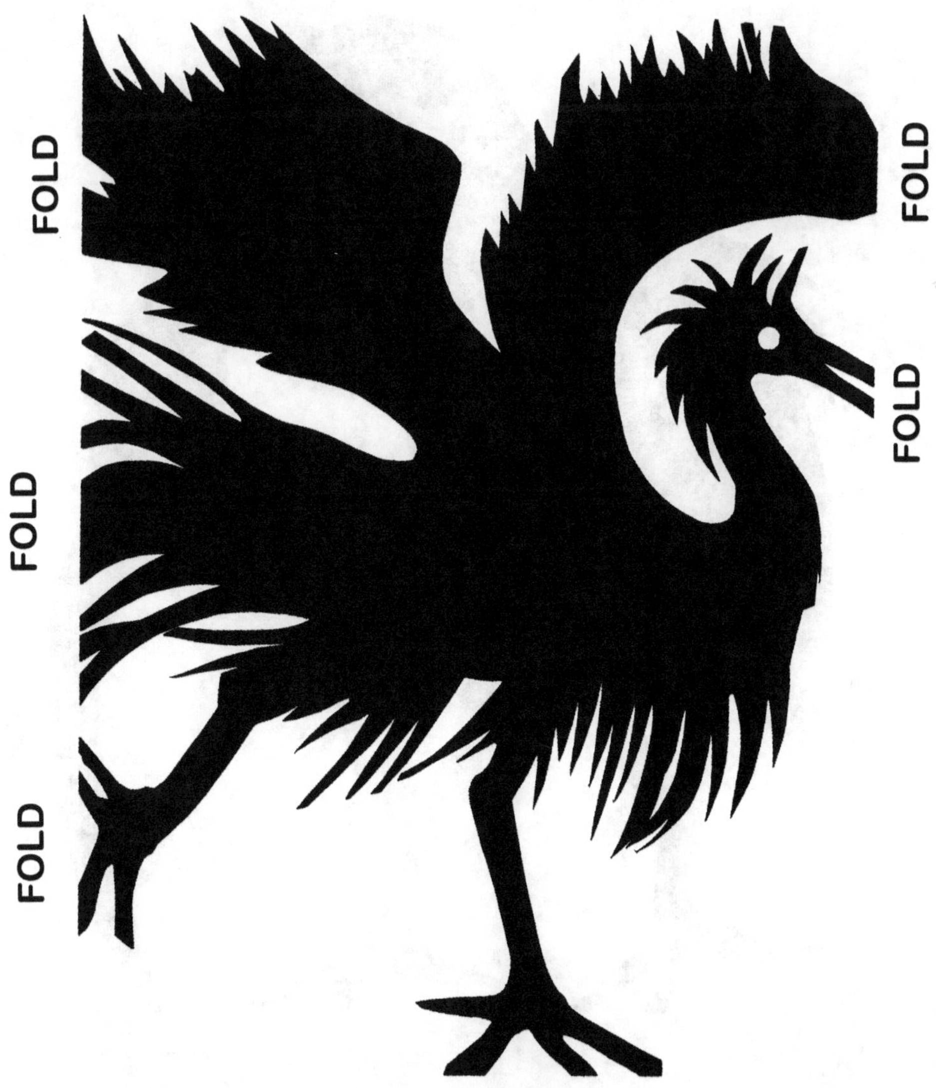

White Ibis

The white ibis is distinguishable by its bright red, long sickle shaped bill and red legs. The plumage is pure white and it probes the mud for aquatic life to feed on.

Birds of Southern Florida, 26
Florida's Fabulous Waterbirds: Their Stories, 37, 38

- ★ Quick and easy.
- ✂ Single or Multi-image.
- ✂ Follow directions on page 5 or 7.
- ✂ Tape the pattern in place or make a light pencil tracing.
- ✂ Use a small paper punch for the eyes.

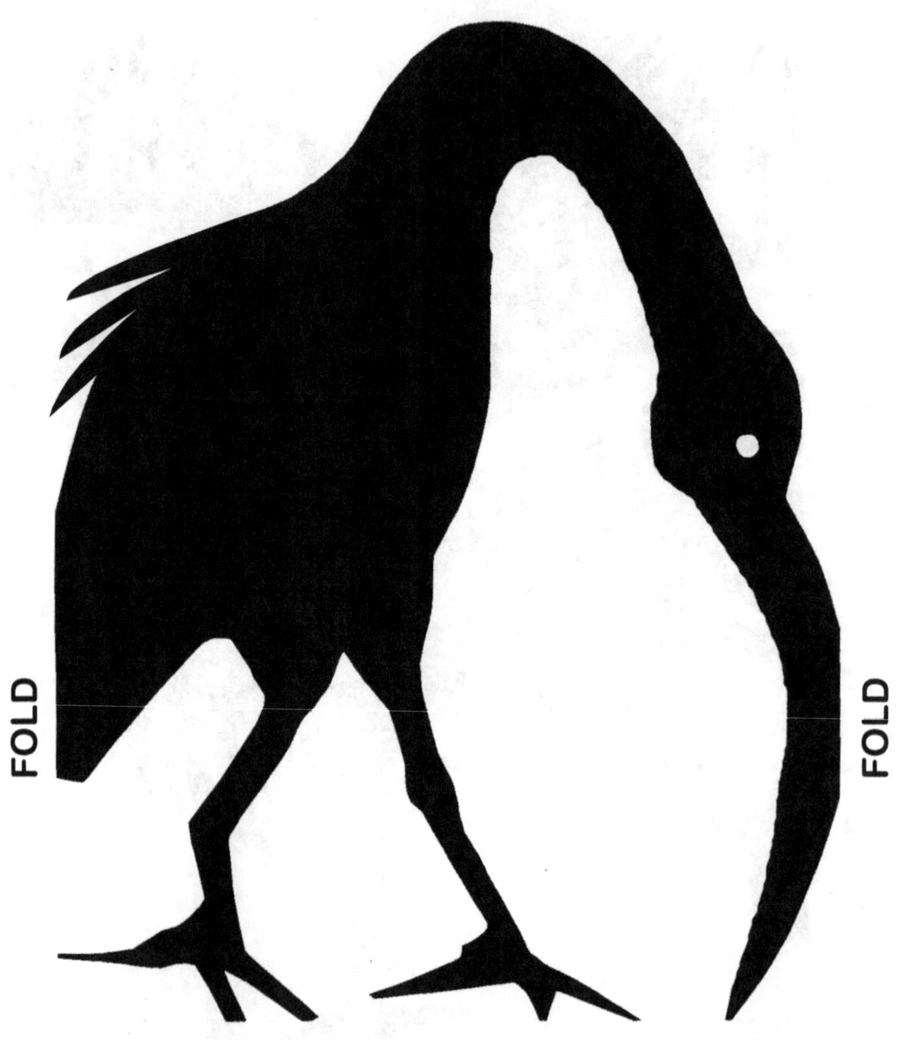

White Ibis Circle

- ★★ Intermediate.
- ✂ Circle fold.
- ✂ Follow directions on page 10.
- ✂ Tape the pattern in place or make a light pencil tracing.
- ✂ Use a small hole paper punch for the eyes.
- ☺ Let your paper do the turning.
- ☺ Cut away the smaller areas first. This gives you more paper area to hold as you cut.

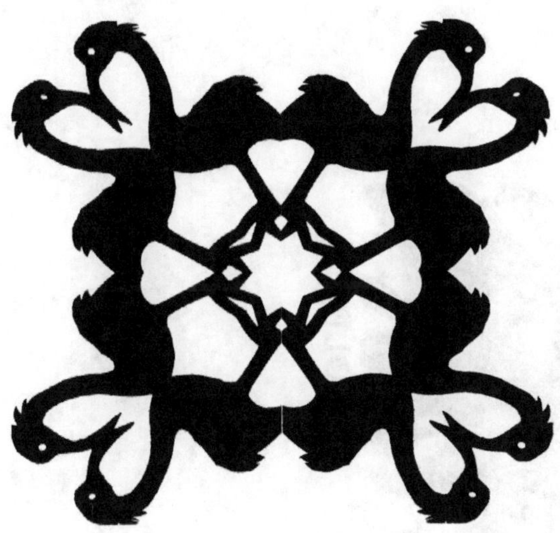

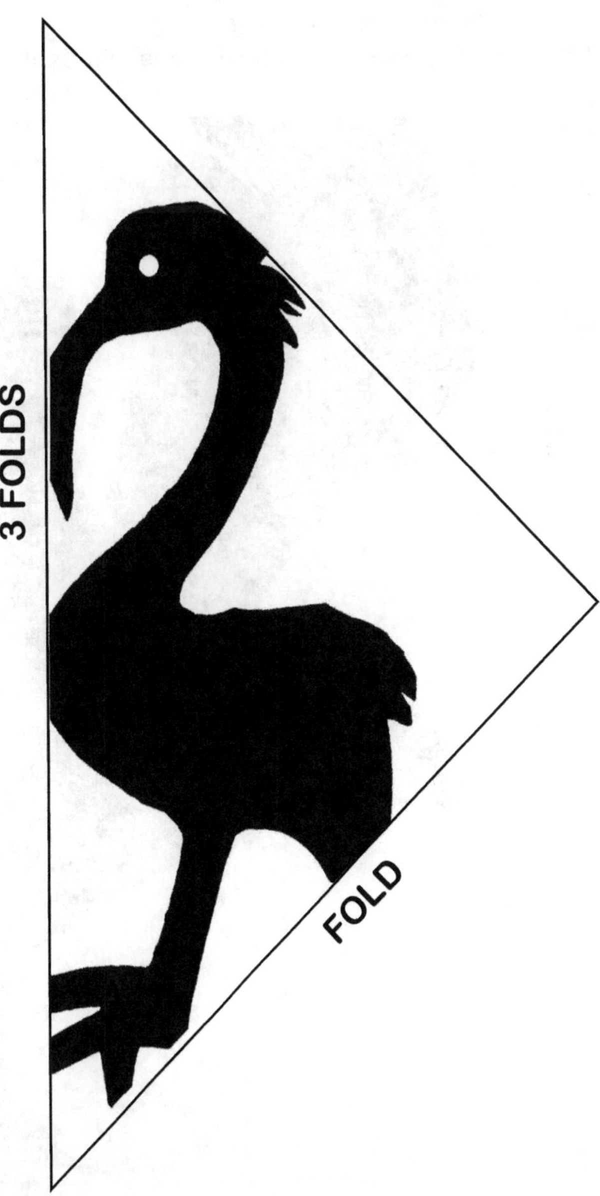

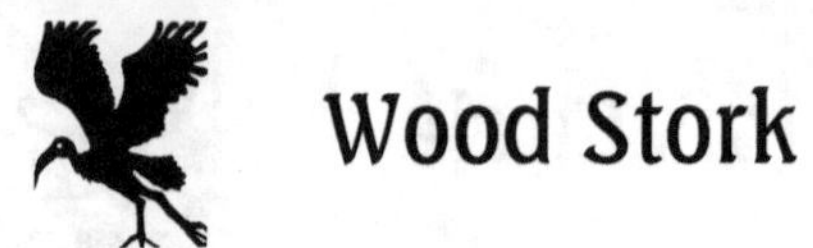

Wood Stork

The wood stork, also known as wood ibis or flint head, is one of the largest wading birds found in Florida and the only stork in the United States. This stork stands more than 3.5 feet tall with a wingspan of more than 5 feet. His body is white except for a short black tail and black feathers that border the wings. The long stout bill is 6-9 inches long and is grayish-black on adult birds, yellowish on young storks. Wood storks are wetland dwellers They feed by touch in shallow ponds, tidal pools, swamps, and marshes.

Birds of Southern Florida, 50
Florida's Fabulous Birds: Land Birds: Their Stories, 12, 13
Florida's Wood Storks
http://edis.ifas.ufl.edu/UW065

★ Easy
✂ Top fold or Side fold image.
✂ Follow directions on page 8.
✂ Tape the pattern in place or make a light pencil tracing.

.

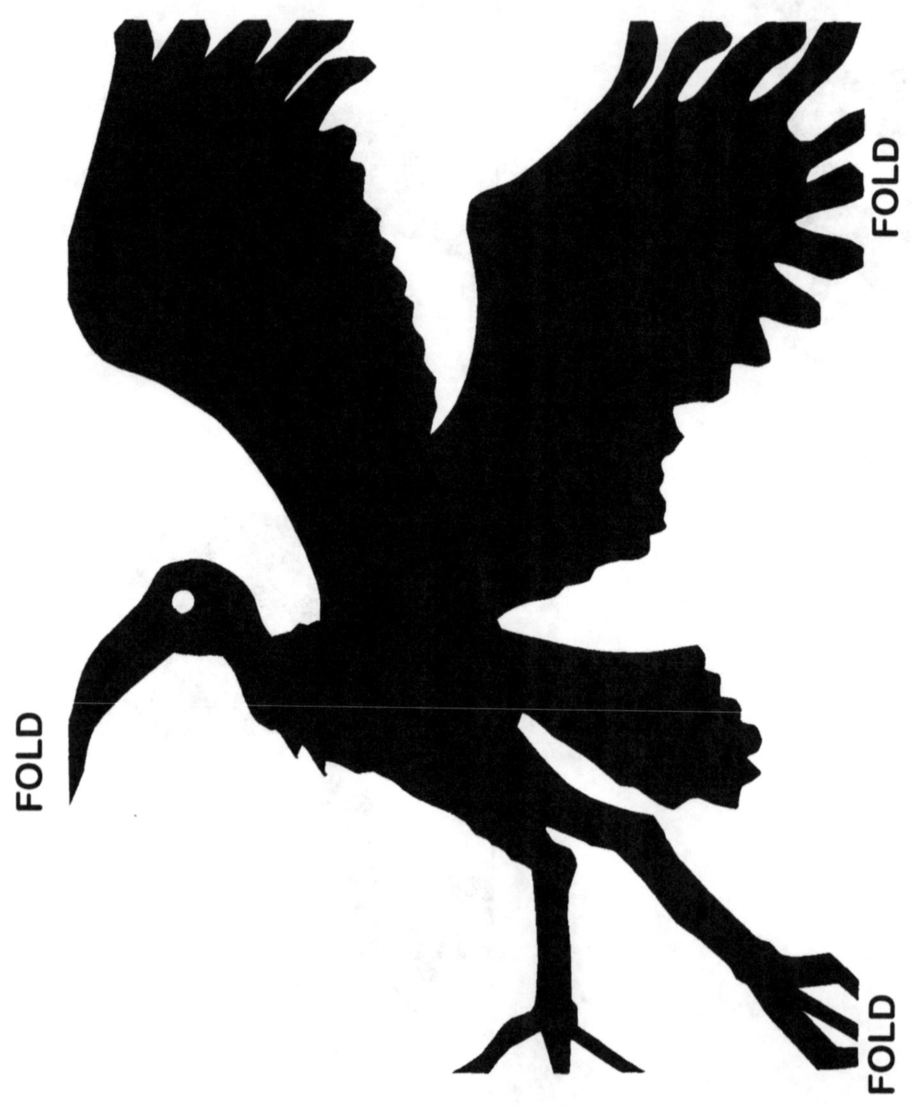

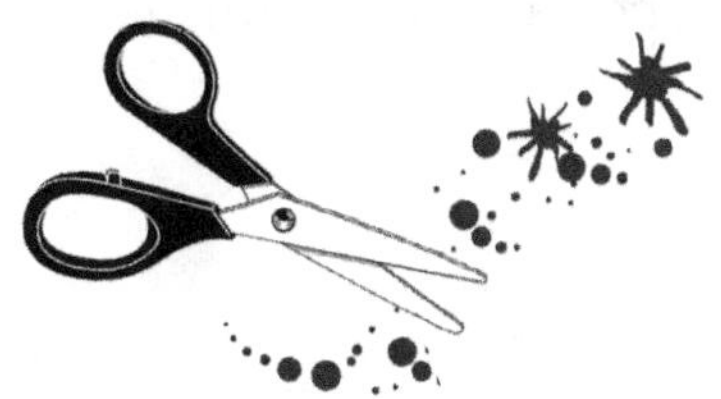

Fish

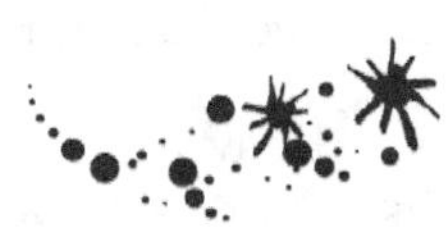

Fish: Most fish commonly have a backbone and are cold blooded. There are over 29,000 different species are in the oceans of the world. They come in all sizes, shapes and colors and need oxygen to live, which they take from the water through their gills. Most fish have teeth. All fish have fins.

Want to learn more? See full references in the Bibliography

FOLD-AND-CUT PATTERNS

Atlantic Cod
Atlantic Spadefish
Catfish
Clownfish
Clownfish Circle
Coral and Fish Circle
Eel
Hammerhead Shark
Lionfish
Sailfish
School of Fish
Seahorse
Seahorse Family
Shark
Starfish
Stingray
Viperfish

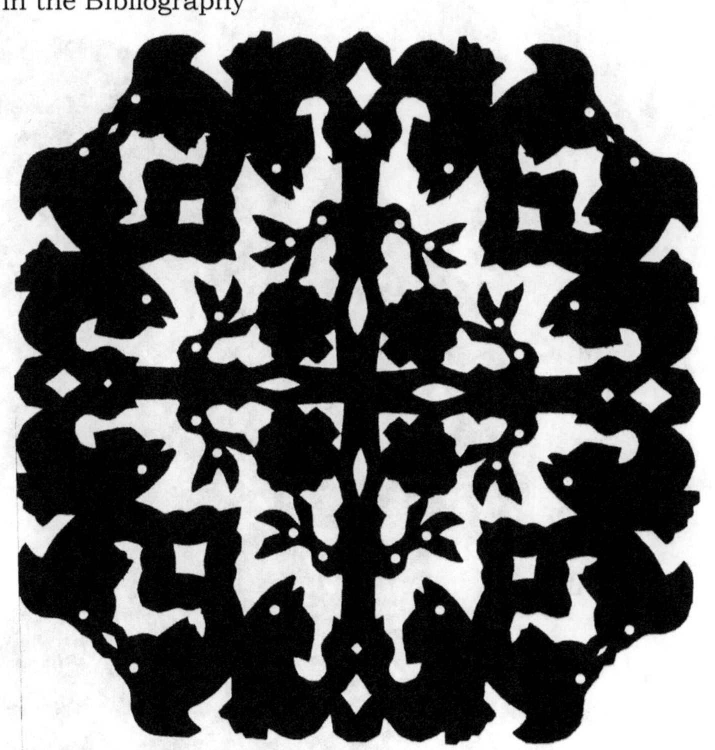

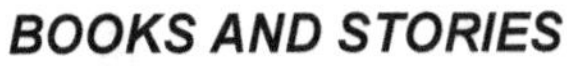

BOOKS AND STORIES

Chomp! A Book About Sharks by Melvin Berger
Coral Reef Hideaway: The Story of Clown Anemonefish by Doe Boyle
Creeps from the Deep by Leighton Taylor
The Fisherman and his Wife an English Folktale
Great White Shark: Ruler of the Sea by Kathleen Weidner Zoehfeld
The Nature of Florida's Ocean Life by Cathie Katz
Neptune's Nursery by Kim Michelle Toftand and Allan Sheather.
Seahorse Reef: A Story of the South Pacific by Sally Walker
Science Under the Sea by Lynn M. Stone
Shark Bait by Graham Salisbury

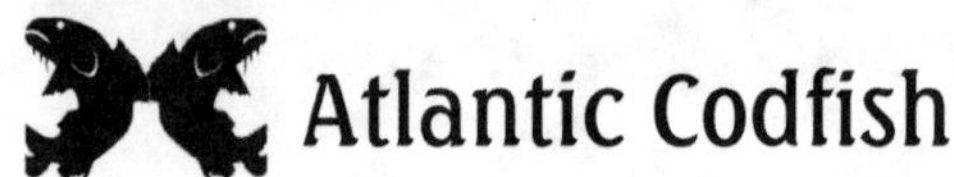

Atlantic Codfish

Cod have multi-colored scales that blend into the habitat they live in. Living in open water they are silvery, and among the seaweed they are mottled in brown and green. The barbell is a touch and taste sensor that hangs down from the chin.

Aquatic Life of the World: Volume 2, 112, 113
www.google.com

★ Easy.
✂ Double or Multi-image.
✂ Follow directions on page 6 or 7.
✂ Tape the pattern in place or make a light pencil tracing.
✂ Use a large hole paper punch for the eyes.
✂ Fold on the dotted line to cut the gills.

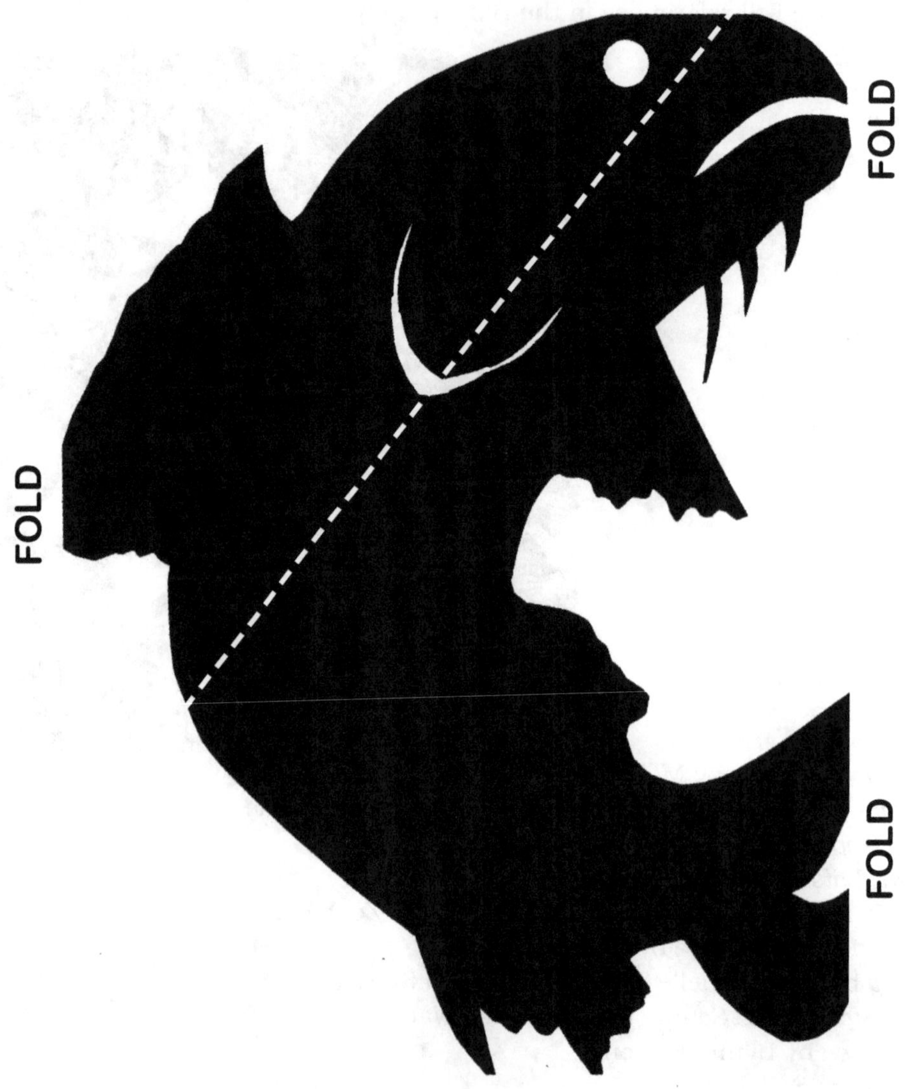

Atlantic Spadefish

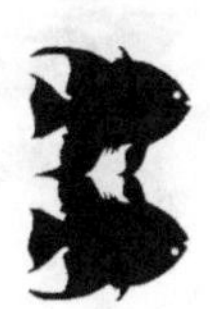

The mouth of this fish is very small and has a blunt snout. The body is silvery, rather flat and disk shaped with black vertical bands. He is a bottom feeder, meaning he feeds on crustaceans, mollusks, sponges, other invertebrates, and occasionally on plankton.

Atlantic Coast Fishes, 192, plate 37
Eye Witness Books: Fish, 11

- ★ Easy
- ✂ Top fold.
- ✂ Follow directions on page 8.
- ✂ Tape the pattern in place or make a light pencil tracing.
- ✂ Fold on the dotted line and cut out crescent shape for the gills.
- ✂ Use a large hole punch for the eye.

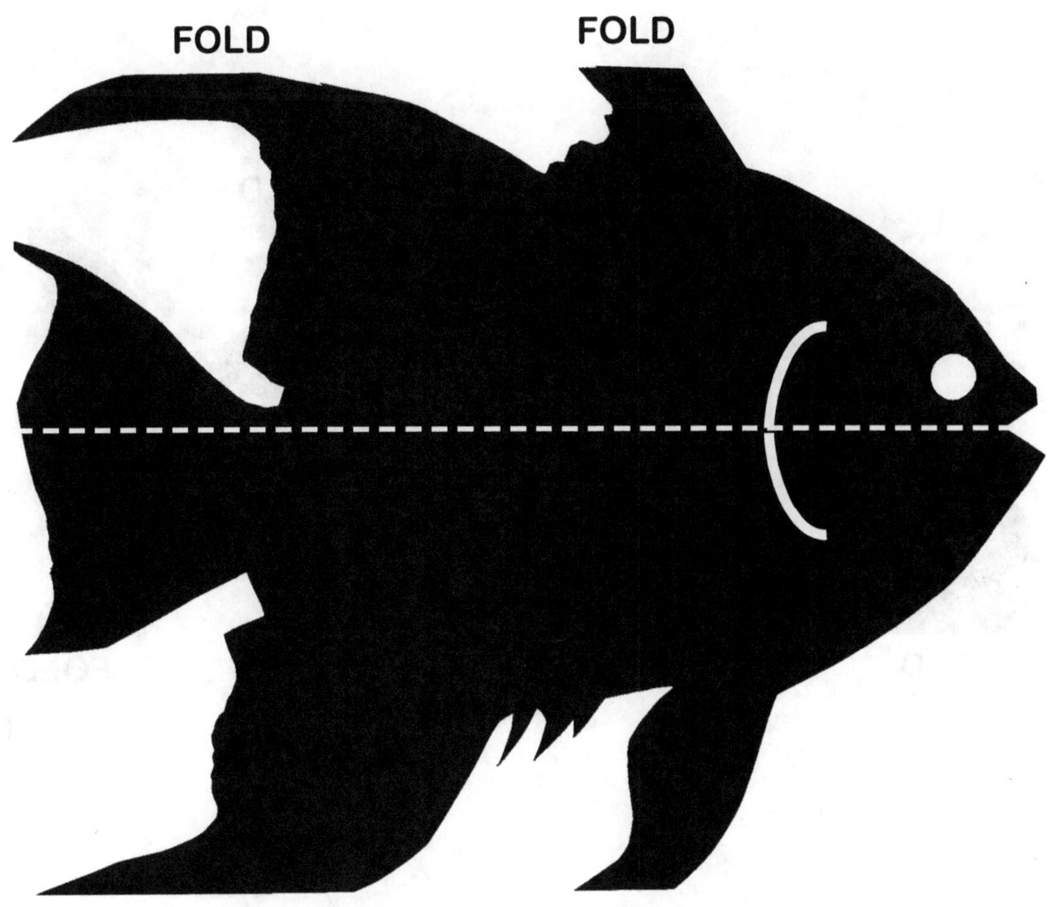

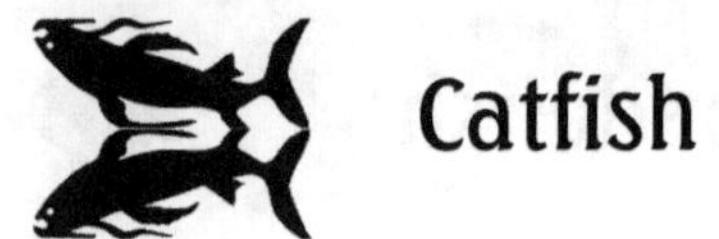

Catfish

These fish like the bottom of the water. Their coloring varies according to the area they are found in. Whisker-like barbells are found extending from the corners of the mouth, under the chin and are used for feeling their way along the murky coastal regions where they feed.

Atlantic Coast Fishes, 83, plate 13
Eye Witness Books: Fish, 18, 19,

★ Easy.
✂ Multi-image.
✂ Follow directions on page 7.
✂ Tape the pattern in place or make a light pencil tracing.
✂ Use a small hole paper punch for the eye.
✂ Fold on the dotted line to cut out the gills.

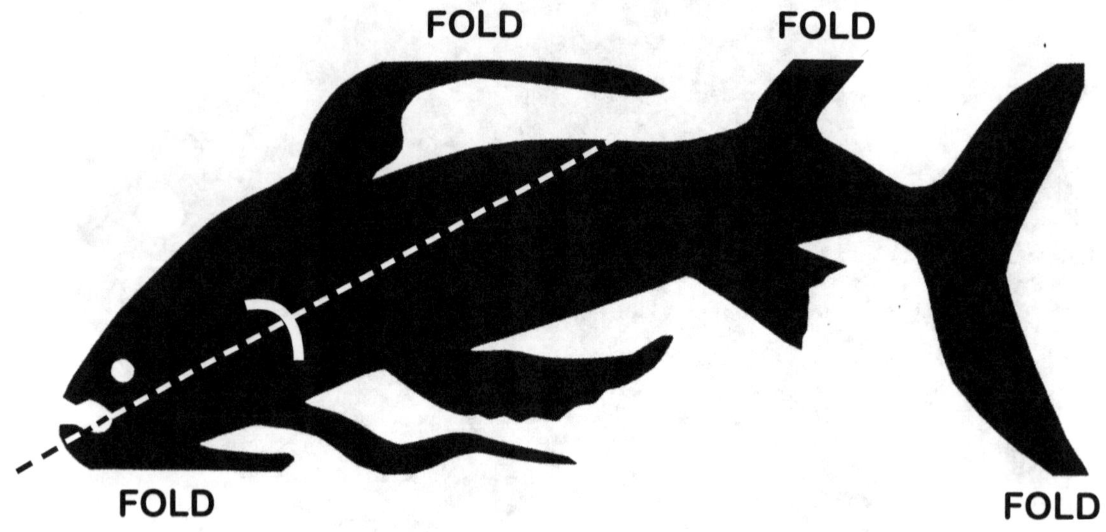

Clownfish 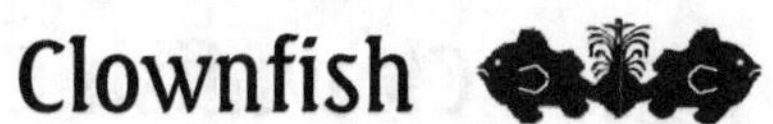

Bright orange, black and white, this colorful fish is found mostly in the warm coral reefs of the tropics. He lives with the sea anemone which has swaying poisonous venom-filled tentacles. They help each other, like friends, feeding and protecting each other from predators.

Eye Witness Books: Fish, 46, 47
Eye Witness Books: Seashore, 49

- ★ Easy.
- ✂ Multi-image.
- ✂ Follow directions on page 7.
- ✂ Tape the pattern in place or make a light pencil tracing.
- ✂ Use a large hole paper punch for the eyes.
- ✂ Fold on the dotted line and cut the shape of the pectoral fin that is close to the eye.

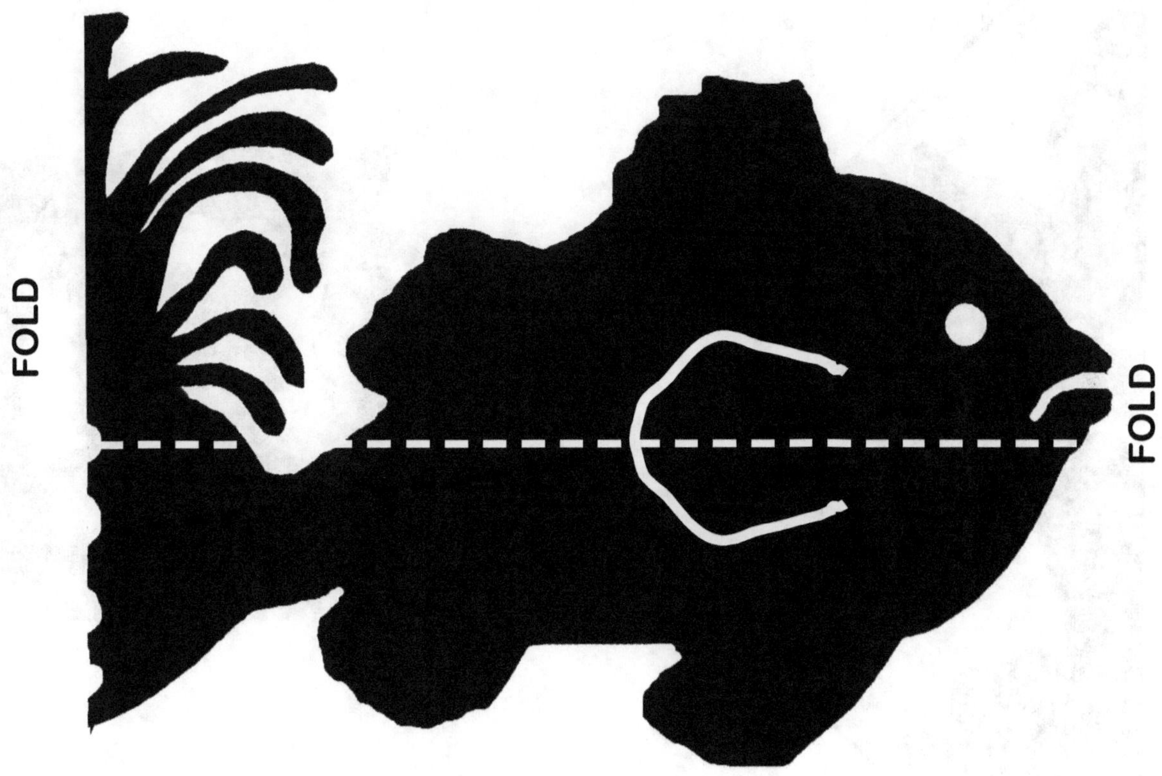

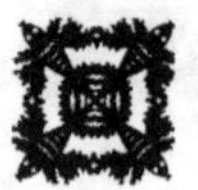

Clownfish Circle

- ★ Easy.
- ✂ Circle fold.
- ✂ Follow directions on page 10.
- ✂ Tape the pattern in place or make a light pencil tracing.
- ✂ Use a large hole paper punch for the eyes.
- ☺ Let your paper do the turning.
- ☺ Cut away the smaller areas first. This gives you more paper area to hold as you cut.

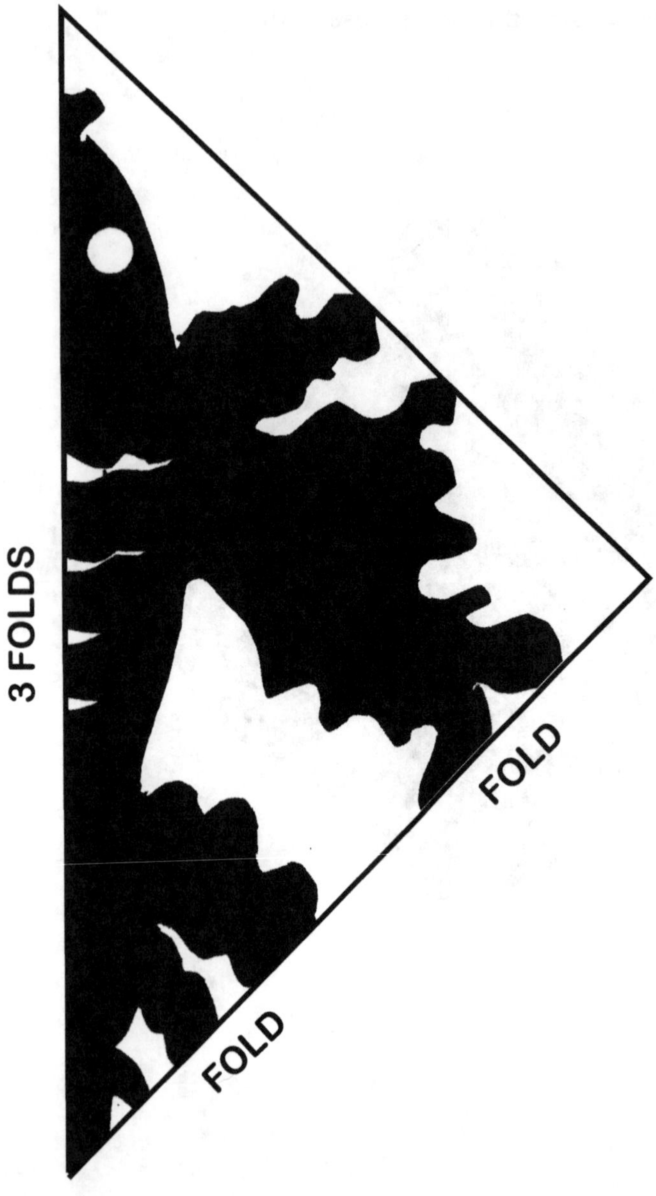

3 FOLDS

FOLD

FOLD

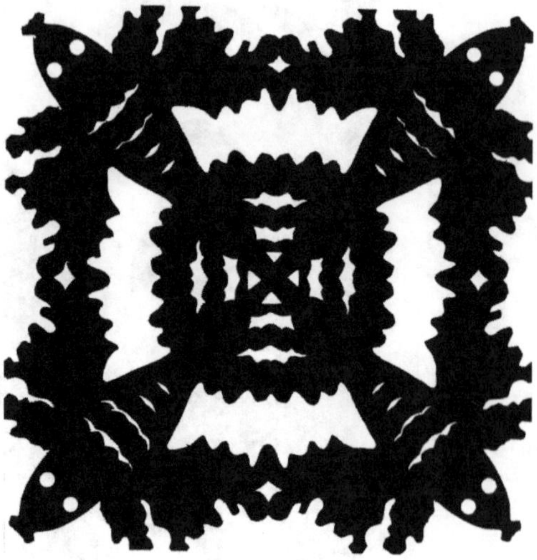

Coral and Fish Circle

- ★ Easy.
- ✂ True circle.
- ✂ Follow directions on page 11.
- ✂ Tape the pattern in place or make a light pencil tracing.
- ✂ Use a small paper punch for the eye.
- ☺ Let your paper do the turning.
- ☺ Cut away the smaller areas first. This gives you more paper area to hold as you cut.
- ☺ Tape colored tissue paper behind the cutouts for an added effect.

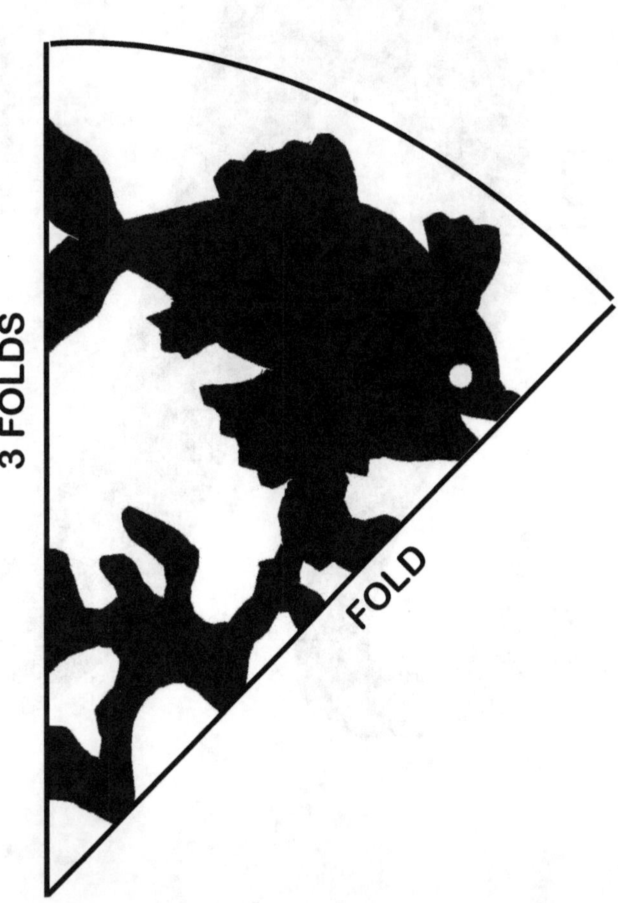

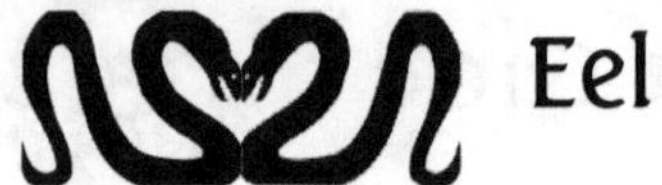

Eel

Eels have a body of mostly muscle and are snakelike, slimy fish. It is a fact that there are over 738 species of eels. And yes, an eel does have teeth. The eel is a boney fish with lots of vertebrae making it long and bendy. They have no scales and grow from 3 to 10 feet long.

Eels, 6-48
Eye Witness Books: Fish, 48, 49

★ Quick and easy.
✂ Multi-image.
✂ Follow directions on page 7.
✂ Tape the pattern in place or make a light pencil tracing.
✂ Use a small hole paper punch for the eyes.

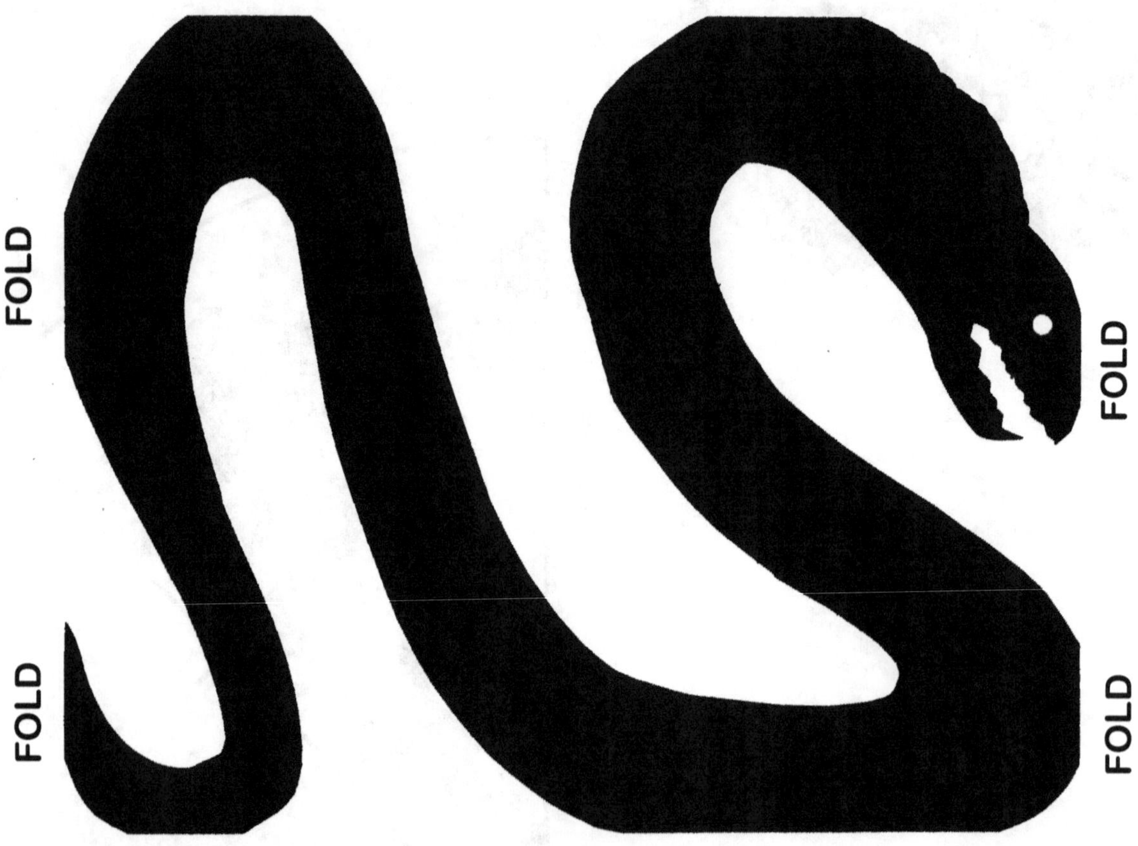

Hammerhead Shark

The head of the hammerhead is at right angles to the body, like a pole. The bulging eyes can be as much as three feet apart at either end of the head. The nostrils are near the eyes and the mouth is set under this strangely formed head.

Eye Witness Dictionaries: The Visual Dictionary of Animals, 18, 19
Sharks, 22, 50, 51

- ★ Quick and easy.
- ✂ Double or Top-fold image.
- ✂ Follow directions on page 6 or 8.
- ✂ Tape the pattern in place or make a light pencil tracing.
- ✂ Fold on the dotted line and cut a curve to make the mouth.
- ✂ Use a large hole punch for the eyes.

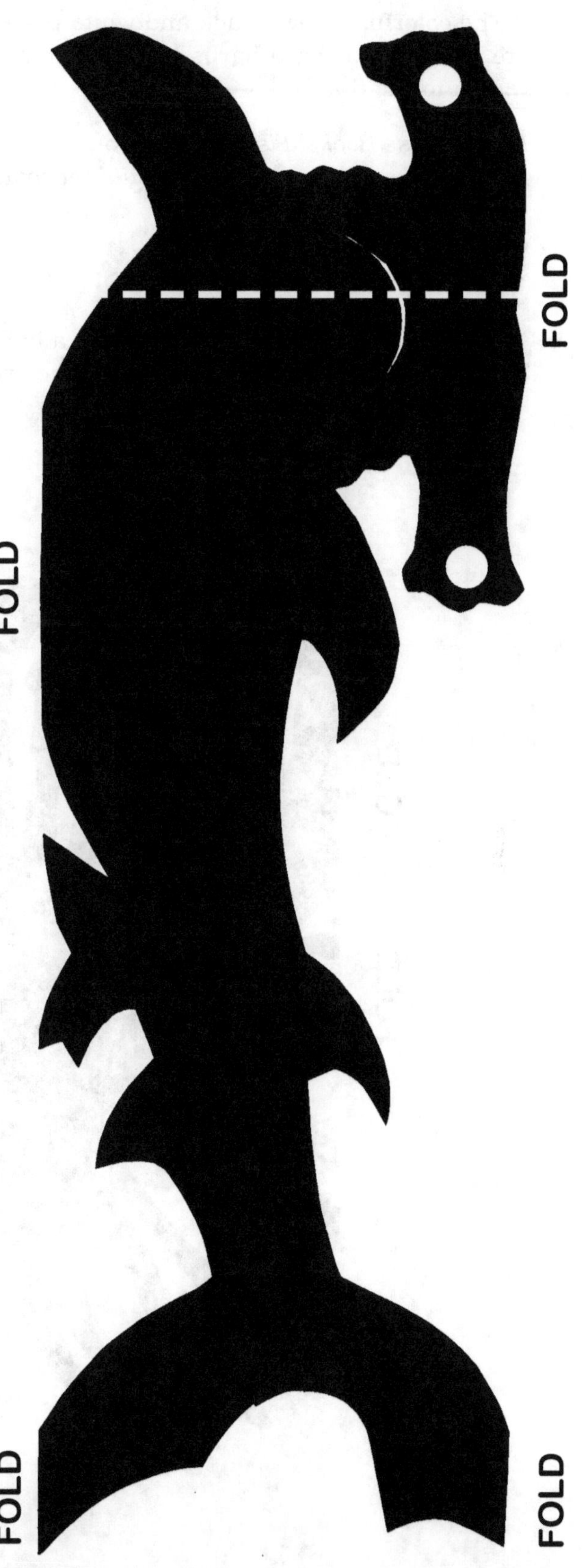

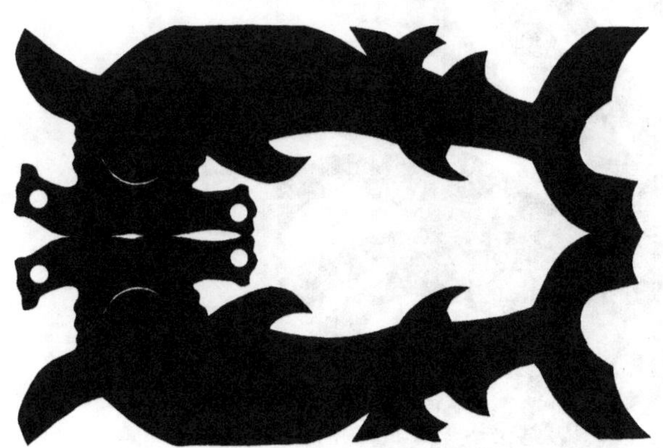

Lionfish

The colorful yellow, black and white pattern of this fish acts as a warning to other fish that they are poisonous. Sharp barbs top the dorsal fin. When there is pressure on the spine it forces the venom to the tip.

Eye Witness Books: Fish, 31, 54, 55
Eye Witness Dictionaries: The Visual Dictionary of Animals, 20, 21

★★★ Advanced.
✂ Single fold image.
✂ Follow directions on page 5.
✂ Tape the pattern in place or make a light pencil tracing.
✂ Use a small hole paper punch for the eye.
✂ Let your paper do the turning.

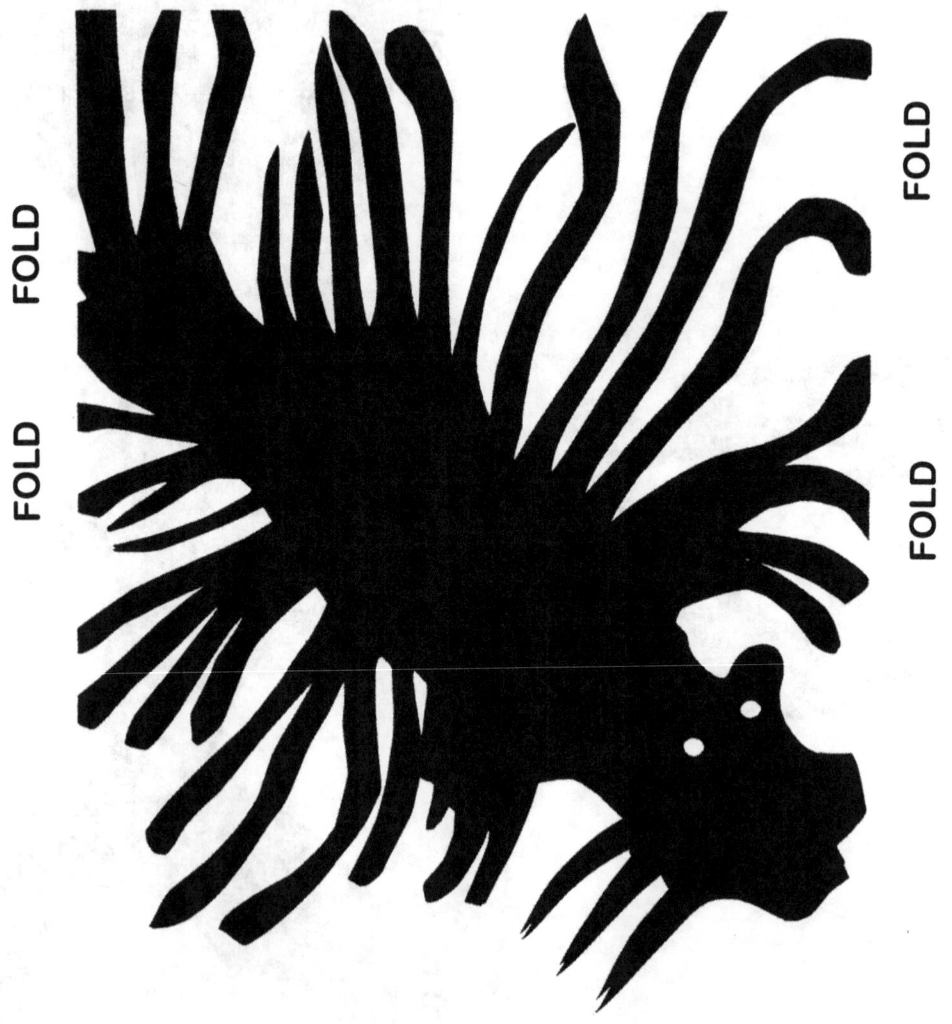

Sailfish

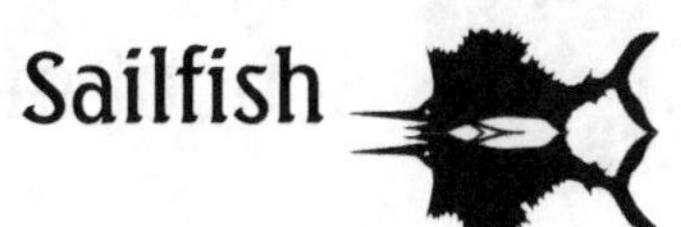

The sailfish is the official Florida state saltwater fish. Its high and long first dorsal fin is like a sail. The top of the body is dark blue and elsewhere it is white with brown spots. It has a long spear-like front jaw twice the length of the lower jaw. It can swim up to 60 miles per hour.

Atlantic Coast Fishes, 226, plate 15
Eye Witness Books: Fish, 11, 30

- ★ Easy.
- ✂ Double or Multi-image.
- ✂ Follow directions on page 6 or 7.
- ✂ Tape the pattern in place or make a light pencil tracing.
- ✂ Use a small hole paper punch for the eyes.
- ☺ Could be a Top Fold to use as a stand-up.

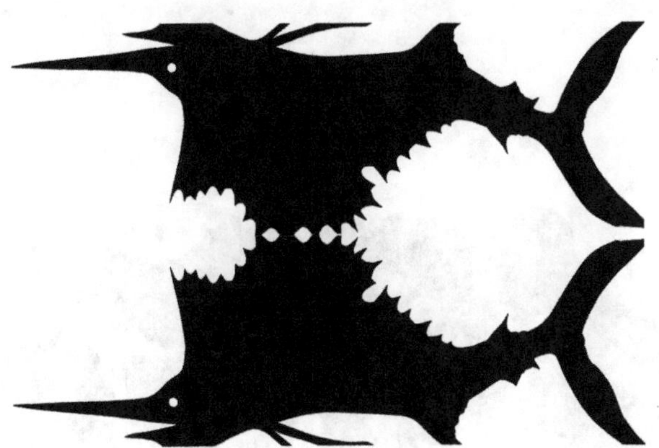

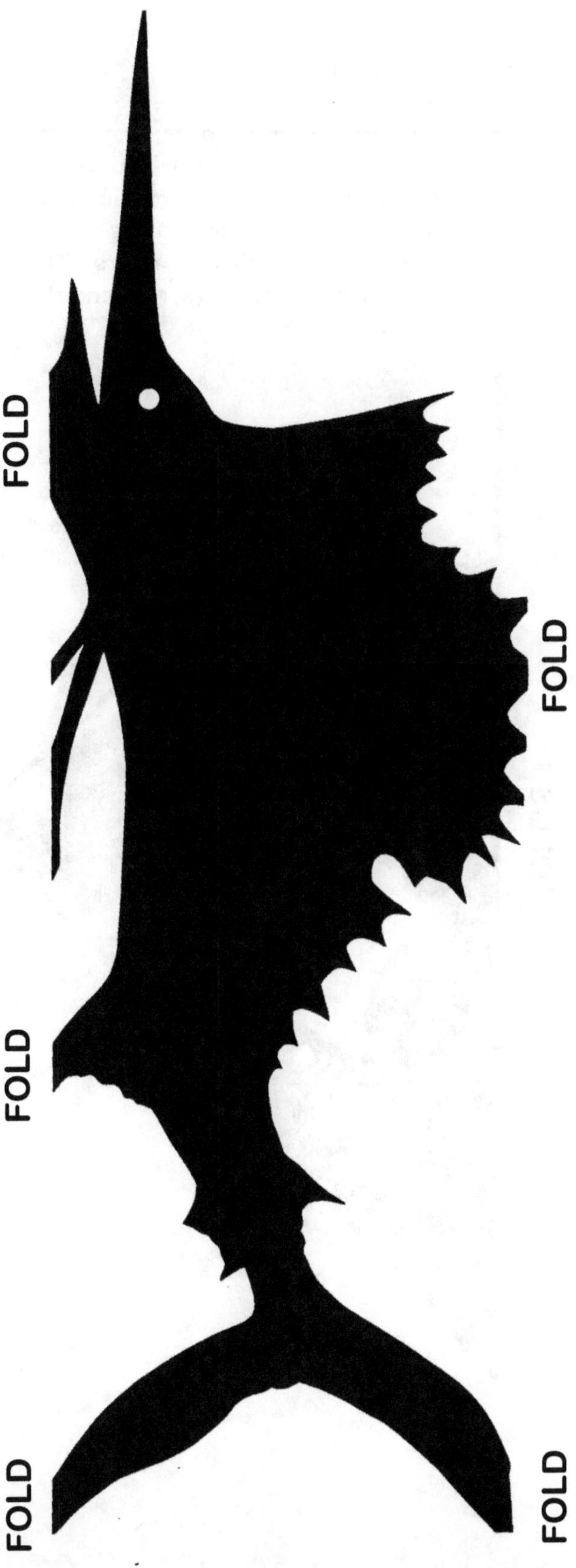

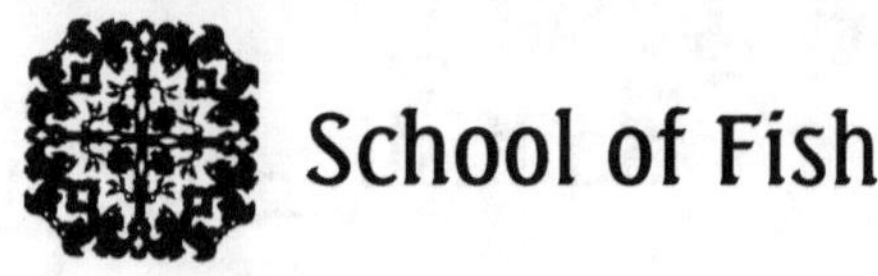

School of Fish

- ★★ Intermediate.
- ✂ Circle fold.
- ✂ Follow directions on page 10.
- ✂ Tape the pattern in place or make a light pencil tracing.
- ✂ Use a small hole punch for the eyes and on the kelp.
- ☺ Let your paper do the turning.
- ☺ Cut away the smaller areas first. This gives you more paper area to hold as you cut.
- ☺ Tape colored tissue paper behind the cutouts for an added effect.

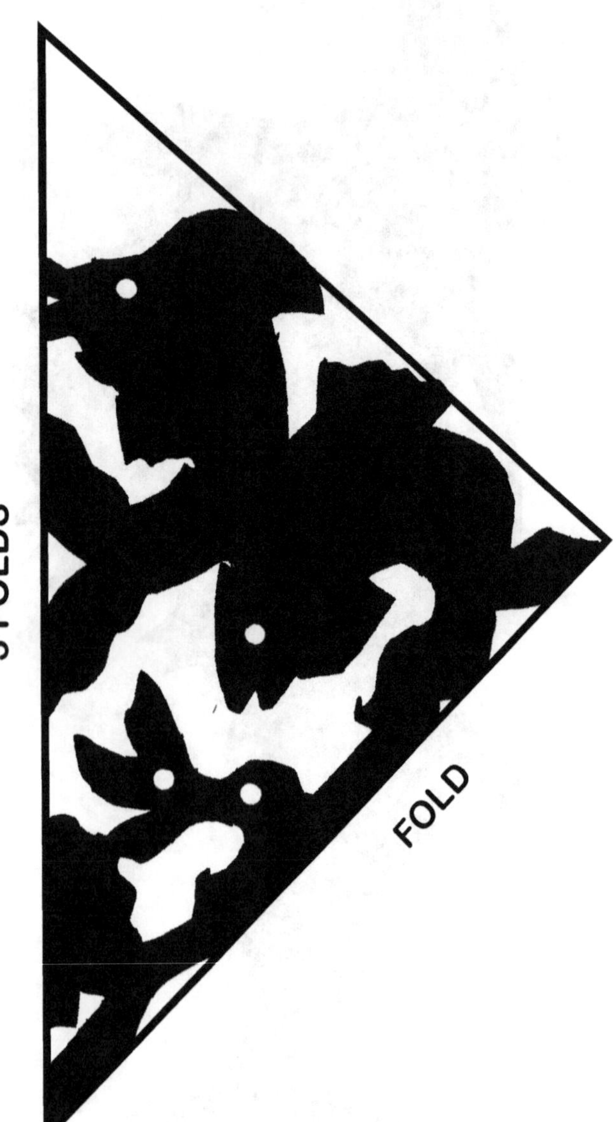

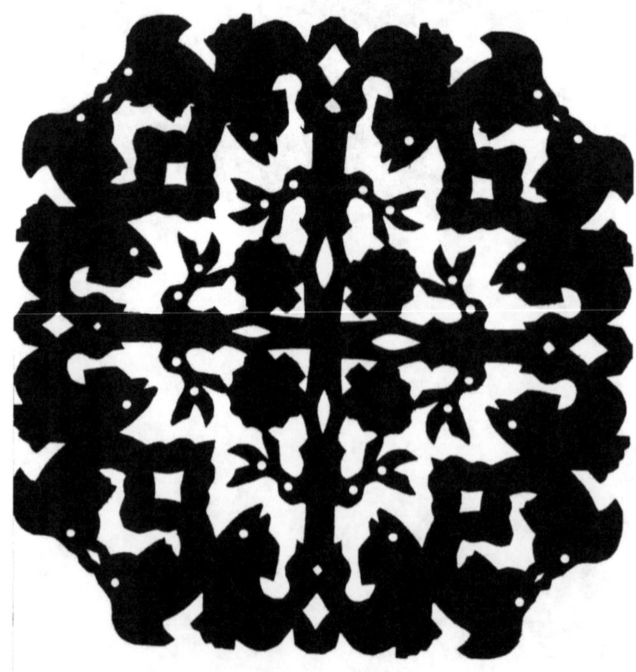

Seahorse

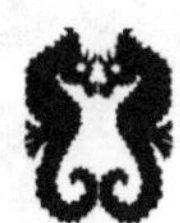

The female seahorse produces the eggs and lays them in the front pouch of the male. He actually gives birth to the young in several weeks. They are carnivores.

Aquatic Life of the World, 456, 500, 501
Eye Witness Dictionaries: The Visual Dictionary of Animals, 20, 21

- ★ Easy.
- ✂ Double or Multi-image.
- ✂ Follow directions on page 6 or 7.
- ✂ Tape the pattern in place or make a light pencil tracing.
- ✂ Use a large hole paper punch for the eyes.

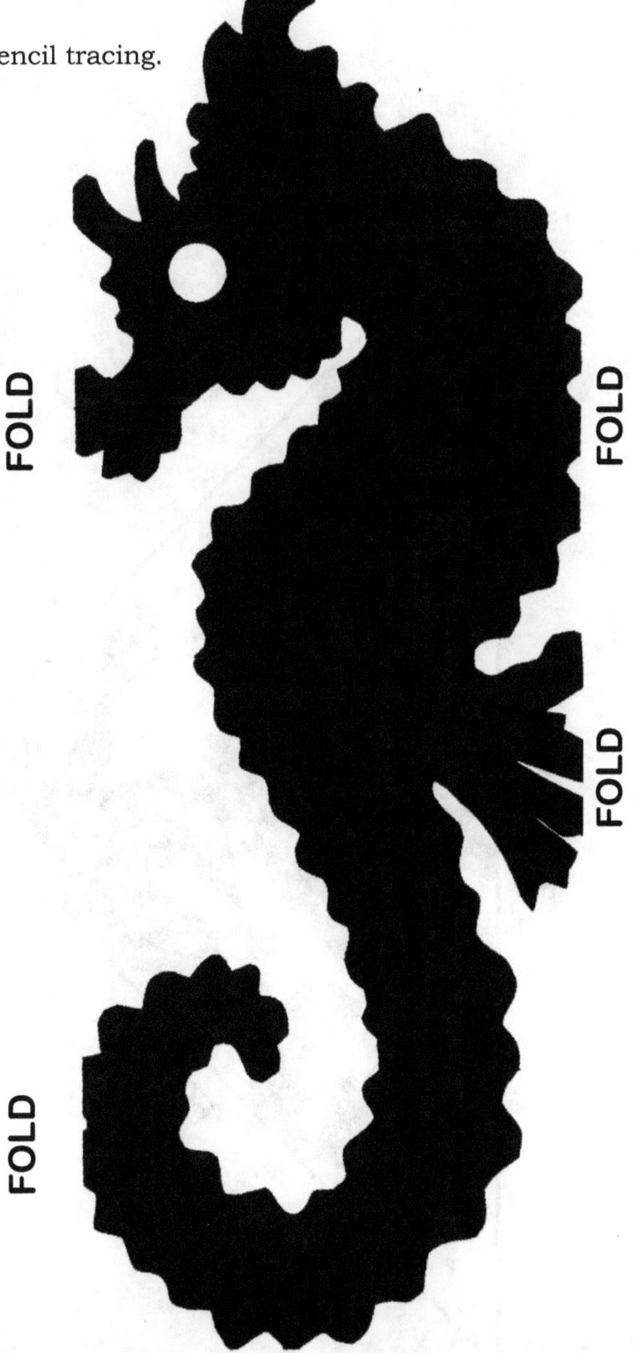

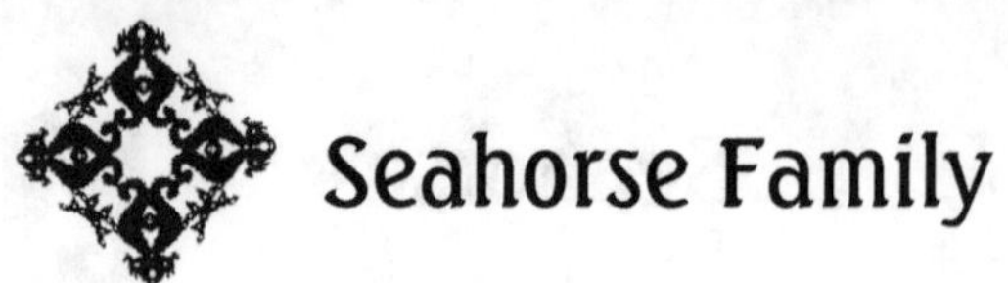

Seahorse Family

- ★★ Intermediate.
- ✂ Circle fold.
- ✂ Follow directions on page 10.
- ✂ Tape the pattern in place or make a light pencil tracing.
- ✂ Use a small hole paper punch for the eye and bubbles on the kelp.
- ☺ Let your paper do the turning.
- ☺ Cut away the smaller areas first. This gives you more paper area to hold as you cut.

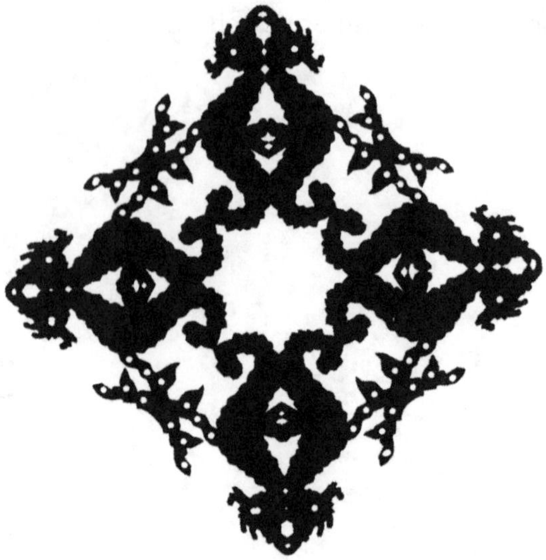

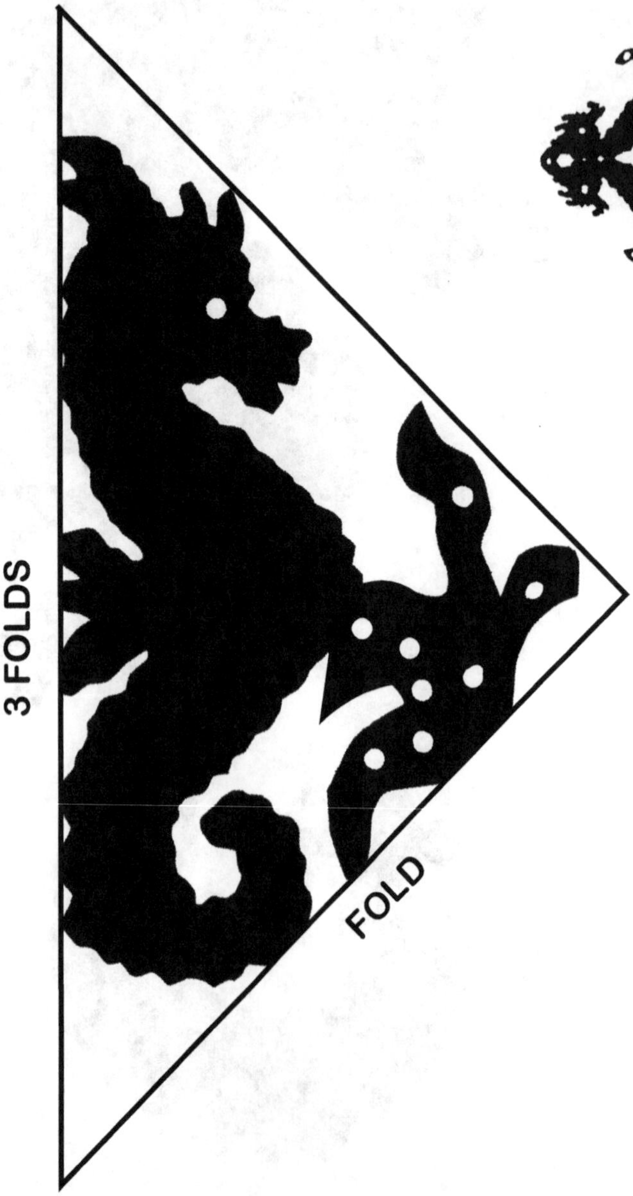

3 FOLDS

FOLD

Shark

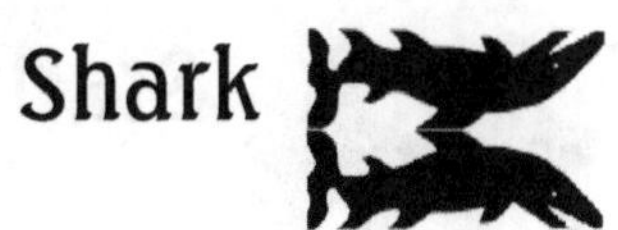

Sharks are predators. They have a keen sense of hearing and smell. They have five rows of teeth and new ones replace those that are lost in a feeding frenzy. Their skeleton is cartilage, not bone. Carpenters have sometimes used shark skin as sandpaper. There are over 300 species of shark in the ocean. (*The great white shark is an endangered species.)

Eye Witness Books: Fish, 58, 59, 60, 61, 65
Eye Witness Dictionaries: The Visual Dictionary of Animals, 18, 19
Sharks, 1-77

- ★ Quick and easy.
- ✂ Double or Multi-image.
- ✂ Follow directions on page 6 or 7.
- ✂ Tape the pattern in place or make a light pencil tracing.
- ✂ Use a small hole paper punch for the eye.
- ✂ Use a rectangular punch for gills.
- ☺ Can be cut as top fold as shown or nose to tail fold.

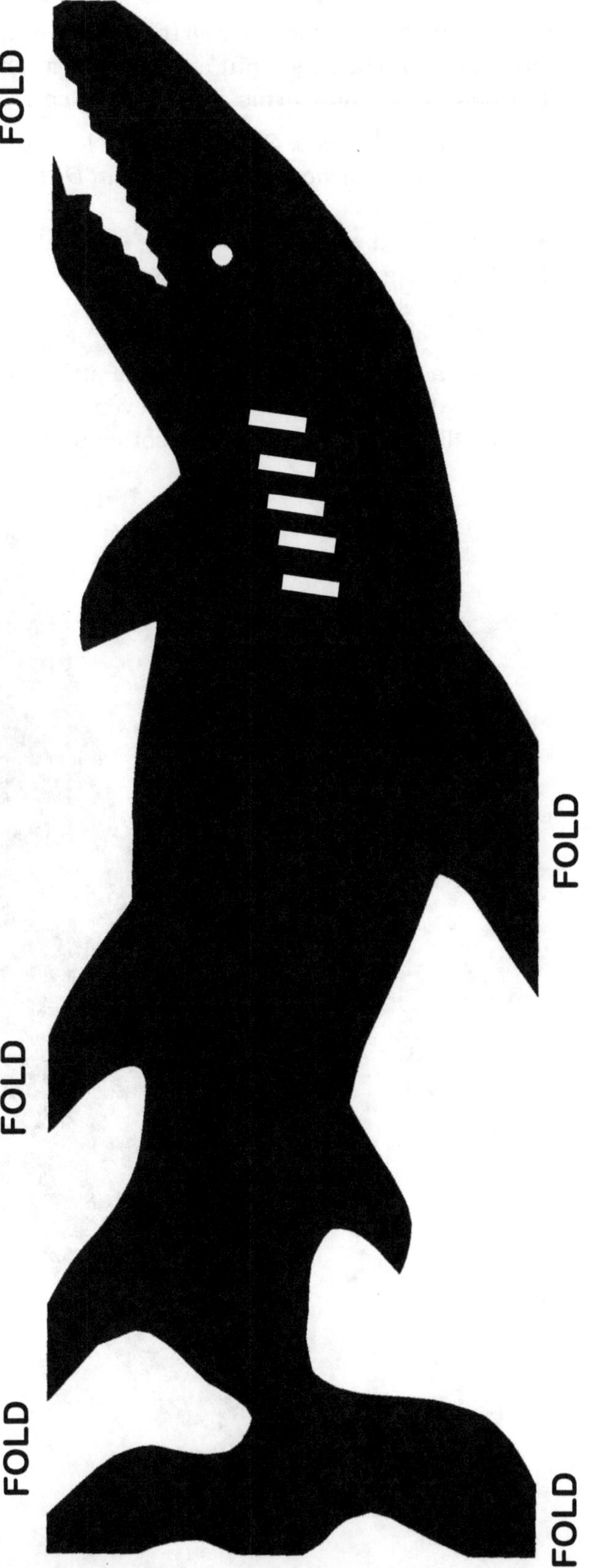

★★ Starfish

The sea star, or starfish, has thousands of tiny protruding little tube feet and no brain. These creatures are not truly fish, but are listed as such, and are very colorful. The starfish has no backbone, but has five or more arms, which if lost can be regrown.

Eye Witness Books: Seashore, 40, 41
Eye Witness Dictionaries: The Visual Dictionary of Animals, 7, 22, 23

- ★ Quick and easy.
- ✂ Double or Multi-image.
- ✂ Follow directions on page 6 or 7.
- ✂ Tape the pattern in place or make a light pencil tracing.
- ✂ Use a small paper punch for the little tube feet all over the starfish if you choose.
- ☺ Use different colors of paper, even paint on the little tube feet, for added effect.
- ☺ Scallop decorative edge scissors may be used to cut out this image.

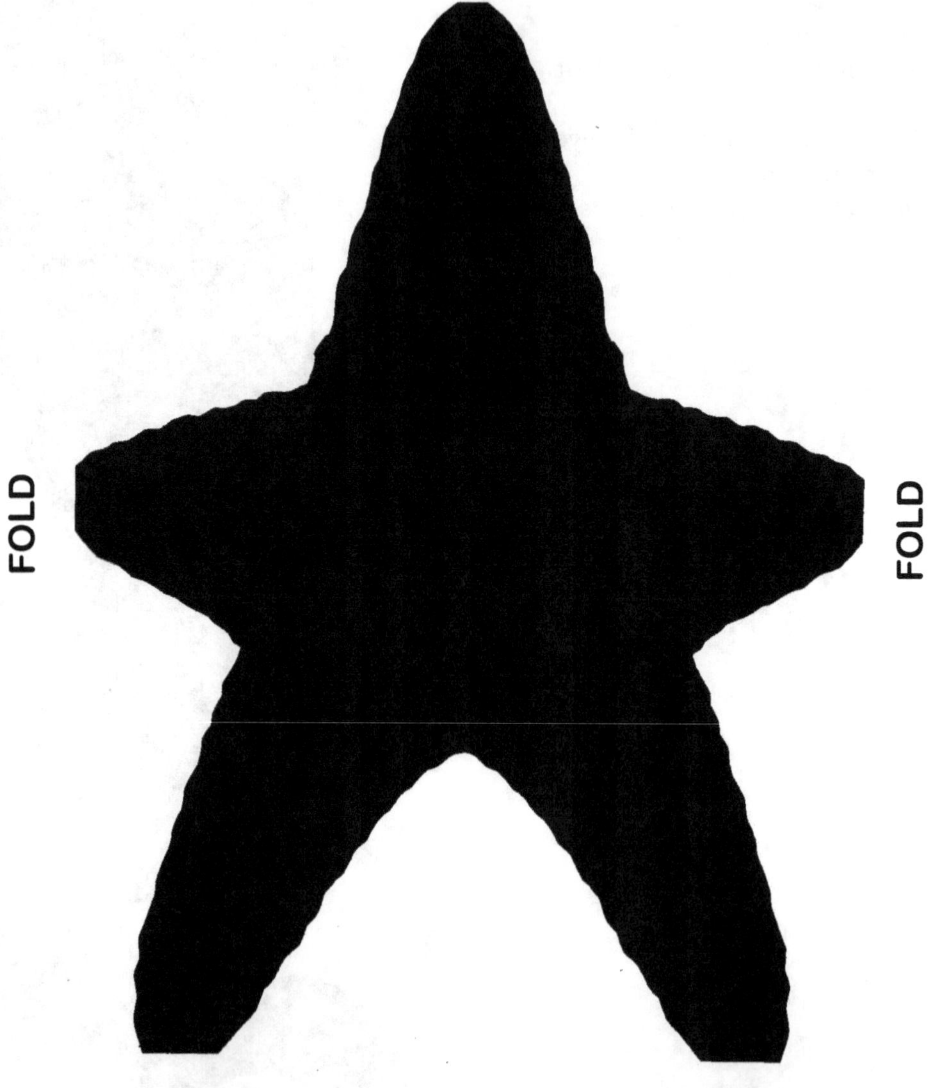

Stingray

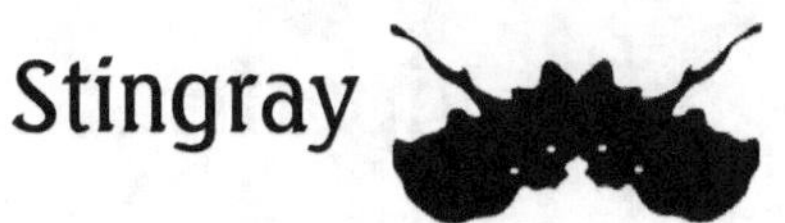

The stingray has a long, flexible whip-like tail, armed near the base with a strong, serrated bony spine with which it can inflict painful, even fatal wounds. They are found in all oceans. The stingray propels itself almost effortlessly with its wing-like fins and spends a lot of time hiding under the sand on the ocean floor.

Aquatic Life of the World: Volume 9, 562, 563
Eye Witness Books: Fish, 23, 54, 55, 56, 57, 59, 71
Sharks, 39, 57, 59, 60

- ★ Quick and easy.
- ✂ Double or Multi-image, 4¼ x 5½.
- ✂ Follow directions on page 6 or 7.
- ✂ Tape the pattern in place or make a light pencil tracing.
- ✂ Use a small hole paper punch for the eyes.

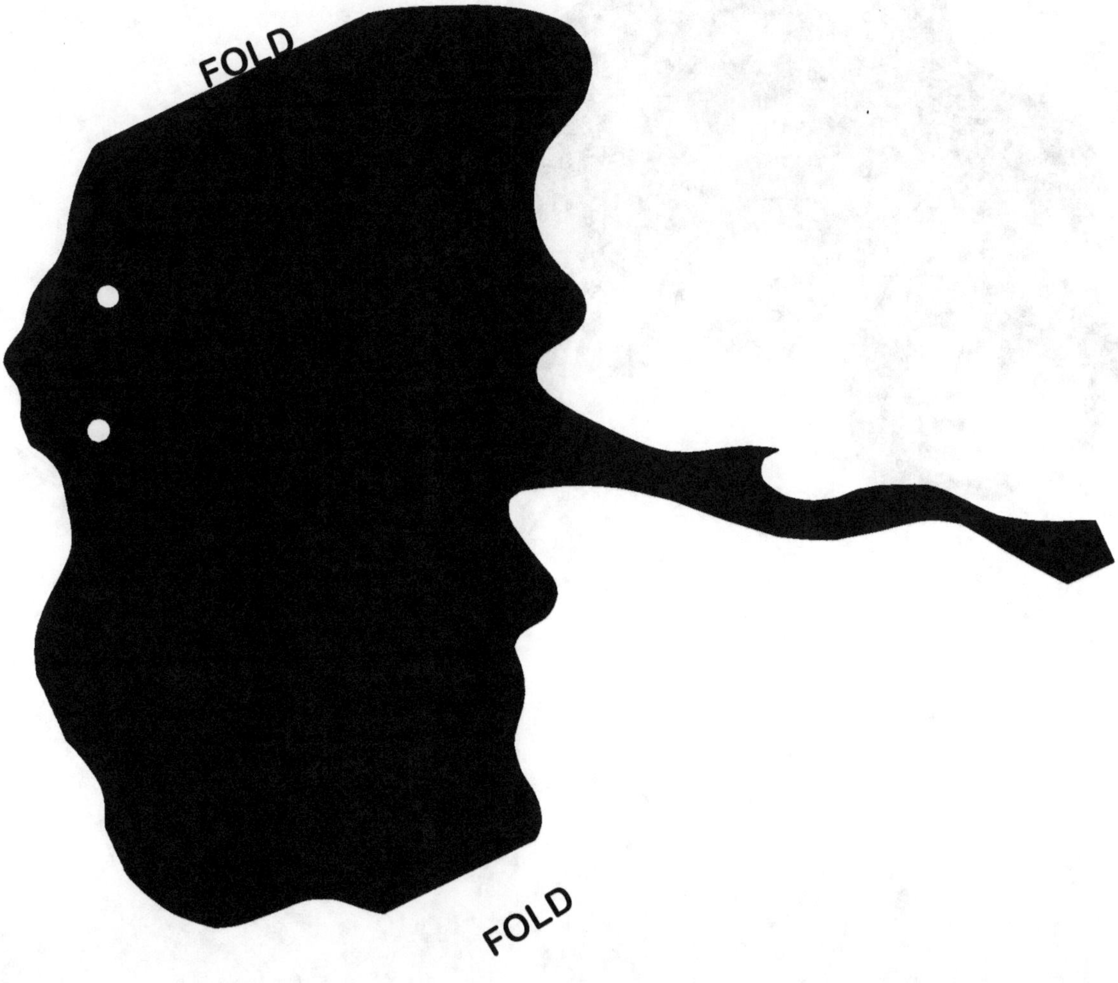

FOLD

FOLD

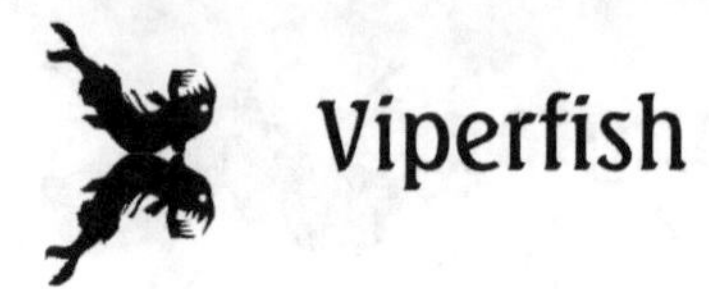

Viperfish

The viperfish is found deep in the Atlantic Basin and elsewhere in the oceans. It has fang-like teeth and a large mouth. It has luminescent organs. It has a long dorsal spine with a photophore, a light-producing organ that acts as a lure to attract smaller fish.

Aquatic Life of the World: Volume, 2, 74, 75, 76, 76, 77
Creeps from the Deep, 24, 25, 27
www.google.com

★ Quick and easy.
✂ Top fold.
✂ Follow directions on page 8.
✂ Tape the pattern in place or make a light pencil tracing.
✂ Use a large hole paper punch for the eyes.

FOLD

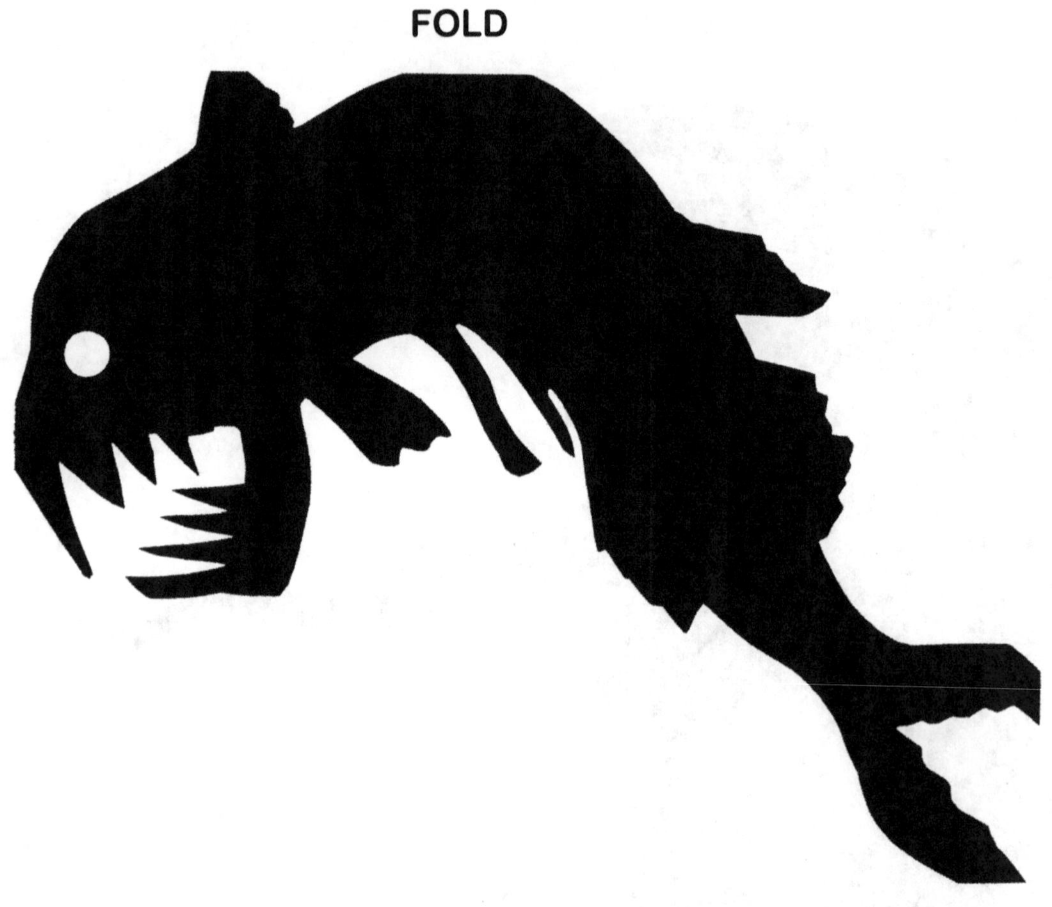

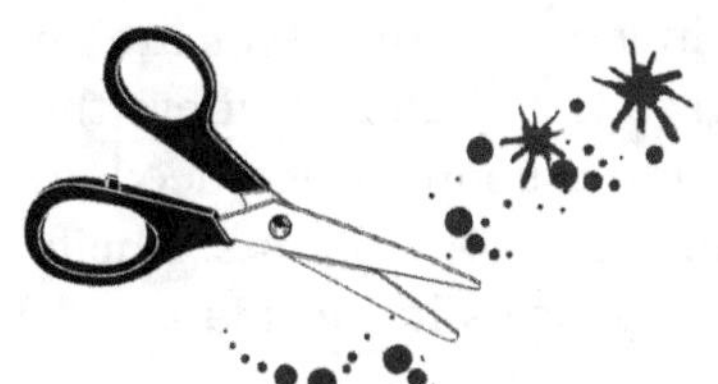

Crustaceans and Mollusks

Crustaceans: Included among these small ocean creatures are the lobsters, crabs, and shrimp. These animals have an exoskeleton, a hard shell (carapace) that provides protection and shape to their body. There are over 40,000 species on the Earth.

Mollusks: These unusual creatures are invertebrates. The octopus and squid have soft bodies with no bones and are large and swift swimmers. The scallop, mussel, and clam, are only a few of the mollusks. We can't even begin to name the 110,000 kinds of shellfish that are found throughout the world. Some grow shells to protect their soft bodies and live on or between the rocks and sandy floor of the ocean. Be considerate of nature when looking for shells. Do not disturb live habitats.

Want to learn more? See full references in the Bibliography!

FOLD-AND-CUT PATTERNS

Crab
Conch
Lobster
Octopus
Scallop
Shrimp
Squid

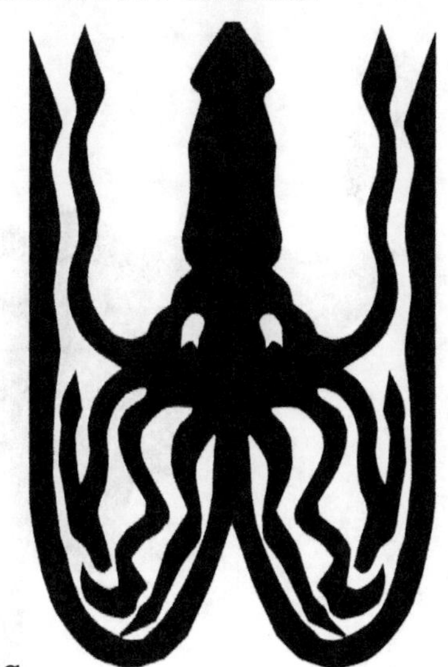

BOOKS AND STORIES

About Crustaceans by Cathryn and John Sill
Animals Without Bones Lobster by Lynn M. Stone
Just So Stories: The Crab that Played with the Sea by Rudyard Kipling
The Lobster and Ivy Higgins by Nancy Buss
The Nature of Florida's Ocean Life by Cathie Katz
Neptune's Nursery by Kim Michelle Toftand and Allan Sheather
Octavia and her Purple Ink Cloud by Donna and Doreen Rathmell
The Octopus: Phantom of the Sea by Mary M. Cerullo
Octopus' Den by Deirdre Langeland
Science Under the Sea by Lynn M. Stone

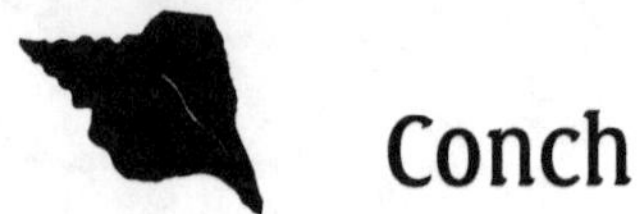

Conch

The Florida Horse Conch, Fighting Conch, Queen, and Hawkwing shells are shell collector's favorites. But remember, a living creature was there first, a mollusk! The Horse Conch is the state shell of Florida and is chalky salmon, orange and white in color, being 20 inches in length. Their eyes are on tentacles on the top of the head. Living on the sandy bottom of the ocean in the shallows where the eelgrass is plentiful, are mollusks in their shells. They have a foot, eyes, and a snout. Some feed on delicate algae while others are carnivores and eat bivalve shells as well as oysters and clams. Shells can become homes for other species when they become empty. (*Protected Species in Florida.)

National Audubon Society First Field Guide Shells, 26, 100, 101
Seashells of the World, 16, 19, 22, 42, 43, 85
Snails, Shellfish and other Mollusks, 10, 11, 17, 28, 29

★ Quick and easy.
✂ Top fold.
✂ Follow directions on page 8.
✂ Tape the pattern in place or make a light pencil tracing.
✂ Fold on the dotted line to cut opening in shell for the mollusk to live in.

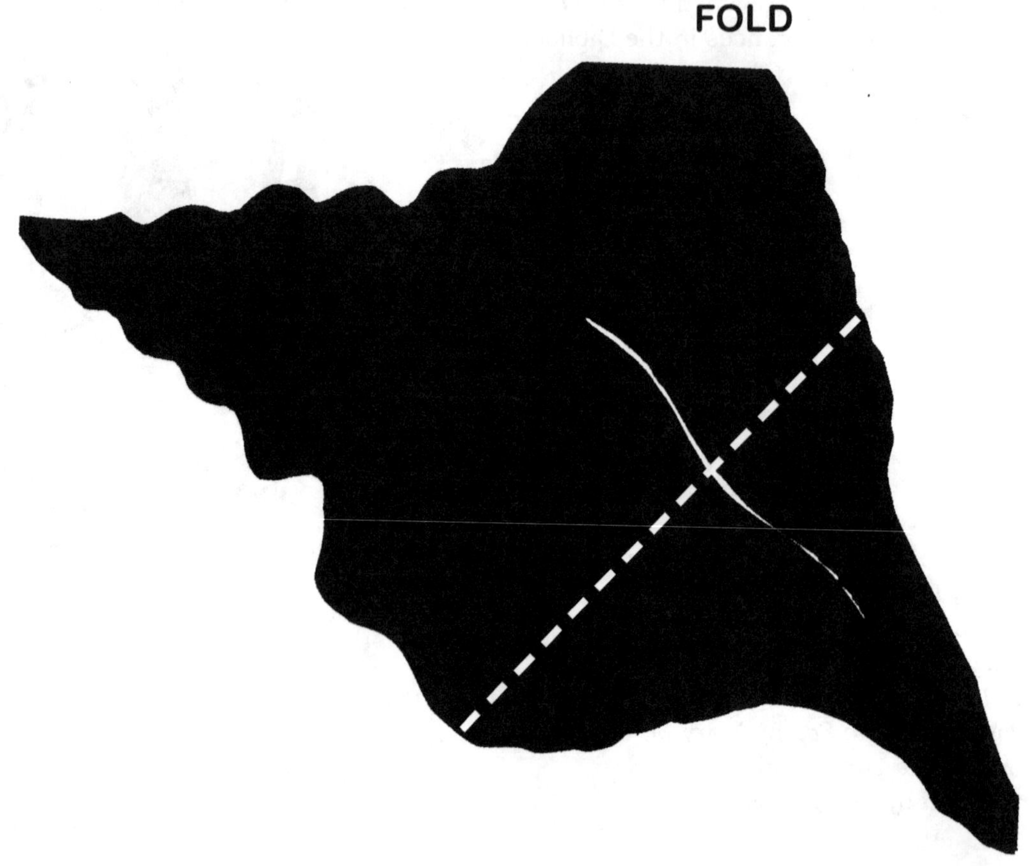

Crab

The carapace is a protective shell that covers most of the crab. A crab has two large pincers for picking up food, and sharp claws on the four other limbs used for walking and swimming. Protruding eyes and two pair of antennae are distinctive.

Eye Witness Books: Seashore, 44, 45, 46, 47, 48, 49
Eye Witness Dictionaries: The Visual Dictionary of Animals, 28

★ Quick and easy.
✂ Double or Multi-image.
✂ Follow directions on page 6 or 7.
✂ Tape the pattern in place or make a light pencil tracing.
✂ Use a large hole paper punch for the eyes.
☺ Can be reduced or enlarged in size. There are red crabs, blue crabs, etc. So check references to see all the colors and shapes. Create your own patterns.
☺ Let your paper do the turning.

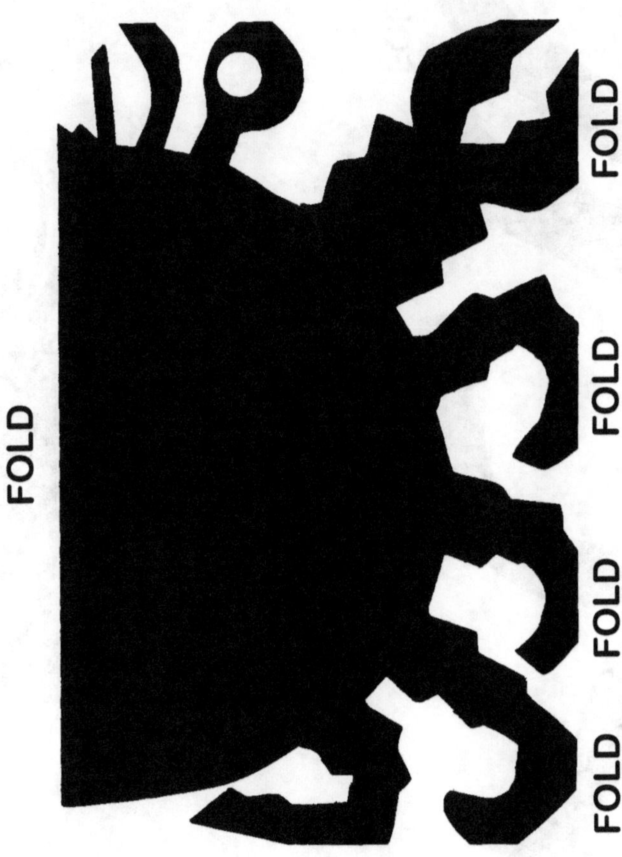

Lobster

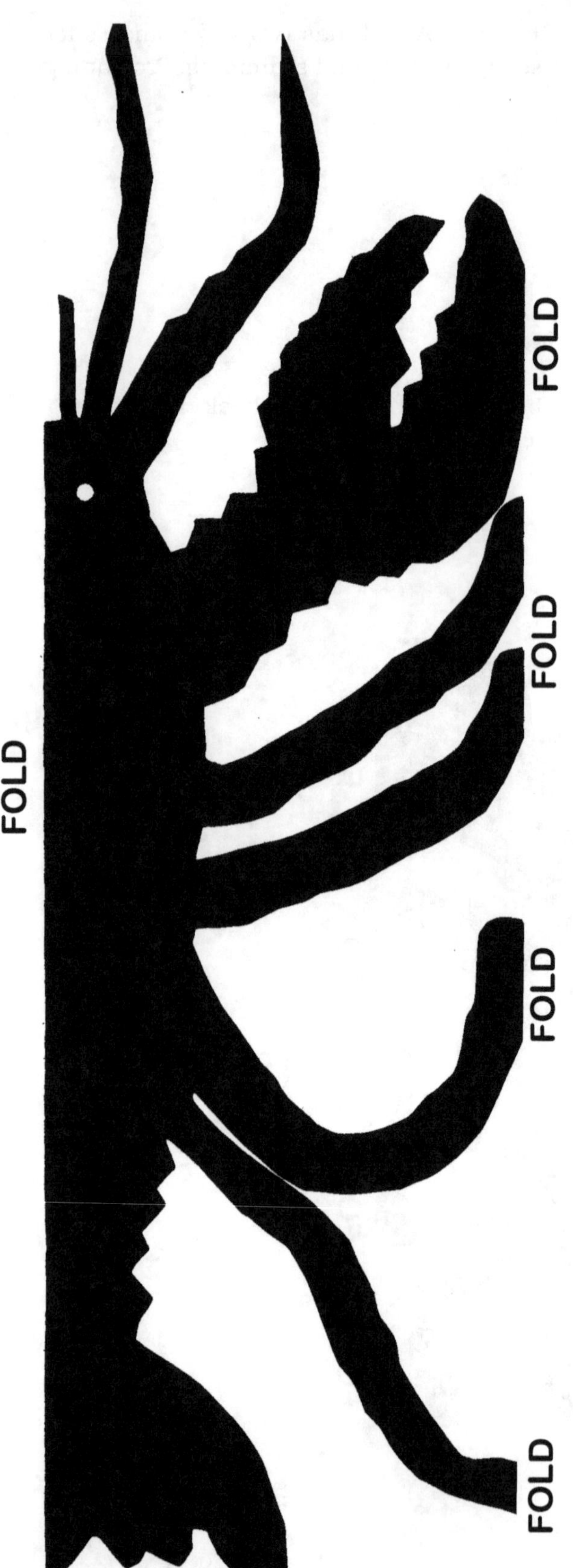

The lobster's eyes are on the top of stalks that protrude from the top of the head. Lobsters use their antennae to detect scents, heat, and vibrations. Their heavy pincer is for crushing shellfish while the other pincer is for slicing fish. They live on the rocky, sandy ocean floor.

Animals without Bones, Lobster, 5-24
Eye Witness Books: Seashore, 44, 45, 46, 47

- ★★ Intermediate.
- ✂ Double image.
- ✂ Follow directions on page 6.
- ✂ Tape the pattern in place or make a light pencil tracing.
- ✂ Use a small hole paper punch for the eyes.
- ☺ Let your paper do the turning.

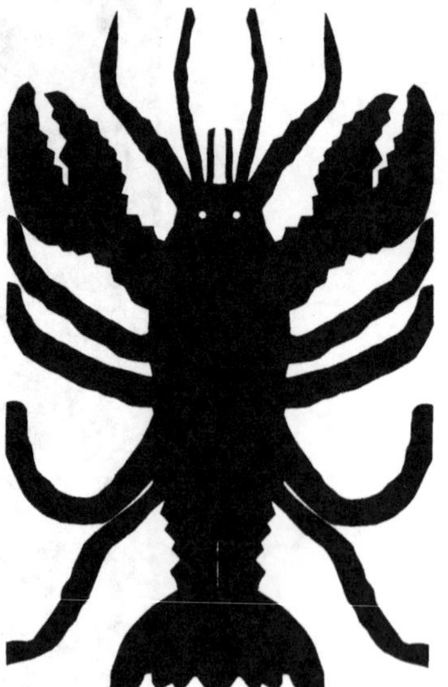

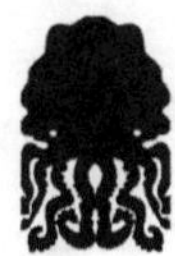

The octopus is a mollusk with eight arms with strong suction cups on the underside that can feel and taste. It can shoot ink into a predator's face, change its color to blend into the surroundings, and can even detach one of its arms, sending it crawling away, in hopes that the predator will chase after the arm instead of the octopus. The limb will grow back.

Aquatic Life of the World, 8,
Snails, Shellfish and other Mollusks, 6, 8, 9, 10, 15, 17, 22, 32, 33, 39, 41, 42

★★ Intermediate.
✂ Double or Multi-image.
✂ Follow directions on page 6 or 7.
✂ Tape the pattern in place or make a light pencil tracing.
✂ Use a large hole paper punch for the eyes.
☺ Let your paper do the turning.

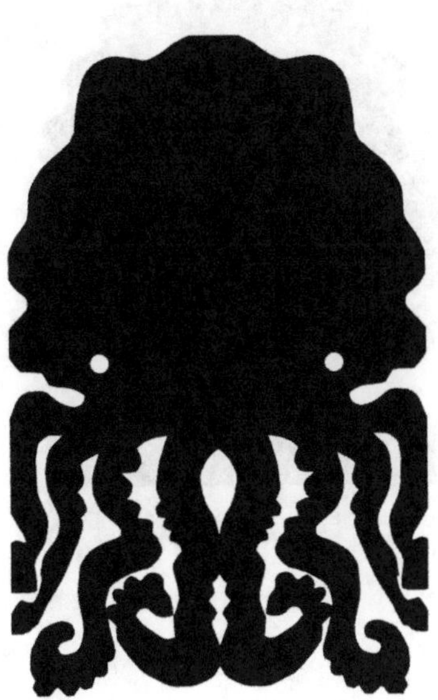

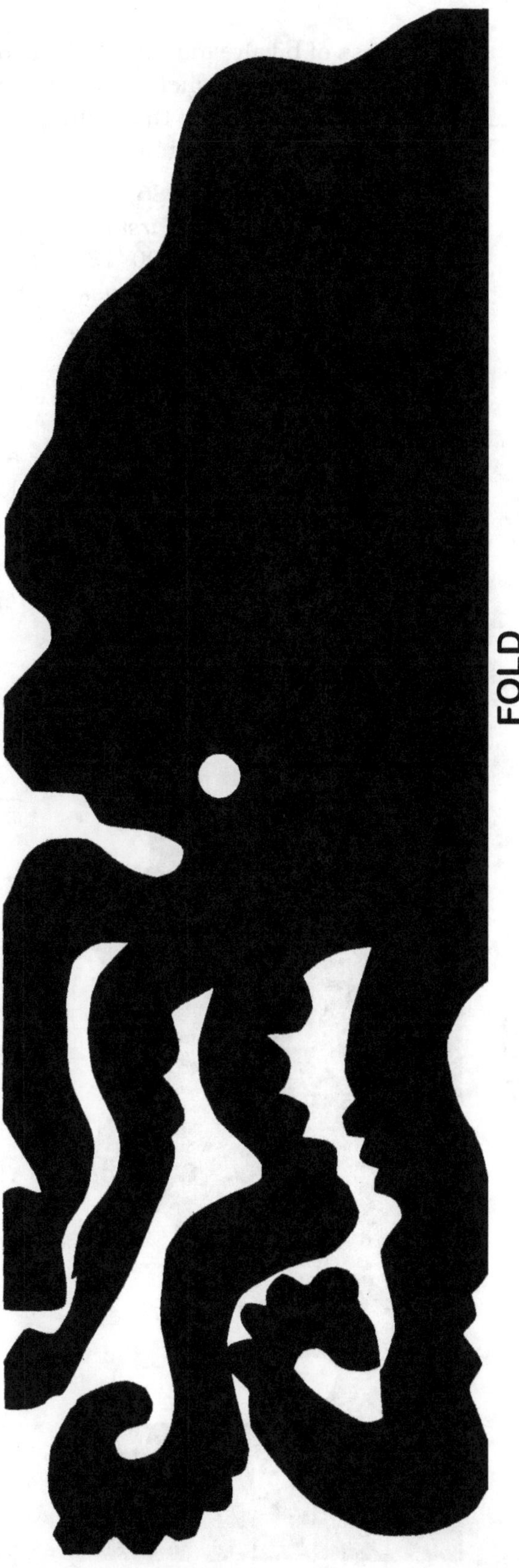

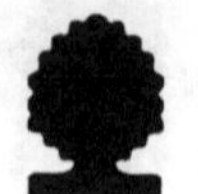

Scallop

This class of bivalve mollusk is defined as a double-shelled creature. They have one hundred little eyes at the edge of the shell opening to scan for prey and predators. There are 19 to 21 ribs on the yellow to purplish shell of the Atlantic calico scallop. These living creatures have a variety of names, classes, and families and may be known by more than one name.

Aquatic Life of the World, 486, 487
National Audubon Society First Field Guide Shells: 19, 29, 48, 49, 58, 59
Seashells of the World, 14, 20, 134-138
Snails, Shellfish and other Mollusks, 10, 11, 15, 19, 30

★ Quick and easy.
✂ Double or Multi-image.
✂ Follow directions on page 6 or 7.
✂ Tape the pattern in place or make a light pencil tracing.
☺ After the scallop is cut you can make folds to represent the ridges.

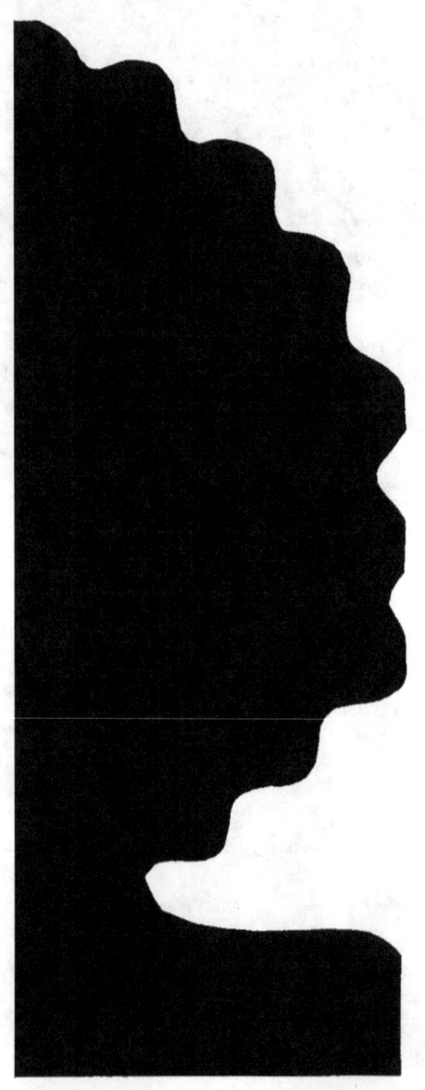

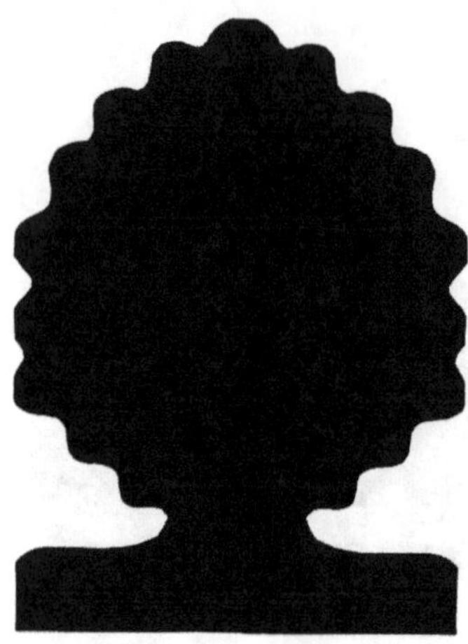

Shrimp

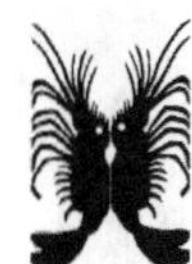

The shrimp is a small ten-limbed crustacean with blunt claws on the first pair of limbs. They are found in tidal pools, living in the sand and among the seaweed. There are 2,000 species in several different groups.

Eye Witness Books: Seashore, 32, 33, 44, 50, 64
Science Under the Sea, 5-24

★★ Intermediate.
✂ Double or Top Fold image.
✂ Follow directions on page 6 or 8.
✂ Tape the pattern in place or make a light pencil tracing.
✂ Use a large hole paper punch for the eyes.
☺ Let your paper do the turning.

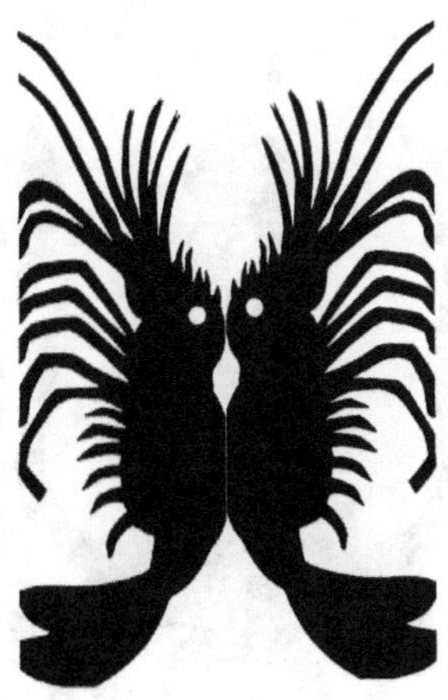

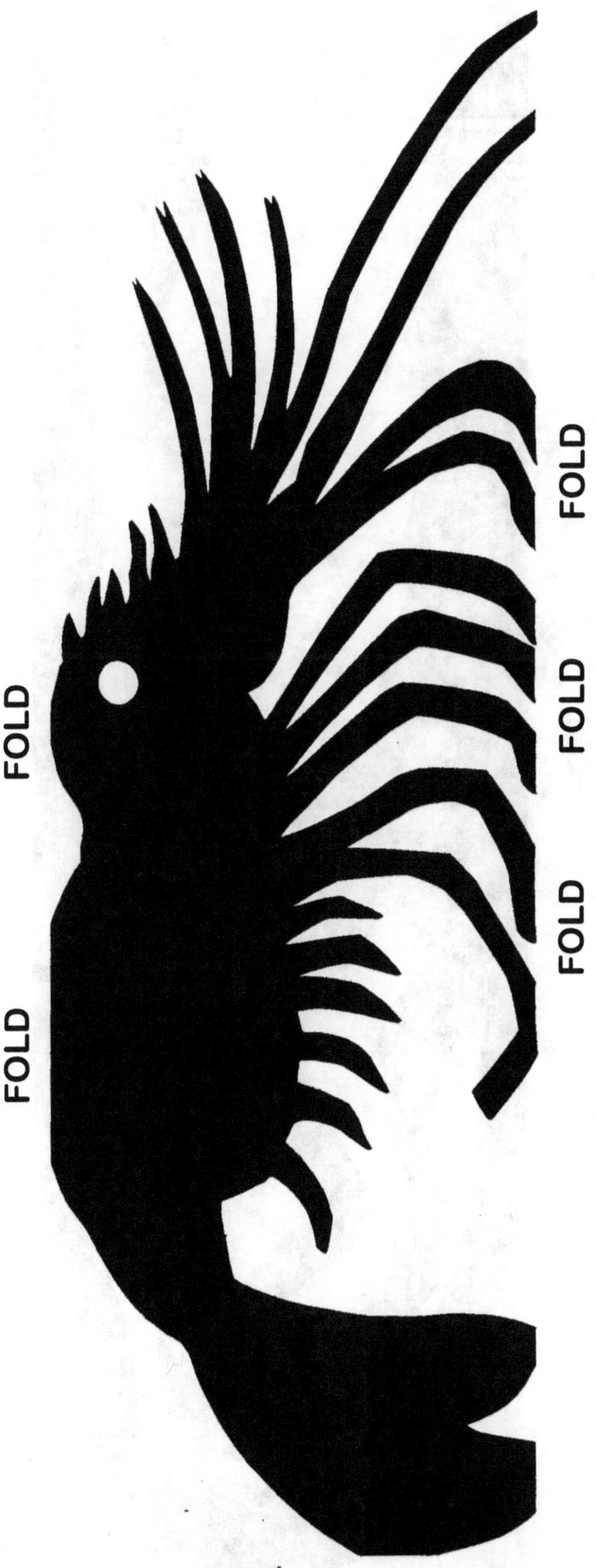

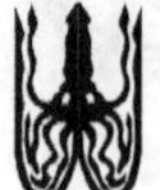

Squid

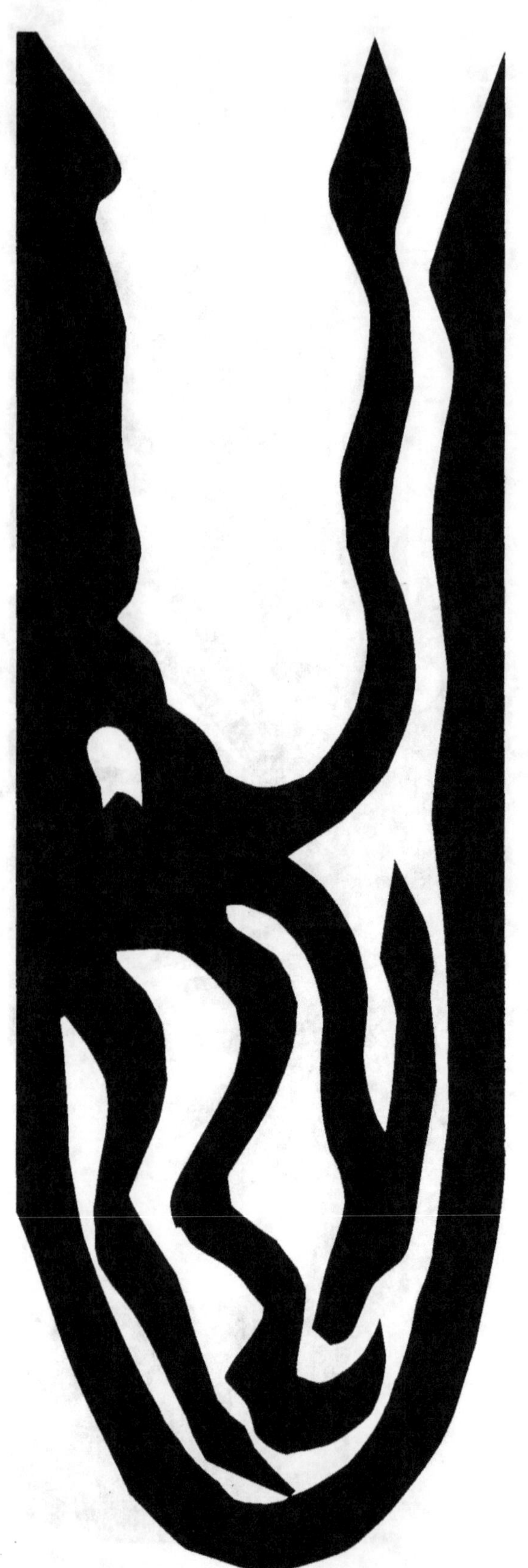

The squid is a mollusk with ten arms, called tentacles, that hang down from the head. Two are longer for use in hunting. They can shoot ink and change color to protect themselves from predators.

Eye Witness Books: Seashore. 26, 33, 38, 39, 56
Snails, Shellfish and other Mollusks, 33, 34, 35

★★★ Advanced.
✂ Double image.
✂ Follow directions on page 6.
✂ Tape the pattern in place or make a light pencil tracing.
✂ Use a large hole paper punch for the eye and small scissors to finish the shape.
☺ When you hold up the squid the long arms will hang down.

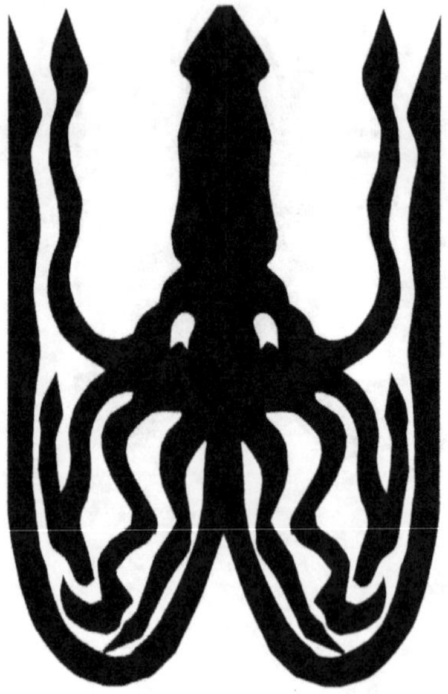

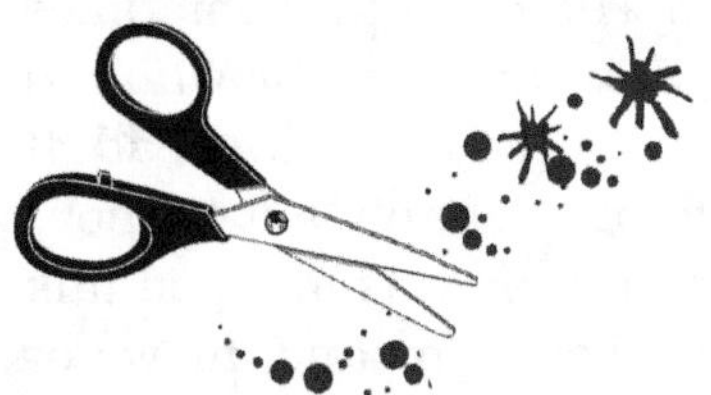

Marine Mammals

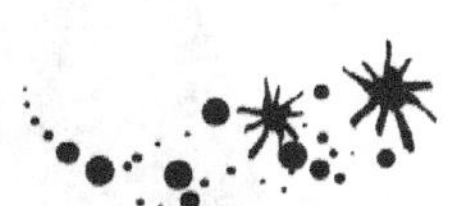

Marine Mammals: A cetacean is a marine mammal having a smooth body, one or two openings in the top of the head for breathing, flippers, a thick layer of blubber that helps them float and a horizontally flattened tail that propels them through the water. Whales, dolphins, manatees, and porpoises are cetaceans. Those listed are only a few of the marine mammals in the oceans of the world.

FOLD-AND-CUT PATTERNS

Bottlenose Dolphin
Manatee
Sea Otter
Seal
Whale

BOOKS AND STORIES

Dolphin Adventure: A True Story by Wayne Grover
Dolphins at Daybreak (Magic Tree House # 9) by Mary Pope Osborne & Sal Murdocca
Here Come the Dolphins by Alice E. Goudey
If a Dolphin Were a Fish by Loran Wiodarski
Just So Stories: How the Whale Got His Throat by Rudyard Kipling
The Lost Seal by Diane McKnight
Otter on His Own: The Story of a Sea Otter by Doe Boyle
Sea Otter Inlet by Celia Godkin
Songs of the Humpback Whale by Jodi Picoult
Water Beds: Sleeping in the Ocean by Gail Langer Karwoski
The Whale is Smiling by Josephine Nobisso

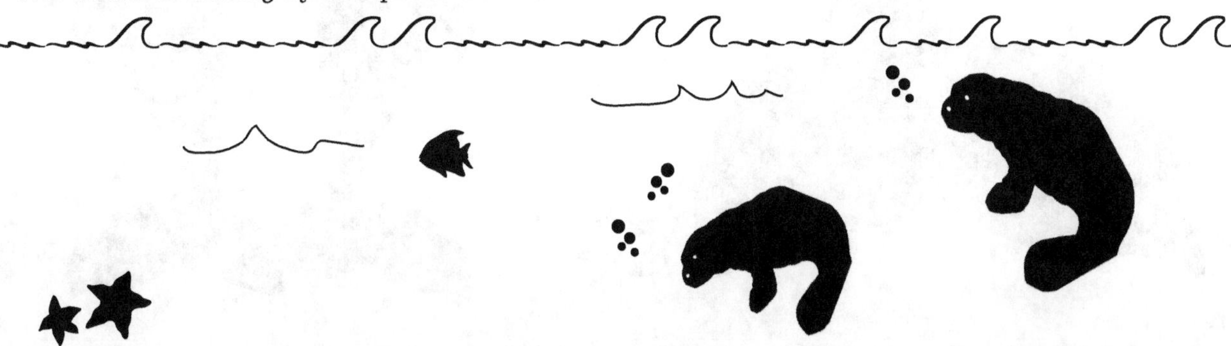

Bottlenose Dolphin

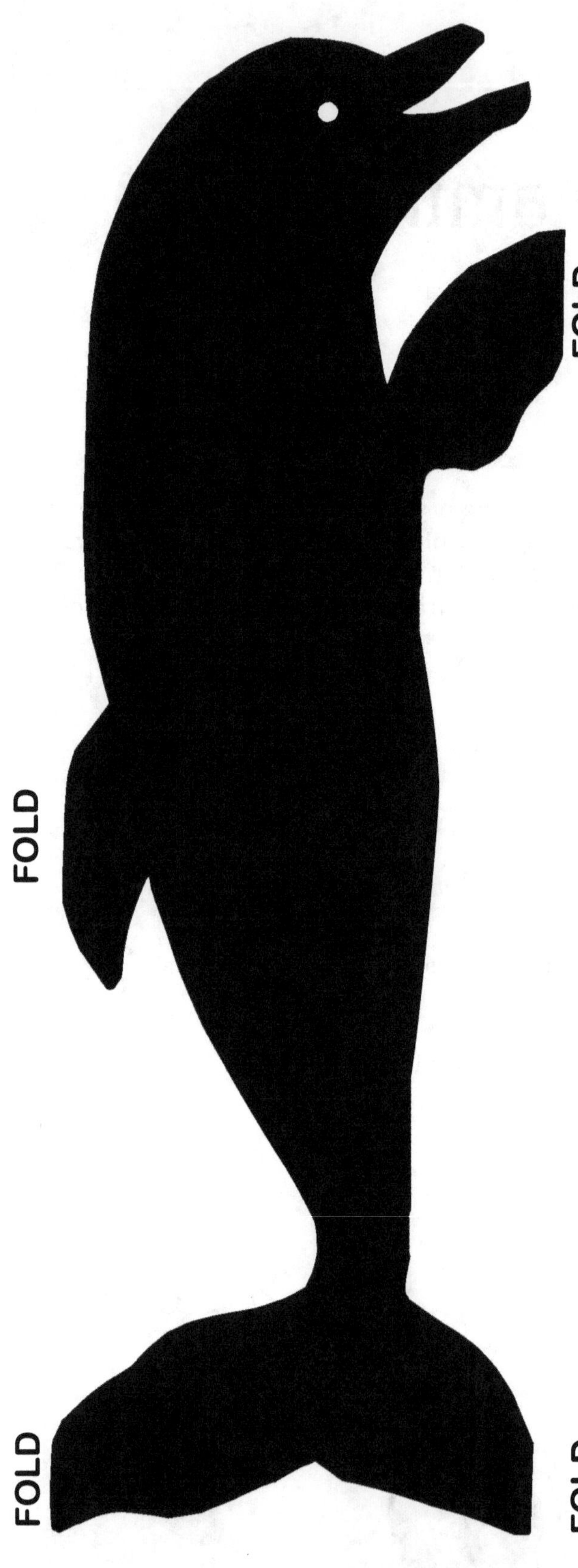

The state of Florida designated the dolphin as its saltwater mammal. The dolphin, sometimes called a porpoise, breathes through a blowhole, a crescent shaped nostril on the top of its head. It has a thin torpedo-like body enabling it to move swiftly through the water. Dolphins in a pod talk to each other by clicks, barks, moans, mews or whistles. They are friendly and trainable. The common dolphin has about 200 teeth.

Animal Fact and File, 50, 51
Eye Witness Dictionaries: The Visual Dictionary of Animals, 52-55, 59
Whales and Dolphins, 106-127

- ★ Quick and easy.
- ✂ Double or Multi-image.
- ✂ Follow directions on page 6 or 7.
- ✂ Tape the pattern in place or make a light pencil tracing.
- ✂ Use a small hole paper punch for the eyes.
- ☺ Reduce the pattern to make the baby dolphin.

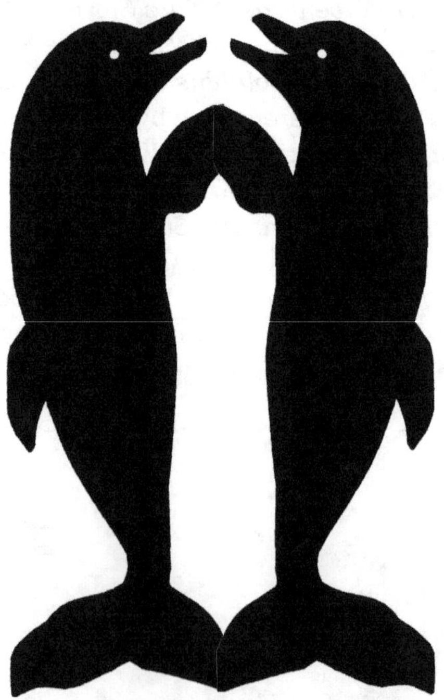

Manatee 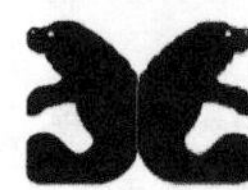

Manatees, also known as sea cows, are gentle plant-eating mammals with front flippers that have nails and a flattened paddle like tail helping them move through the water. They can grow to ten feet long, weighing over 1,000 pounds. The manatee lives in the warm Florida waters and is the state marine mammal for Florida. Mother manatees are very protective of their young. The baby plays, swims and feeds close to the mother. Urban expansion, boats, pollution, and propellers endanger them, with humans being their worst enemy. (*Endangered Species)

Animal Fact and File, 104, 105
Eye Witness Dictionaries: The Visual Dictionary of Animals, 59
The Vanishing Manatee, 1-64

- ★ Quick and easy.
- ✂ Double or Multi-image.
- ✂ Follow directions on page 6 or 7.
- ✂ Tape the pattern in place or make a light pencil tracing.
- ✂ Use a small hole paper punch for the eyes.
- ☺ Enlarge this pattern to make the mother manatee.

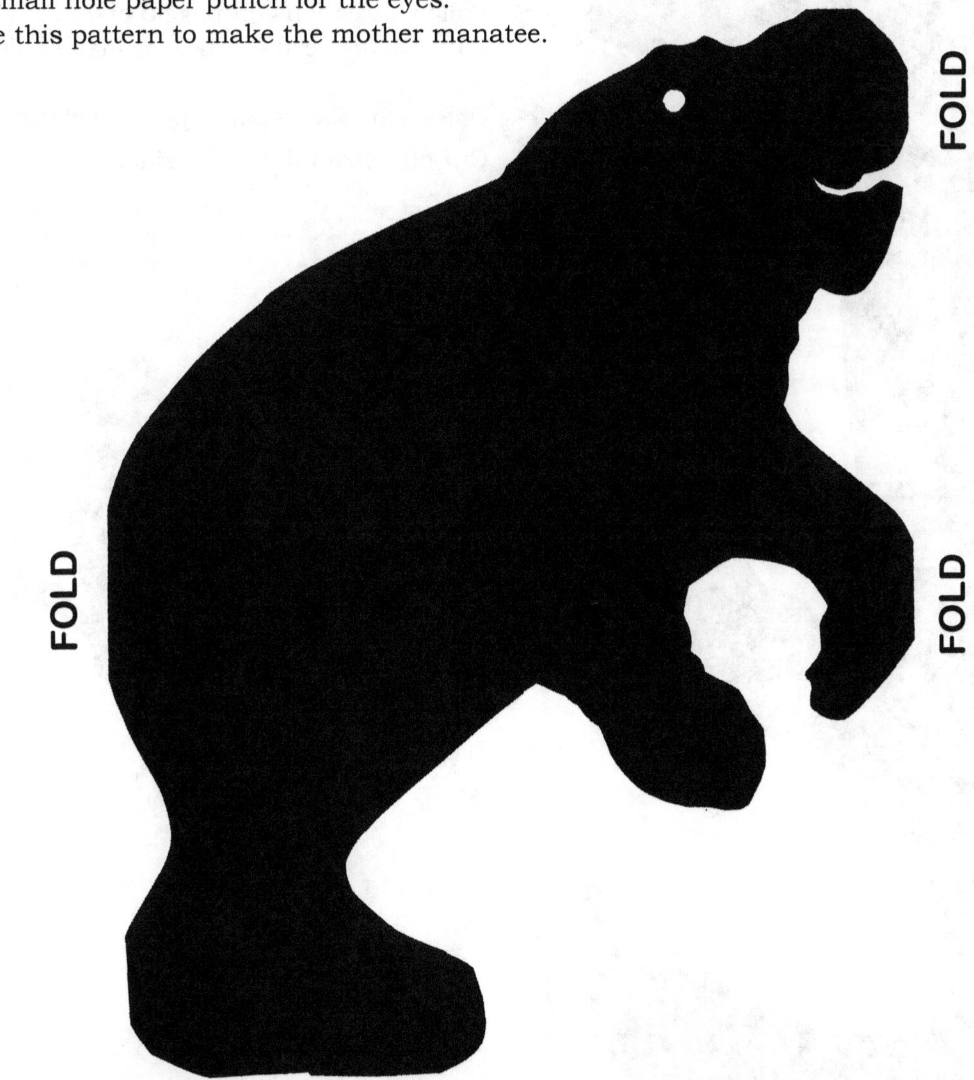

Sea Otter

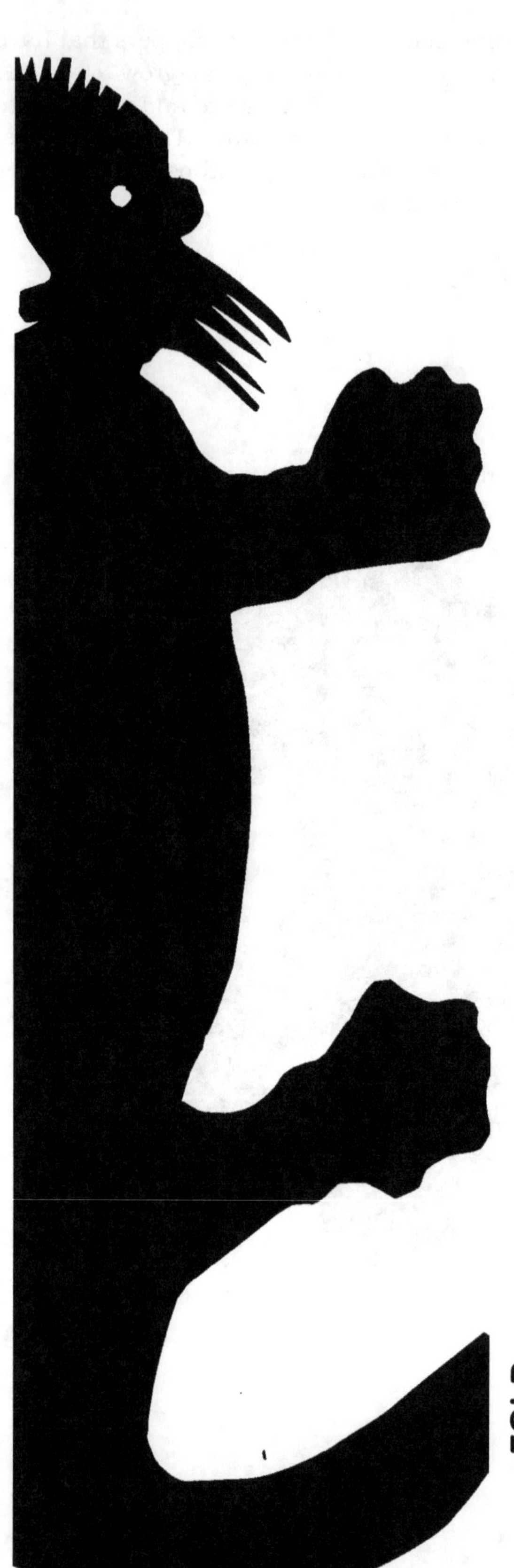

The sea otter of the Northern Pacific has large fully webbed hind feet. The front paws have fingers that are nearly fused. They have long stiff whiskers on the face, throat and elbows. They eat, sleep, and live floating on their backs in kelp beds in the ocean. Weighing between 40 to 60 pounds, they are the smallest of the marine mammals. They eat a variety of seafood, preferring sea urchins, crabs and abalone. (*Endangered Species)

Aquatic Life of the World 8, 508, 509, 510
Eye Witness Books: Seashore, 22, 24-25, 56
Water Beds: Sleeping in the Ocean, 1-32

★ Easy.
✂ Double or Multi-image.
✂ Follow directions on page 6 or 7.
✂ Tape the pattern in place or make a light pencil tracing.
✂ Use a small hole paper punch for the eyes.
☺ Cut off extra tail on one side.

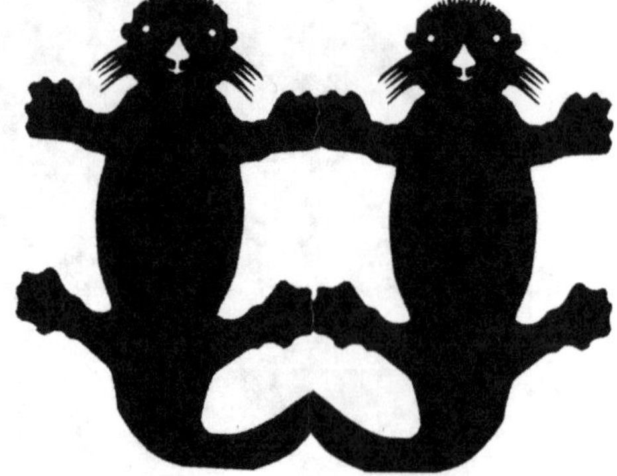

Seal

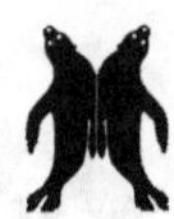

A carnivorous aquatic mammal with a sleek streamlined body, the seal has front flippers for swimming with elongated hind flippers for moving around on land. They can hold their breath for up to an hour underwater. Their diet consists mainly of fish, squid, octopuses, krill, crabs and shrimp. (*Endangered Species)

Animal Fact and File, 44, 45
Aquatic Life of the World, 56, 57
Eye Witness Dictionaries: The Visual Dictionary of Animals, 52-55, 59

★ Quick and easy.
✂ Double or Multi-image.
✂ Follow directions on page 6 or 7.
✂ Tape the pattern in place or make a light pencil tracing.
✂ Use a small hole paper punch for the eyes and nose.
☺ Enlarge the pattern to create a different size seal.

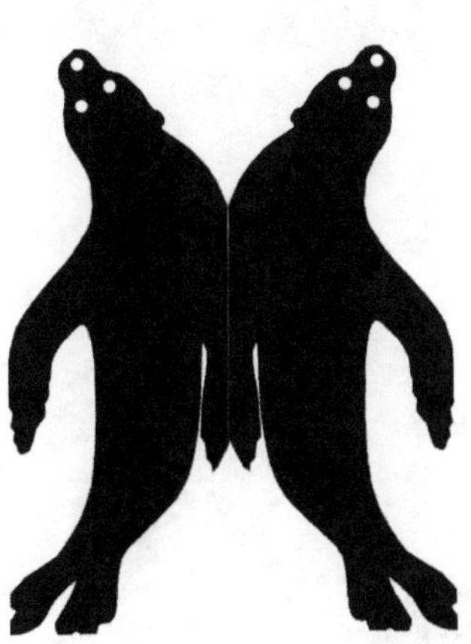

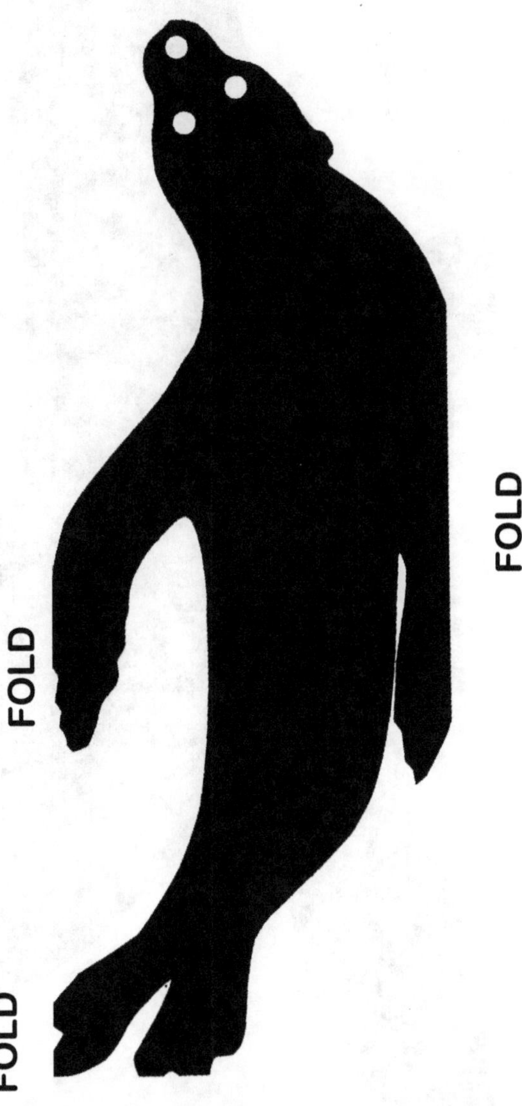

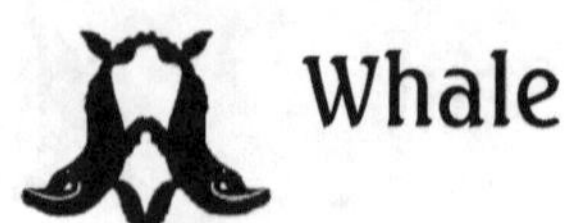

Whale

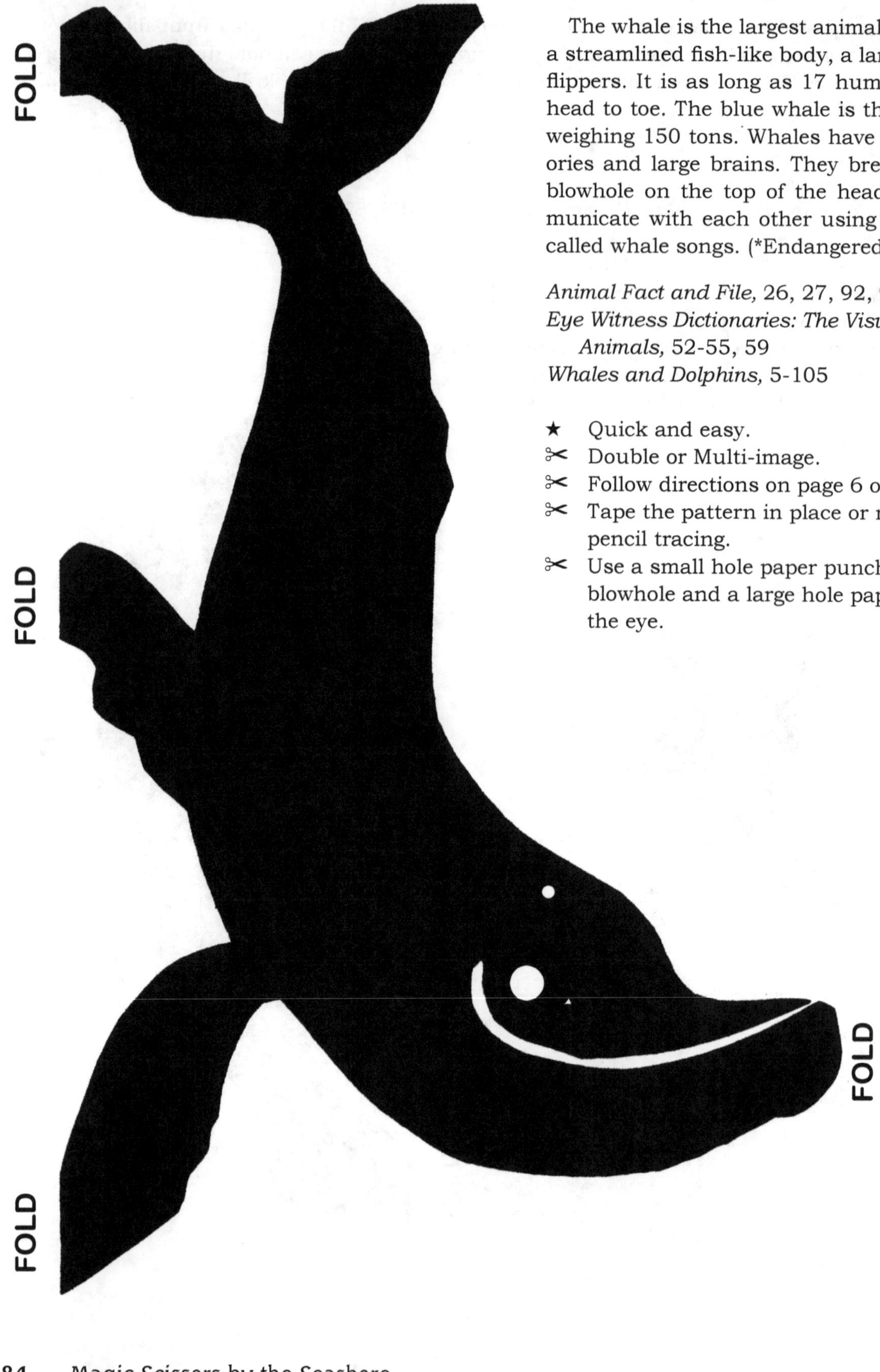

The whale is the largest animal of all time with a streamlined fish-like body, a large flat tail, and flippers. It is as long as 17 human adults lying head to toe. The blue whale is the largest whale weighing 150 tons. Whales have excellent memories and large brains. They breathe through a blowhole on the top of the head. Whales communicate with each other using lyrical sounds, called whale songs. (*Endangered Species)

Animal Fact and File, 26, 27, 92, 93, 164, 165
Eye Witness Dictionaries: The Visual Dictionary of Animals, 52-55, 59
Whales and Dolphins, 5-105

- ★ Quick and easy.
- ✂ Double or Multi-image.
- ✂ Follow directions on page 6 or 7.
- ✂ Tape the pattern in place or make a light pencil tracing.
- ✂ Use a small hole paper punch for the blowhole and a large hole paper punch for the eye.

FOLD

FOLD

FOLD

FOLD

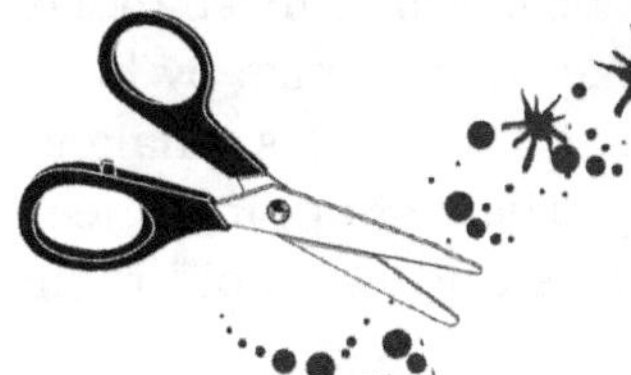

Seaside Mammals

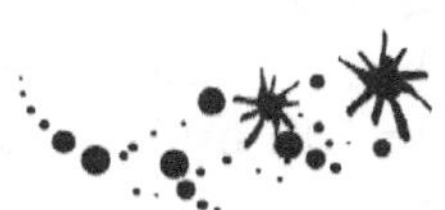

Mammals: The mammal world has perhaps 10 million different types, or species, of animals in the world. Human beings are also classified as mammals. Each type of animal is grouped by family, order and class. All mammals are warm-blooded, have fur or hair, and belong to one class, Mammalia. Mammals give birth to live young and feed their newborn offspring on milk that the mammary gland produces, hence the term mammal. They use their senses to interact, communicate, identify danger, locate food, and live in almost every habitat on earth.

FOLD-AND-CUT PATTERNS

Armadillo
Armadillo Burrowing
Florida Black Bear
Florida Panther
Perdido Key Beach Mouse

BOOKS AND STORIES

The Astonishing Armadillo by Dee Stuart
A Bear Named Trouble by Marion Dane Bauer
A Black Bear's Story by E. Liers
Bears in the Wild by Ada and Frank Graham
Don't Ever Cross That Road! An Armadillo Story by Conrad J. Storad & Nathaniel P. Jensen
It's a Mouse by D. M. Souza
Just So Stories: The Beginning of the Armadillo by Rudyard Kipling
Kratt's Creatures: Where're the Bears? By M. Kratt and C. Kratt
Moon in Bear's Eyes by Stephen R. Swinburne
The Strange Armadillo by Wyatt Blassingame
Unraveling Threads: Armadillo Odyssey by Anji

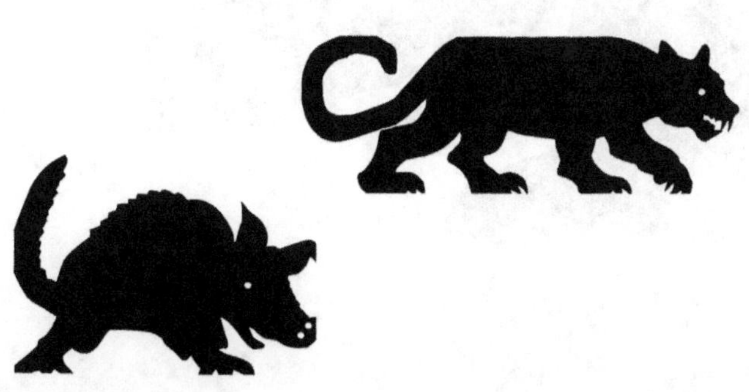

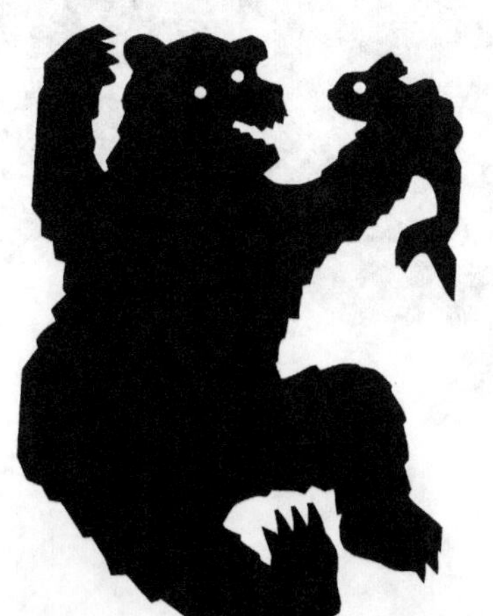

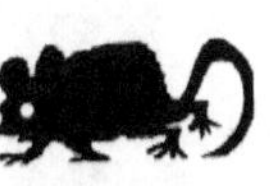

Armadillo

From the tip of the nose, which looks like the snout on a hog, to the rat-like tail, this is one unique creature. A head like a lizard, eyes like a pig, a mule's ears and claws like a bear, this nine-banded mammal is encased in carapace, a boney shell much like a turtle. They make their homes by burrowing underground where they sleep and raise their young. They eat worms, ants, beetles, snakes, grubs, termites, roots, fruit, and berries. There are 20 species of Armadillo. Their short front feet have long powerful claws. They can curl into a tight ball to protect themselves and can hold their breath underwater for six minutes.

Animal Fact and File, 20, 21
The Astonishing Armadillo, 5-47
The Strange Armadillo, 9-64

- ★ Quick and easy.
- ✂ Double or Multi-image.
- ✂ Follow directions on page 6 or 7.
- ✂ Tape the pattern in place or make a light pencil tracing.
- ✂ Use a small hole paper punch for the eye and nose.

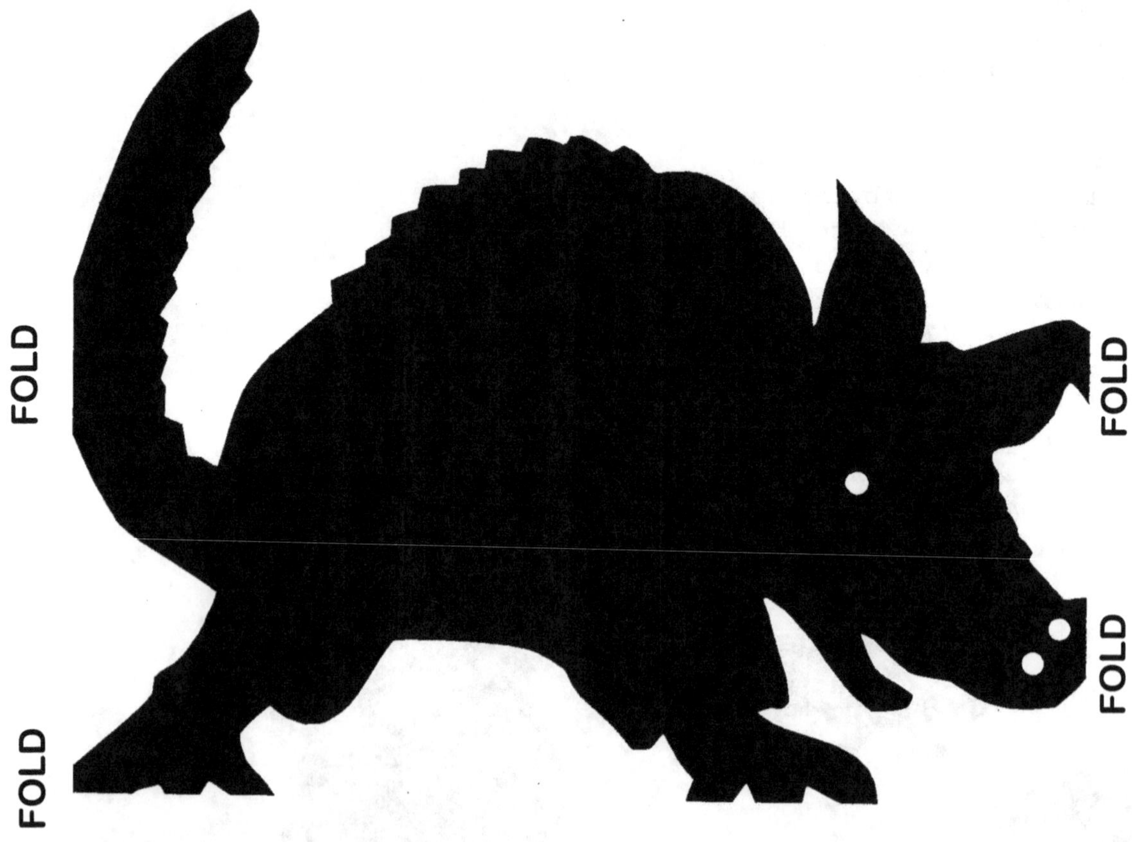

Armadillo Burrowing

★★ Intermediate
✂ Circle fold-and-cut.
✂ Follow directions on page 10.
✂ Tape the pattern in place or make a light pencil tracing.
✂ Use a small hole paper punch for the eye and nose.
☺ Let your paper do the turning.
☺ Cut away the smaller areas first. This gives you more paper area to hold as you cut.

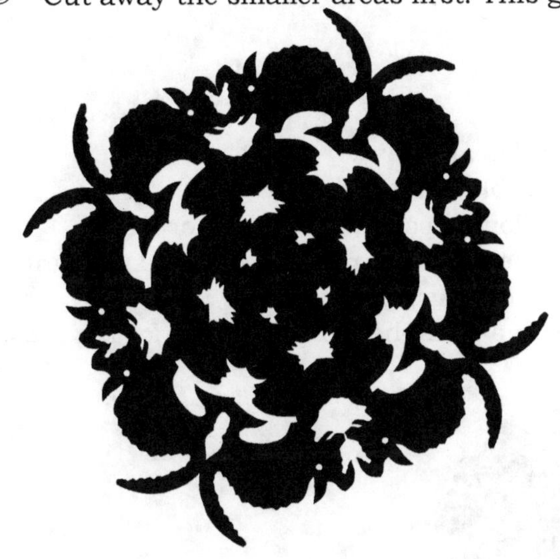

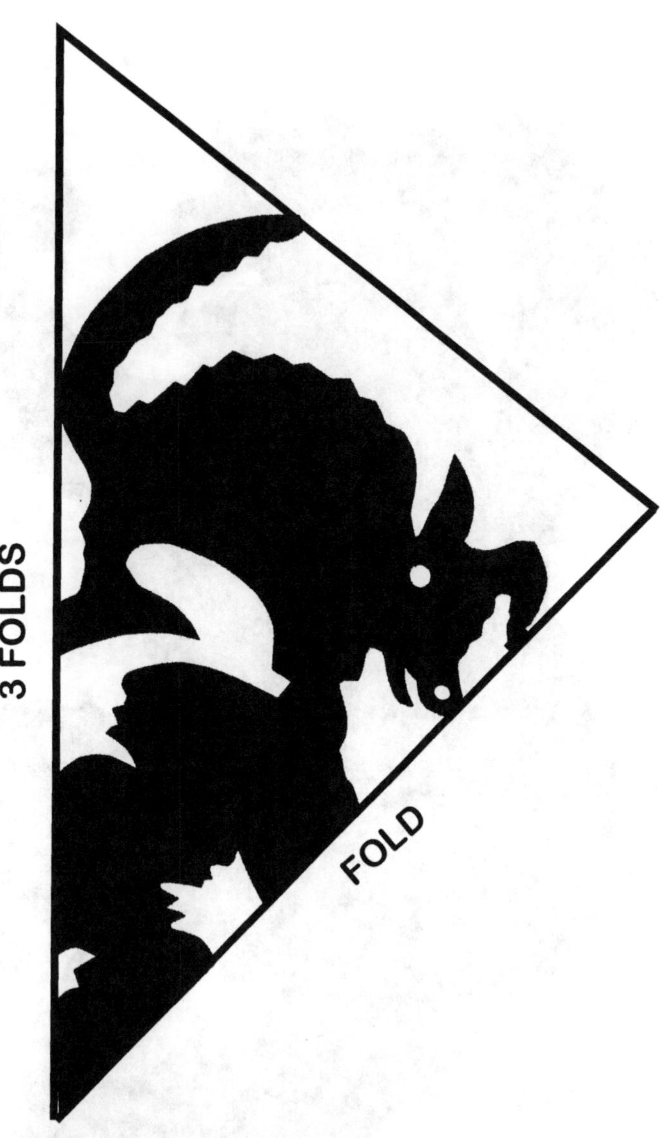

Florida Black Bear

The Florida black bear is the smallest of North American bears at only 5 to 6 feet tall. Their long, sharp, heavily curved claws are used to climb trees and forage for food such as berries, fish, honey, roots, armadillos, grass and Sabal Palm fruit. These bears are still large, powerful mammals with rounded ears, a short stubby tail, and five-toed paws. They also have large canine teeth. Bears are normally shy. Because of increased land development the bears habitat is disappearing. (*Threatened Species)

Animal Fact and File, 24, 25
The Threatened Florida Black Bear, 9-64
www.bearwatch.org
www.myflwc.com/educator/blkbear.htm

- ★ Quick and easy.
- ✂ Double or Multi-image.
- ✂ Follow directions on page 6 or 7.
- ✂ Tape the pattern in place or make a light pencil tracing.
- ✂ Use a small hole paper punch for the eyes.

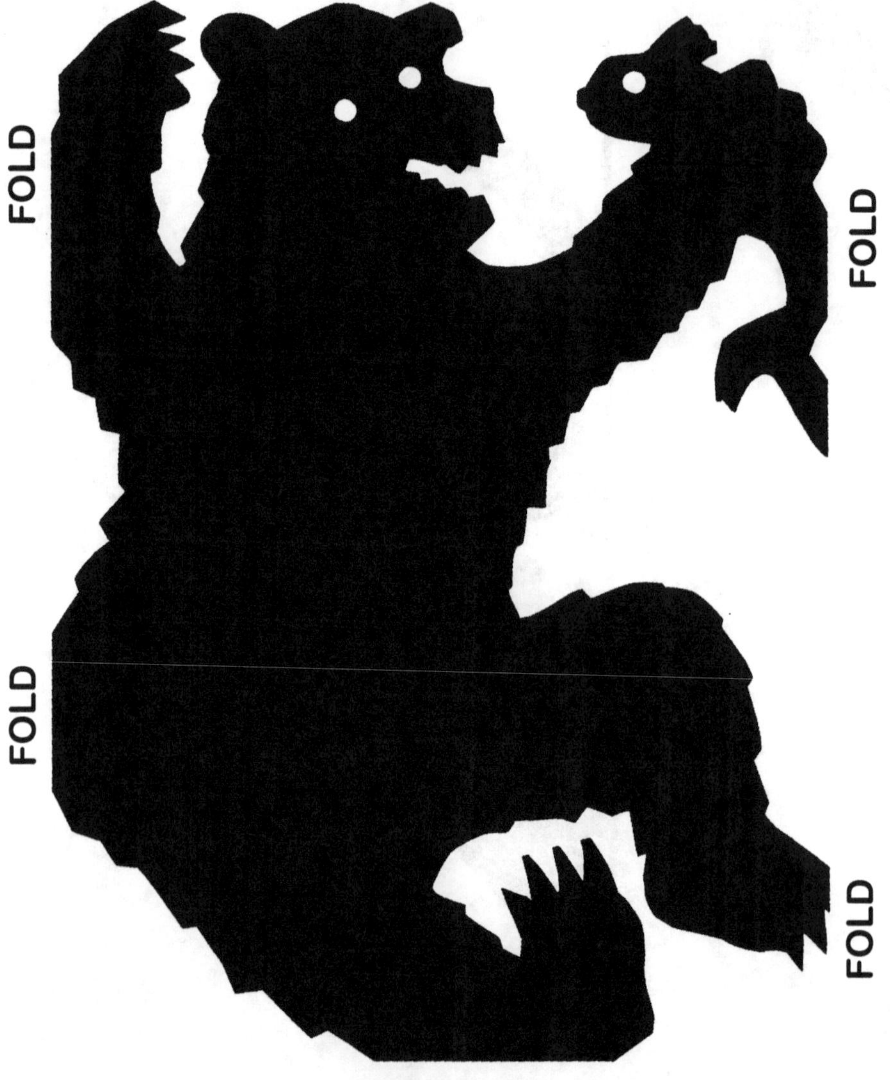

Florida Panther

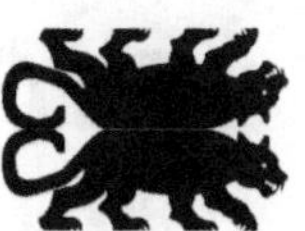

The panther is the state animal of Florida. The fur of the Florida panther is tawny brown on the back and pale gray on the underside. They have very sharp claws, used for climbing trees. Their tails are long. They might be seen at the edge of the pinelands along the shore. Panthers communicate through sounds like purrs, screams, growls, peeps, whistles, moans and hisses. They are strictly carnivores. Perhaps only 70 to 100 remain alive today. Their habitat is being destroyed daily. (*Endangered Species)

Animal Fact and File, 98, 99
www.flheritage.com/facts
www.myfwc.com/panther/

- ★ Quick and easy.
- ✂ Top fold.
- ✂ Follow directions on page 8.
- ✂ Tape the pattern in place or make a light pencil tracing.
- ✂ Use a small hole paper punch for the eyes.
- ☺ Great stand-up figures to prowl across the bookshelf.

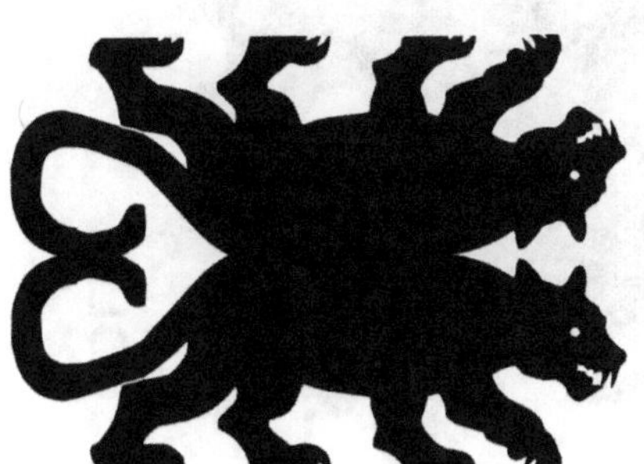

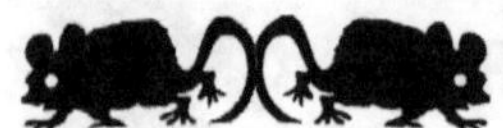

Perdido Key Beach Mouse

This small white and gray mouse lives in a burrow in the sandy dunes of Perdido Key, on the beaches. These beach mice mate for life. They hold their food with their front paws and sit back on their hind legs. (*Endangered Species)

It's a Mouse, 3-40
www.nps.gov/archive/guis/gothabitat/mouse.htm
www.google.com/images

★ Quick and easy.
✂ Top or Side fold image.
✂ Follow directions on page 8.
✂ Tape the pattern in place or make a light pencil tracing.
✂ Use a large hole paper punch for the eyes.

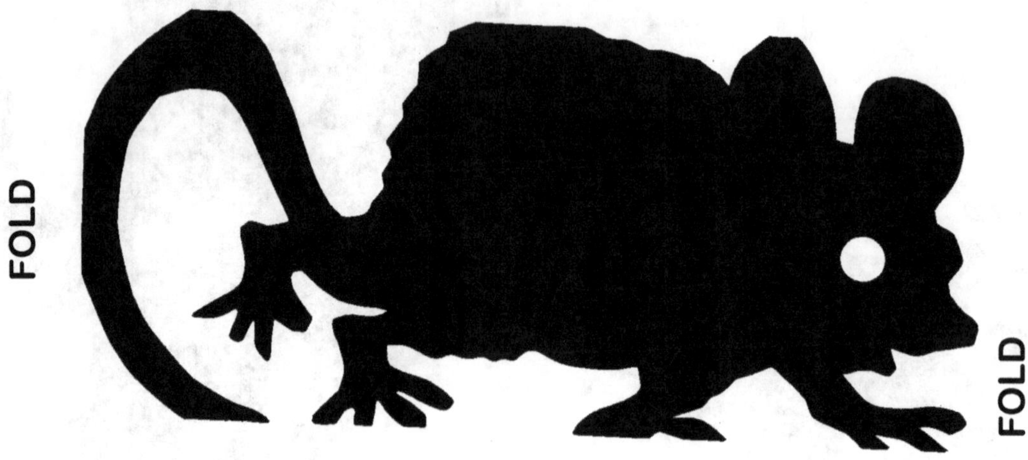

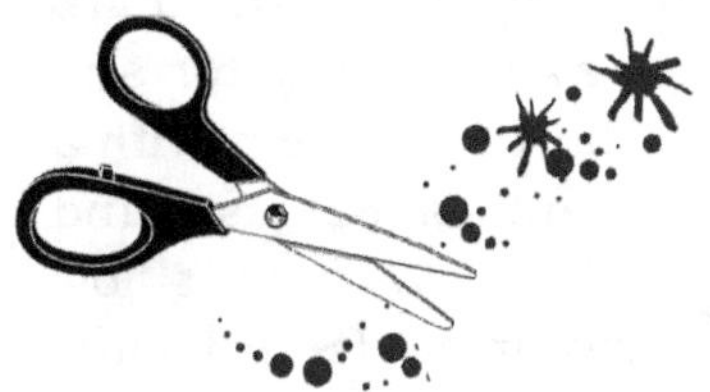

Reptiles

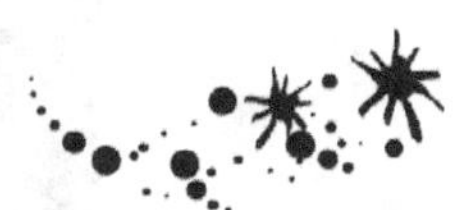

Reptiles have backbones and are classified as vertebrates. All reptiles breathe air and those who live in the water are able to submerge for a time but must rise to the surface to breathe.

Reproduction by reptiles is by bearing their young alive or by laying shelled eggs on land. There are over 8,000 known species of reptiles.

Want to learn more? See full references in the Bibliography!

FOLD-AND-CUT PATTERNS

Alligator
Green Sea Turtle
Green Sea Turtle Hatchling
Tortoise (Land Turtle)
Tortoise Hatchling

STORIES AND BOOKS

The Alligator Book by C.C. Lockwood
Alligators, Sharks and Panthers: Deadly Encounters with Florida's Top Predator-Man by Charles Sobczak
Carolina's Story: Sea Turtles Get Sick Too! by Donna Rathmell
Sea Turtles (Our Wild World) by Lorraine A. Jay
A Series of Unfortunate Events #2: The Reptile Room by Lemony Snicket
There's a Frog on a Log in the Bog by Robert and Linda Day
Tortoise and the Hare by Aesop
The Tortoise and the Jackrabbit by Susan Lowell & Jim Harris
Tudley Didn't Know by John Himmelman
Turtle Summer: A Journal for my Daughter by Mary Alice Monroe
Turtles in my Sandbox by Jennifer Keats Curtis
Who Lives in an Alligator Hole? by Anne Rockwell & Lizzy Rockwell

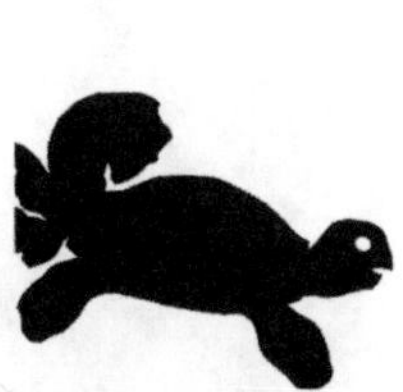
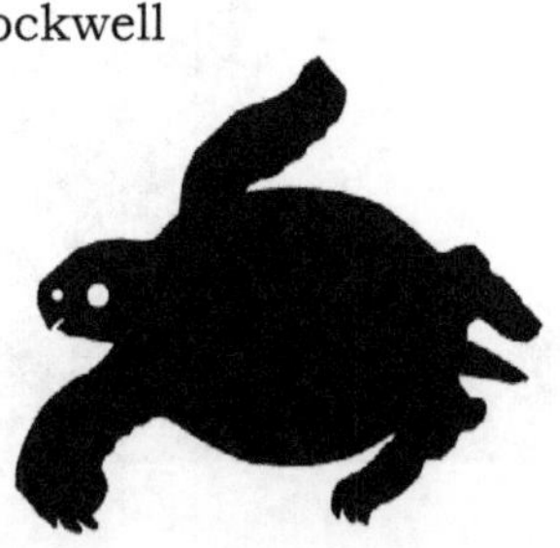

Alligator

The alligator is the state reptile of Florida. An American alligator's head is broad, with sharp teeth and a huge jaw. It is a fierce predator and very aggressive. It has four short strong legs with a long powerful tail. Alligators are sometimes found on the shores and waters of the rivers that flow into the sea. They can grow up to 18 feet long. (*Threatened Species)

Firefly Encyclopedia of Reptiles and Amphibians, 110, 111, 212-223

Reptiles and Amphibians: Birth and Growth, 12, 22-24

Wild Life and Plants of the World, 26, 27

★ Easy.
✂ Top fold image.
✂ Follow directions on page 8.
✂ Tape the pattern in place or make a light pencil tracing.
✂ Use a small hole paper punch eye.
☺ Use green paper.

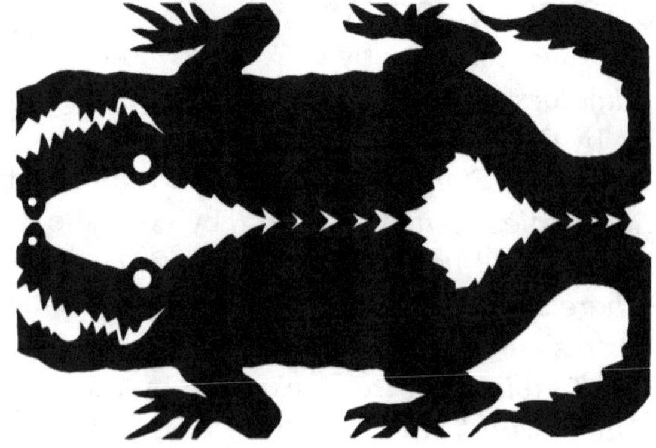

Green Sea Turtle

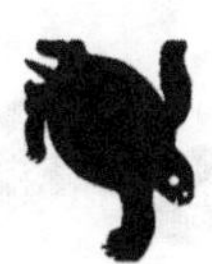

The green sea turtle can be found in all the five oceans except the Arctic. They have no teeth. The seas also contain the loggerhead (*threatened), black sea turtle, flatback, kemp's ridley (*most endangered), hawksbill (*endangered), olive ridley (*endangered), and leatherback (*threatened). There are about 293 different species of turtles. A sea turtle is not able to pull in its head or long flippers into its shell also called a carapace.

The female returns to the shore of her birth to deposit the eggs in the sand, and then returns to the sea. The hatchlings dig their way out of their sandy nest and hurry to the sea. One day the survivors will travel hundreds of miles to return to the sandy shore where they were born to lay their eggs. (*Endangered Species)

Aquatic Life of the World, 458-461
Eye Witness Books: Seashore, 56
Firefly Encyclopedia of Reptiles and Amphibians, 118-137
Reptiles and Amphibians; Birth and Growth, 6, 25, 26, 31
Turtle Summer: A Journal for my Daughter, 1-32
www.seaturtles.org

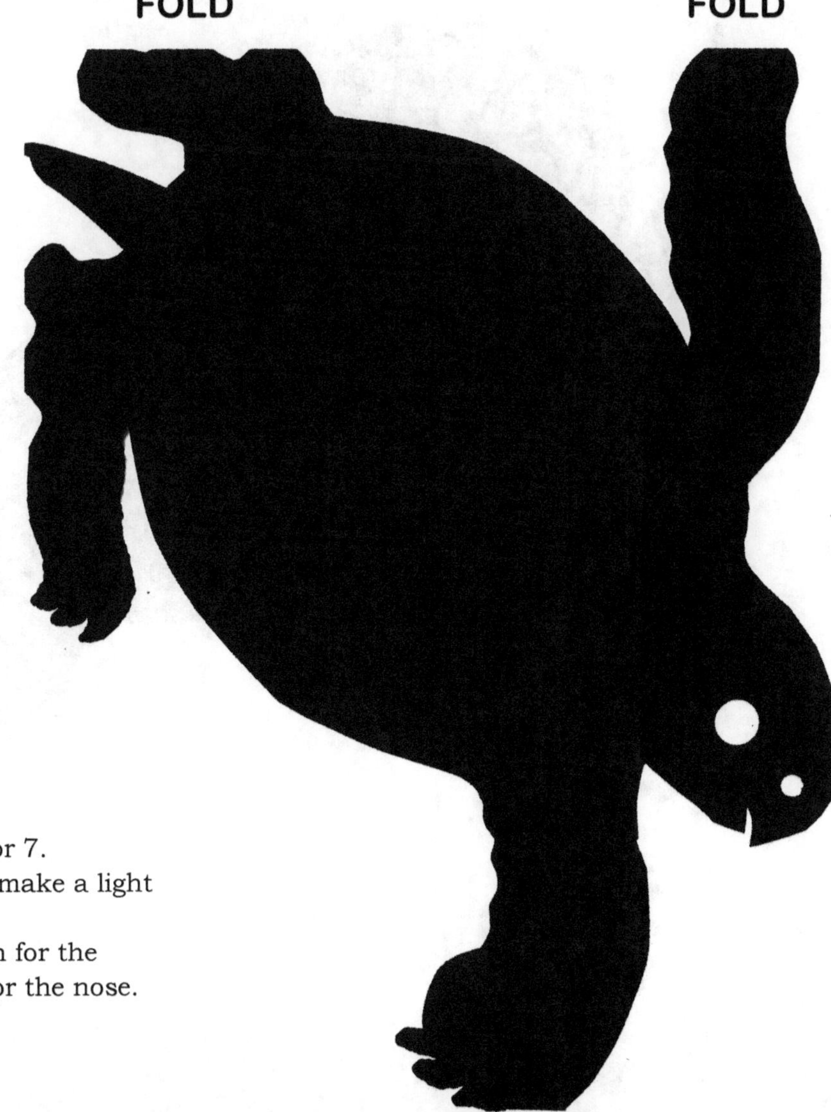

- ★ Quick and easy.
- ✂ Double or Multi-image.
- ✂ Follow directions on page 6 or 7.
- ✂ Tape the pattern in place or make a light pencil tracing.
- ✂ Use a large hole paper punch for the eyes and small hole punch for the nose.
- ☺ Use green or brown paper.

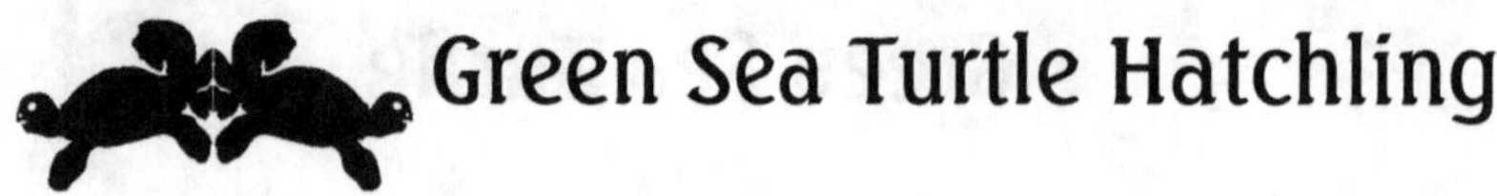

Green Sea Turtle Hatchling

- ★ Quick and easy.
- ✂ Double or Multi-image, 5½ x 4¼.
- ✂ Follow directions on page 6 or 7.
- ✂ Tape the pattern in place or make a light pencil tracing.
- ✂ Use a large hole paper punch for the eye and small hole paper punch for the nose.
- ☺ Use green or brown paper.

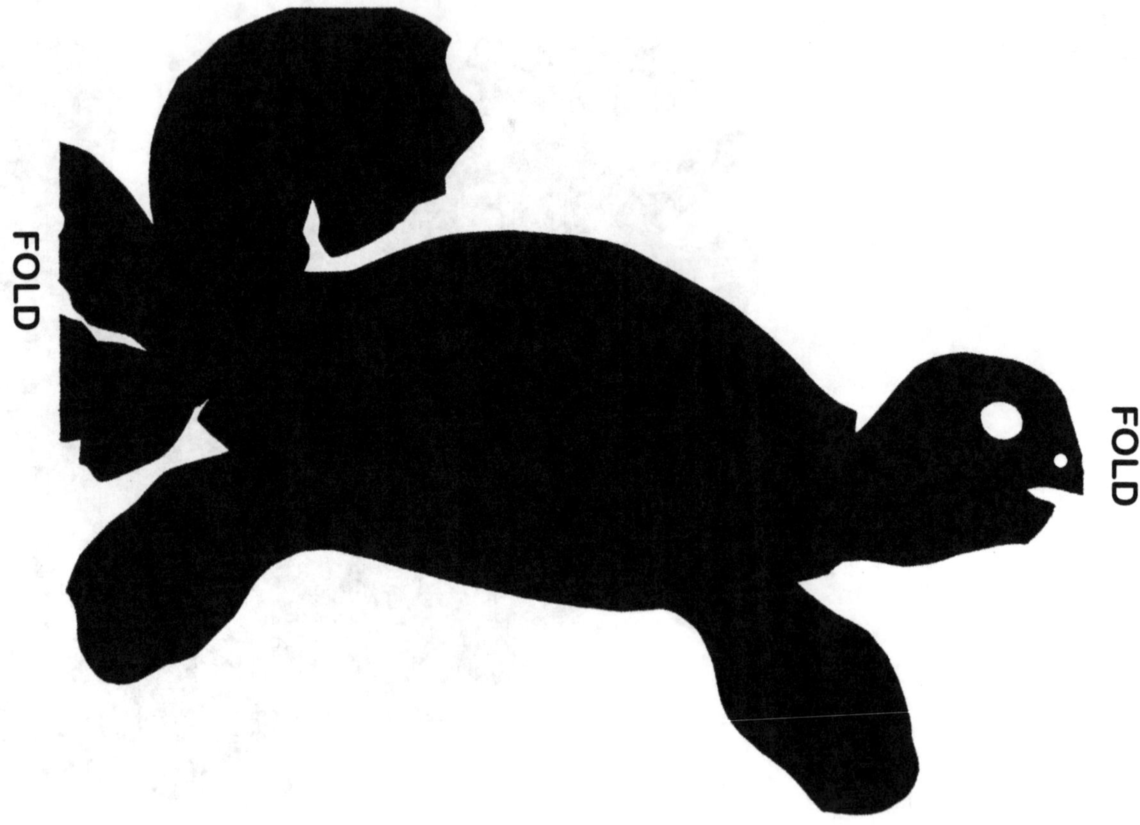

Tortoise (Land Turtle)

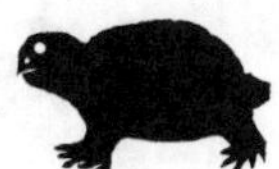

The tortoise and the turtle are reptiles, which means they are cold blooded. They have scaly skin, breathe air, and lay their eggs in the sand. The bony top shell is called a carapace and their skeleton is attached to it. The bottom shell is called plastron. Tortoises cannot leave their shell, however they can pull in their head, arms, legs, and tail. Their toes are short and have no webbing. They have no teeth but do have a vicious bite. The tortoise also lays eggs and buries them. They have a long, fat tail.

Eye Witness Dictionaries: The Visual Dictionary of Animals, 35
Firefly Encyclopedia of Reptiles and Amphibians, 118-137
Reptiles and Amphibians: Birth and Growth, 10-13, 21, 25, 31

- ★ Quick and easy.
- ✂ Double or Multi-image, 5½ x 4¼
- ✂ Follow directions on page 6 or 7.
- ✂ Tape the pattern in place or make a light pencil tracing.
- ✂ Use a large hole paper punch for the eye and small paper punch for the nose.

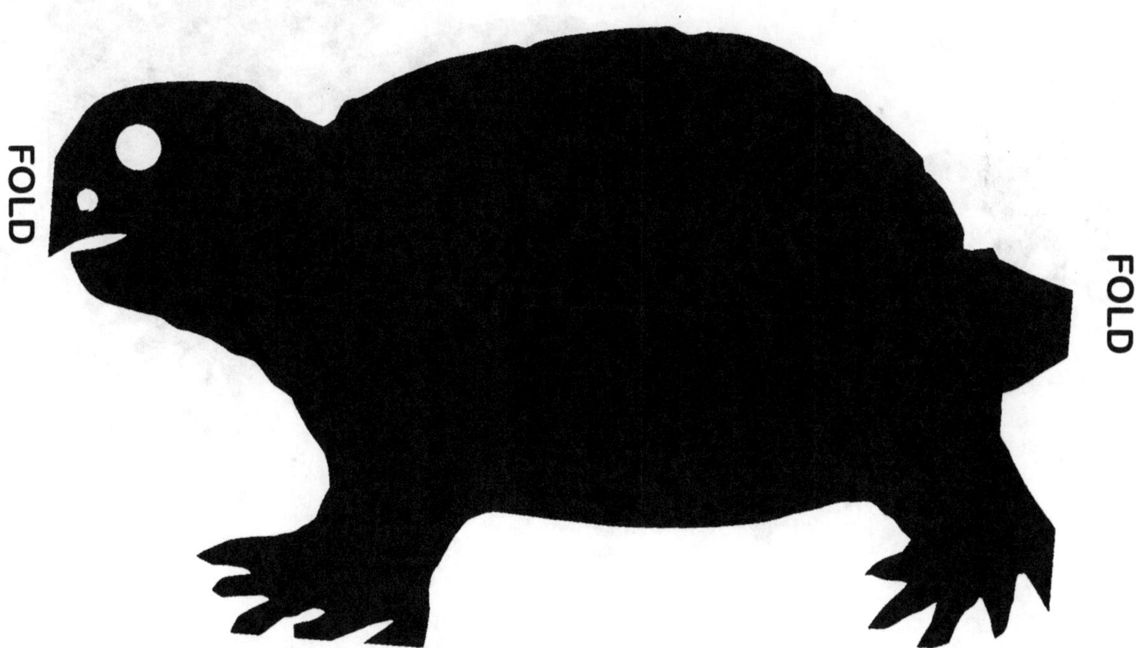

Tortoise Hatchling

- ★ Quick and easy.
- ✂ Double or Multi-image, 5½ x 4¼.
- ✂ Follow directions on page 6 or 7.
- ✂ Tape the pattern in place or make a light pencil tracing.
- ✂ Use a large hole paper punch for the eye and small paper punch for the nose.

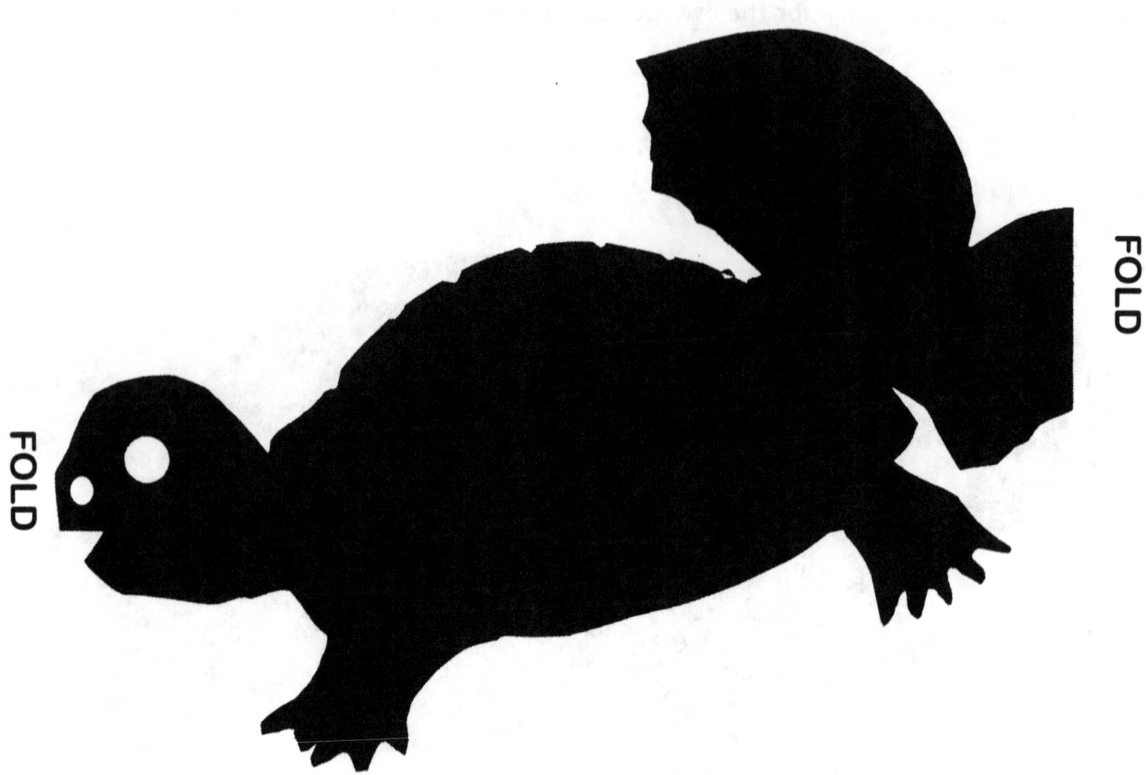

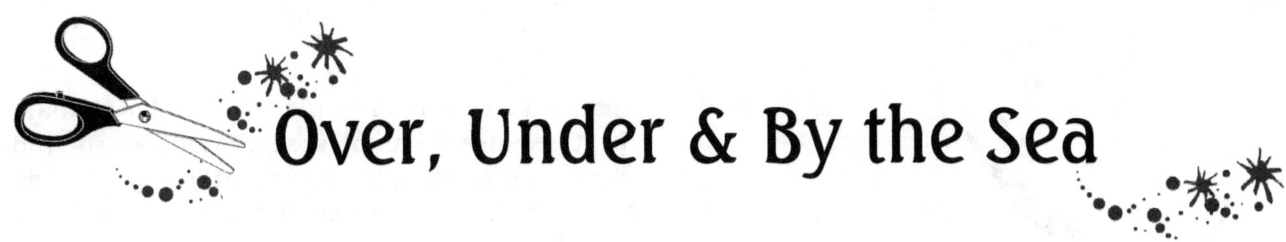

Over, Under & By the Sea

Our list is varied from divers to the space shuttle, dune flowers to speedboats, and banana trees to buoys. All these subjects are found on the seashore, on the sea or in the ocean.

FOLD-AND-CUT PATTERNS

Seaside Trees, Flowers & Butterfly

Banana Trees at Sunset
Beach Morning Glory
Beach Sunflower
Coreopsis Wildflower
Hibiscus
Indian Blanket
Orange Blossoms
Palm Tree
Sabal Palm
Saw Palmetto
Zebra Longwing Butterfly

Seaside Faring

Anchor
Bathysphere
Buoy
Deep Sea Diver (Jim Suit)
Kelp (Seaweed)
Powerboat
Sailboat
Seaplane
Scuba Diver
Space Shuttle
Submarine
Waves

BOOKS AND STORIES

A Series of Unfortunate Events #11: The Grim Grotto by Lemony Snicket
Backyard Sunflower by Elizabeth King
Boats, Ships, Submarines and Other Floating Machines by Ian Graham
Buzz the Little Seaplane by Wendy Cheyette Lewiston
Can You Hear a Shout In Space? by Melvin Berger and Gilda Berger
Disasters in Space Exploration by Gregory L. Vogt
First on the Moon by Hyperion Books for Children
The Great Ships by Patrick O'Brien
Meet My Grandmother: She's a Deep Sea Explorer by Lisa Tucker McElroy
On Board the Space Shuttle by Ray Spangenburg and Kit Moser
Ride the Wind: Airborne Journey of Animals and Plants by Seymour Simon
Rockets and Satellites by Franklin Branley
Sailboat Storybook: Sarah's Boat by Douglas Alvord
Seaplanes: And Naval Aviation (The Story of Flight) by Ole Steen Hansen
Submarines by Kate Petty
Submersibles by Harvey Weiss
Twenty Thousand Leagues Under the Sea by Jules Verne
The Very Hungry Caterpillar by Eric Carle
Waves: From Surfing to Tsunami, Drew Kampion and Jeff Peterson
Wings Over Water: A Chronicle of The Flying Boats and Amphibians of the Twentieth Century by David Oliver

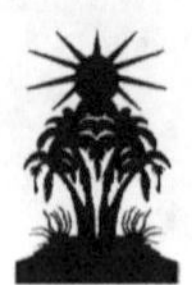

Banana Trees at Sunset

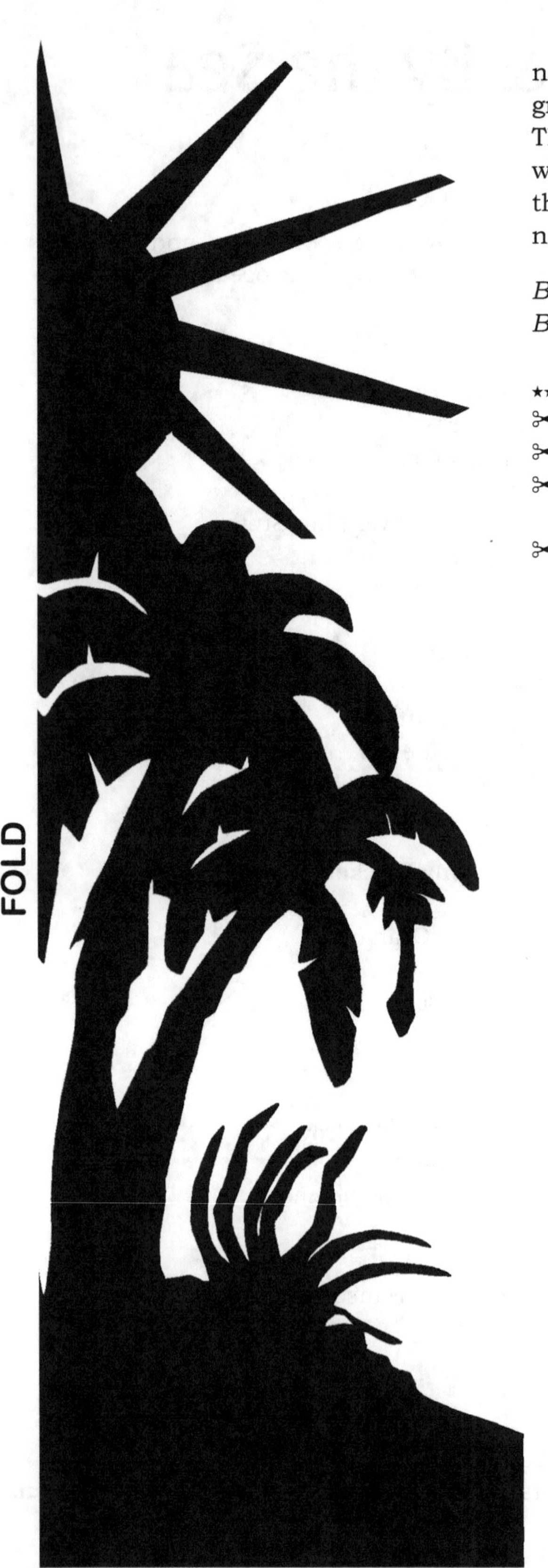

The banana tree is really a plant. The yellow banana is not a fruit because it has no seeds. A bud starts underground from an existing banana plant (so-called "trees"). That "bud," made up of leaves that are wrapped tightly, will push through the ground and start a new "tree". All the leaves together make up the trunk, although there is no wood in this plant.

Banana, xi-xix, 9-14, 243-246
Bananas: An American History, 210

- ⋆⋆⋆ Advanced.
- ✂ Double or Multi-image.
- ✂ Follow directions on page 6 or 7.
- ✂ Tape the pattern in place or make a light pencil tracing.
- ✂ Just cut up along the palm leaves to open areas to make it easier to cut.

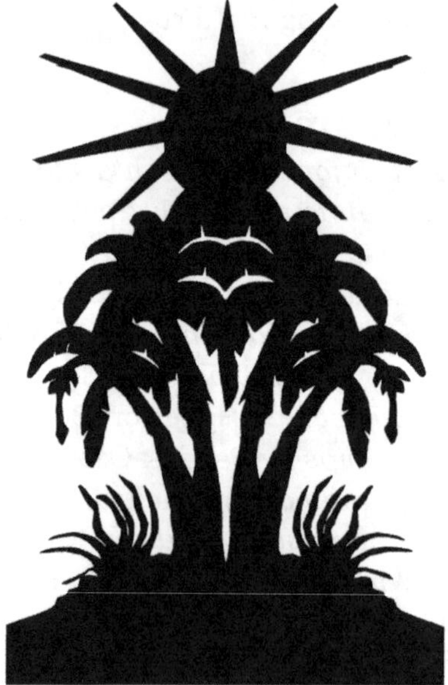

Beach Morning Glory

A hardy creeping tropical vine that is salt tolerant, the beach morning glory has flower petals that are shades of rosy pink with 2-inch large lobed leaves. It is primarily a sand stabilizer to protect the dunes from erosion. The seeds are unaffected by salt water and will float.

A Gardener's Guide to Florida Native Plants, 286

- ★ Quick and easy.
- ✂ Double or Multi-image.
- ✂ Follow directions on page 6 or 7.
- ✂ Tape the pattern in place or make a light pencil tracing.
- ✂ Use a small hole paper punch for the center of the flower.

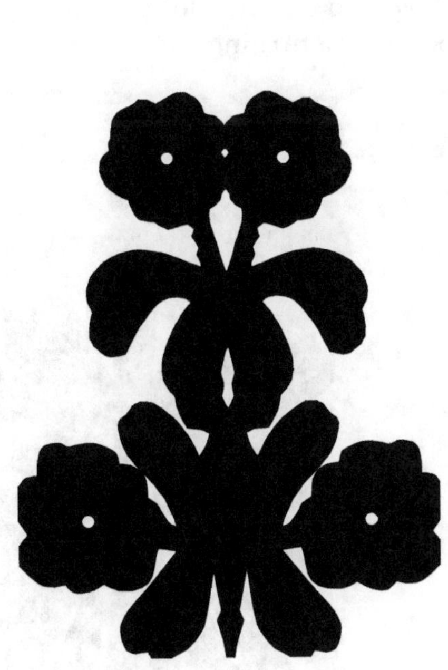

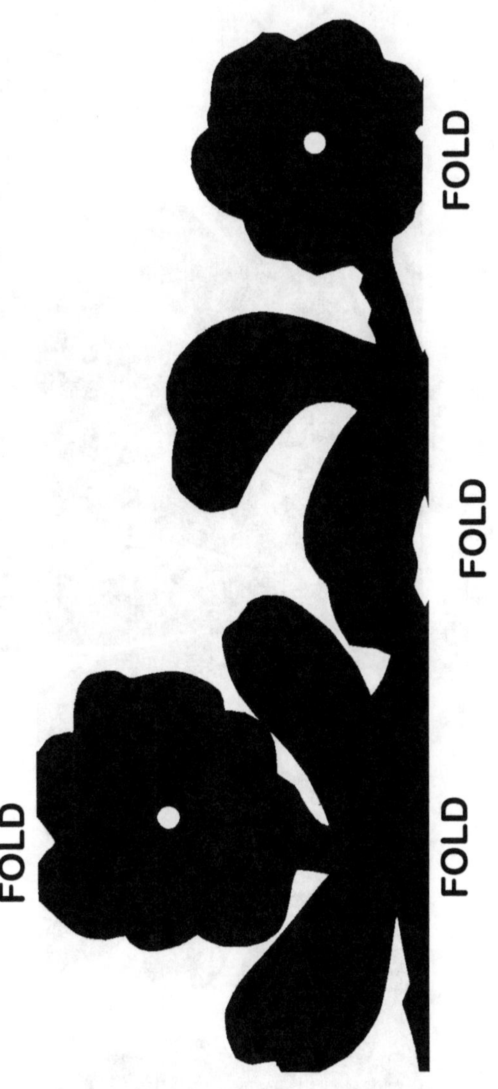

Beach Sunflower

Beach sunflower may be erect, three to four feet tall, or a much-branched, prostrate, spreading plant less than eighteen inches tall, but covering a couple square feet or more. The leaves are sand-papery coarse, heart-shaped, two to four inches long and almost twice as wide at their widest. The flowerhead is about three inches across, slightly nodding, and quite attractive. The petals are bright yellow, numbering 11-21, and about one inch long. The center of the beach sunflower is usually red-purple and about one inch in diameter. Most authorities recognize two subspecies of beach sunflower occurring naturally on beaches and dunes from southeast Texas to the east coast of Florida.

A Garden of Wildflowers, 7, 9, 138-139
A Gardener's Guide to Florida Native Plants, 62
www.floridata.com/ref/H/heli_deb.cfm

- ★ Easy.
- ✂ Double or Multi-image.
- ✂ Follow directions on page 6 or 7.
- ✂ Tape the pattern in place or make a light pencil tracing.
- ✂ Use a small hole paper punch for the center of the flower.
- ☺ Let your paper do the turning.

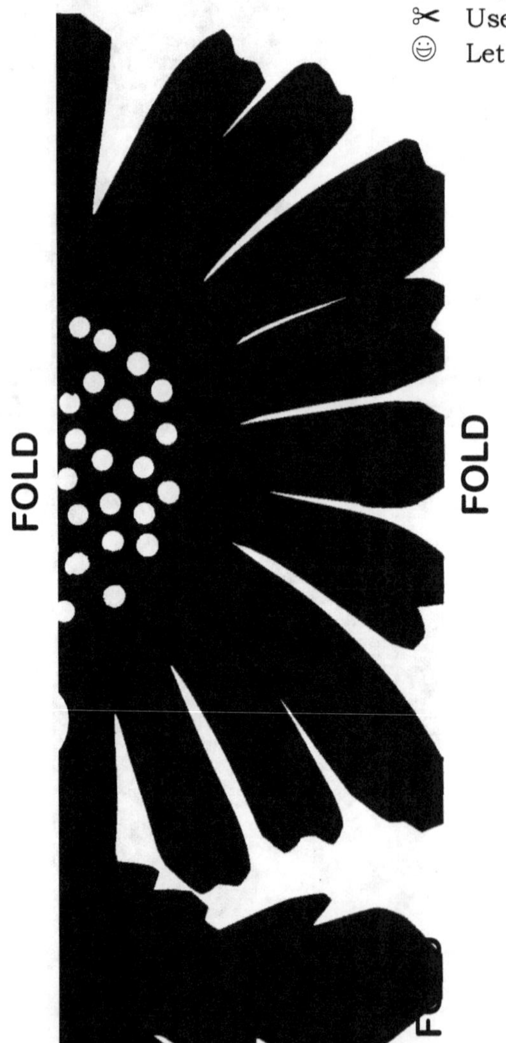

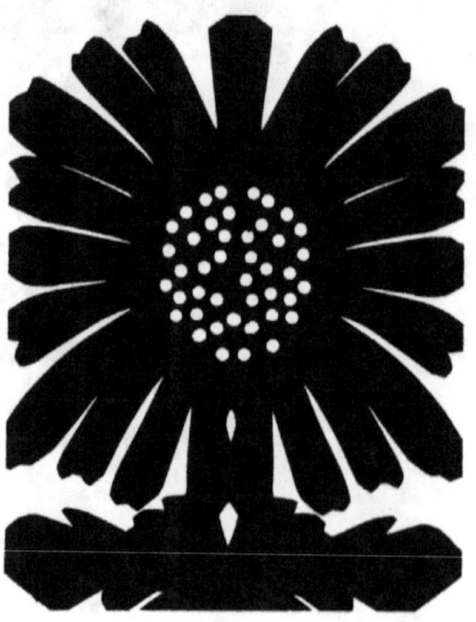

Coreopsis Wildflower

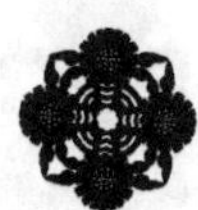

The coreopsis is the wildflower symbol of the state of Florida. The flowers range from golden to pink. The seeded center of the flower is a favorite for seed-eating birds and is used to beautify the roadways.

Wildflowers, 119-121, 127

★ Quick and easy.
✂ True Circle fold.
✂ Follow directions on page 11.
✂ Tape the pattern in place or make a light pencil tracing.
✂ Use a small paper punch to make the seeded center.
☺ Cut away the smaller areas first. This gives you more paper area to hold as you cut.
☺ Let your paper do the turning.

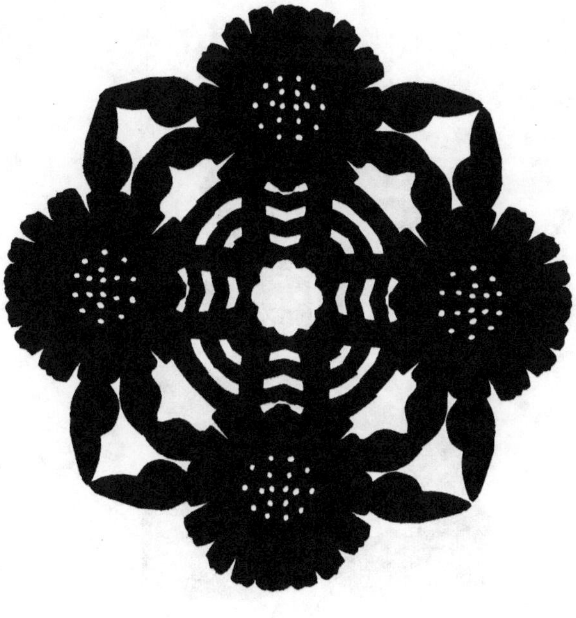

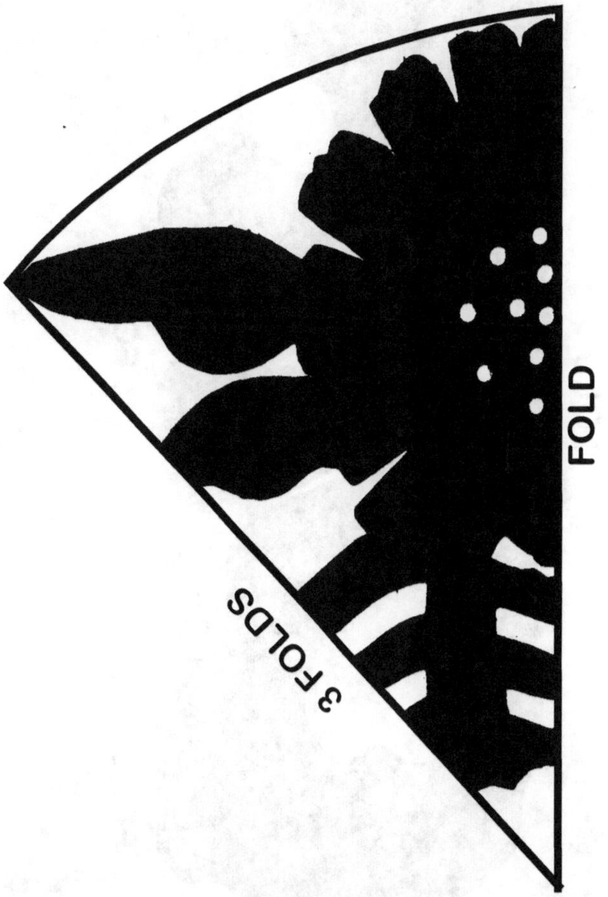

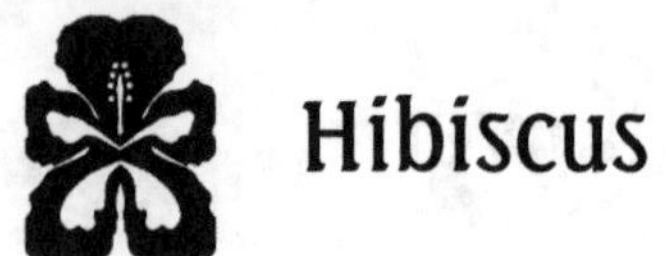

Hibiscus

The hibiscus is a colorful flowering shrub with trumpet shaped petals. It has single as well as double blooms with colors of white, pink, red, purple or yellow. The hibiscus is used for many purposes such as shampoo, medicine, herbal teas, jams, and in making some papers. It is a member of the mallow family.

A Gardener's Guide to Florida Native Plants, 60, 61
The Subtropical Garden, 115, 116, 117
Wildflowers, 124

★ Quick and easy.
✂ Double, Multi-image or 3-Dimensional.
✂ Follow directions on page 6, 7 or 9.
✂ Tape the pattern in place or make a light pencil tracing.
✂ Use a small hole paper punch for the stamen.
☺ Use different colors of paper to create a kaleidoscope of flowers.

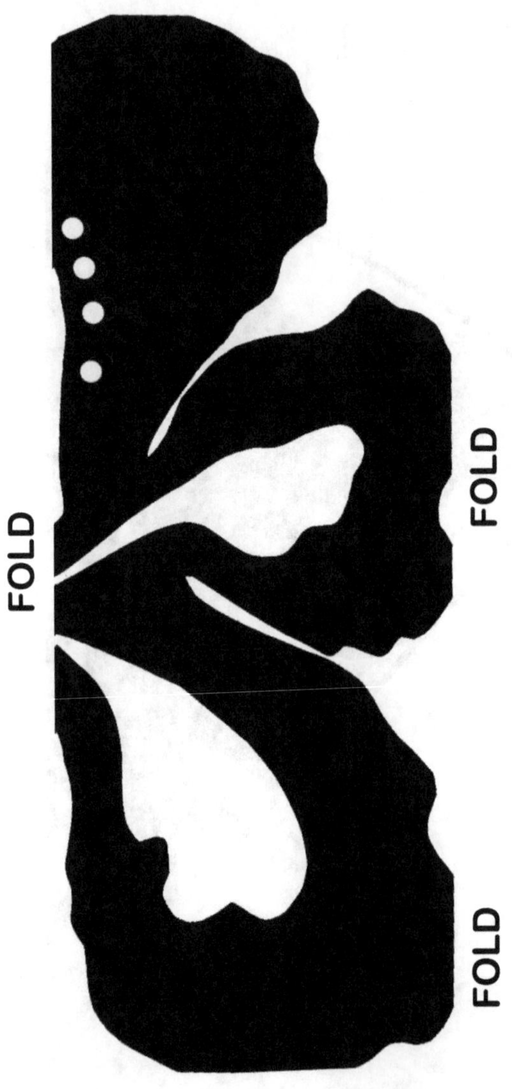

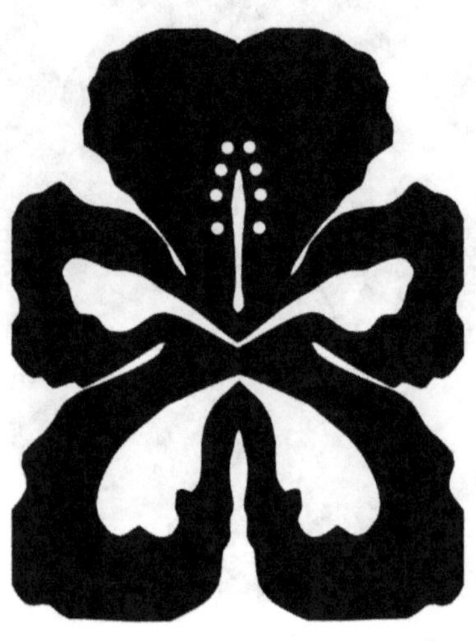

Indian Blanket

Indian blanket is known for its brilliant, daisy-like flowers. The large centers of the flowers are rose-purple and the dense, frilly petals are yellow, orange, crimson or copper scarlet. Indian blanket grows in 14-to-24 inch high mounds with a spread of about 12 inches. It is a drought resistant plant. There are more than two dozen species, most of these are native to North America. One variety (G. pulchella) is found from Virginia to Florida and westward to Colorado and New Mexico, extending south into Mexico.

A Garden of Wildflowers, 7, 9, 138, 139
A Gardener's Guide to Florida Native Plants, 62
www.floridata.com/ref/G/gaillad.cfm

- ★ Easy.
- ✂ True Circle fold.
- ✂ Follow directions on page 11.
- ✂ Tape the pattern in place or make a light pencil tracing.
- ✂ Use a small hole paper punch for the center of the flowers.
- ☺ Let your paper do the turning.
- ☺ Cut away the smaller areas first. This gives you more paper area to hold as you cut.

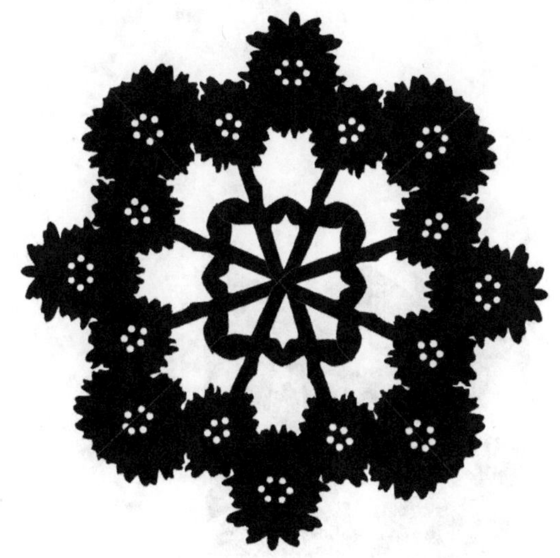

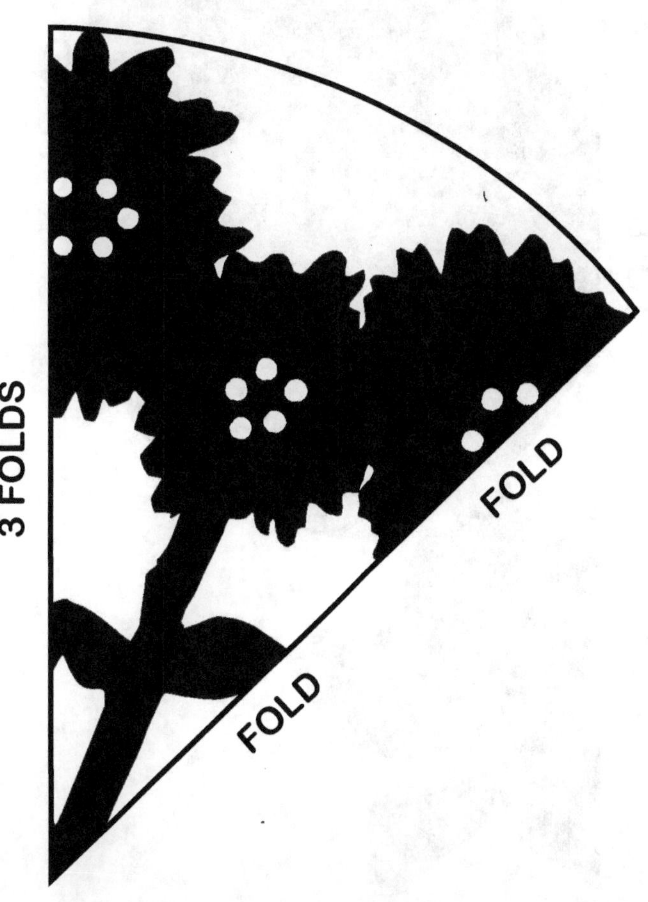

Orange Blossoms

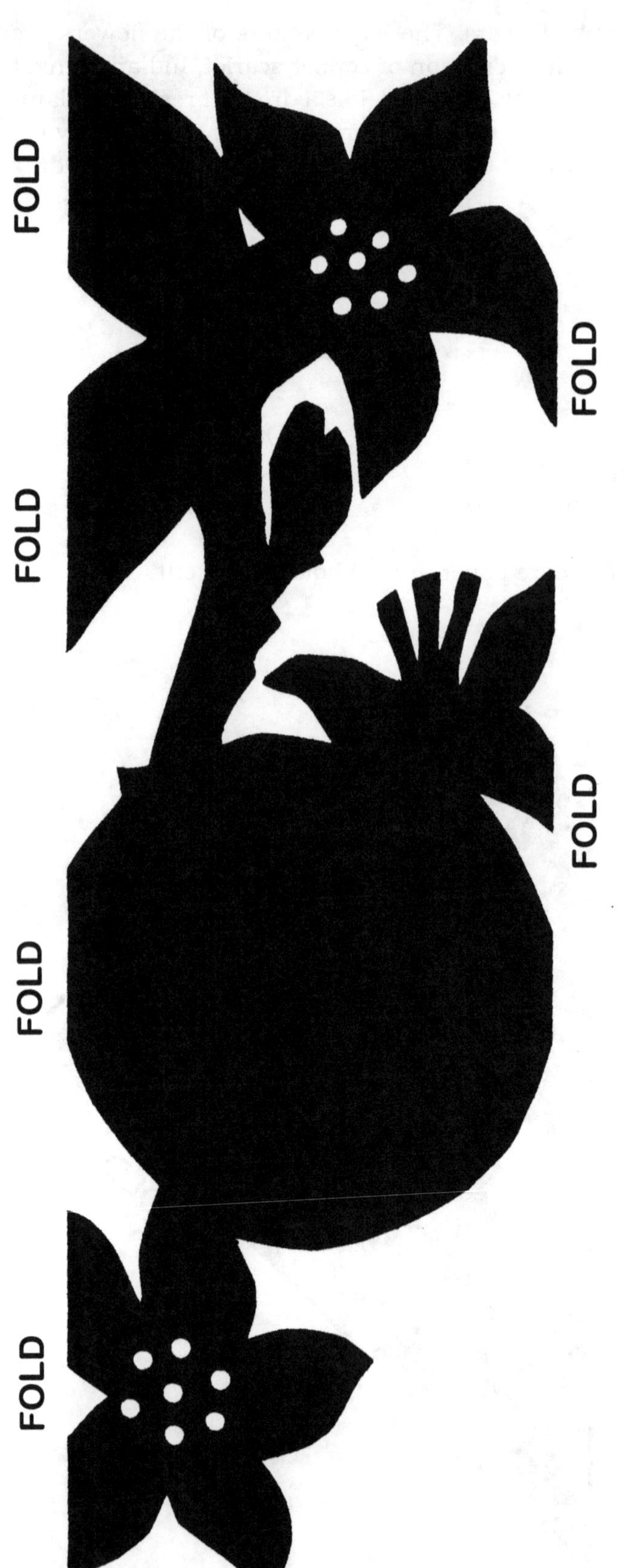

The orange blossom is the official state flower of Florida. It is the citrus blossom of the orange tree. A very fragrant flower with five white petals that blossoms into an orange. Orange trees can display blossoms and fruit at the same time.

Citrus: A History, plate 7, plate 12
Citrus Fruits, 6

- ★ Quick and easy.
- ✂ Double or Multi-image.
- ✂ Follow directions on page 6 or 7.
- ✂ Tape the pattern in place or make a light pencil tracing.
- ✂ Use a small hole paper punch for the blossom center.

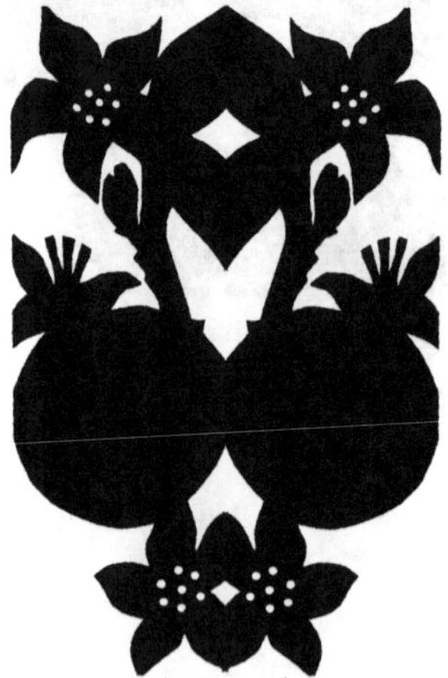

Palm Tree

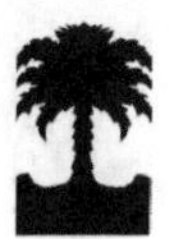

Some palms can grow over 70 feet high. They grow in warm places that have lots of sunshine. The leaves grow close to the top and look like big feathers. There are thousands of species of palm trees.

Berock's Guide to Landscape, 68
The Trees of Florida, 13, 14, 130, 132, CP 8
www.PalmTreesInfo.com

- ★ Quick and easy.
- ✂ Double or Multi-image.
- ✂ Follow directions on page 6 or 7.
- ✂ Tape the pattern in place or make a light pencil tracing.
- ☺ Makes a beautiful border, quilt pattern or picture page for photographs.

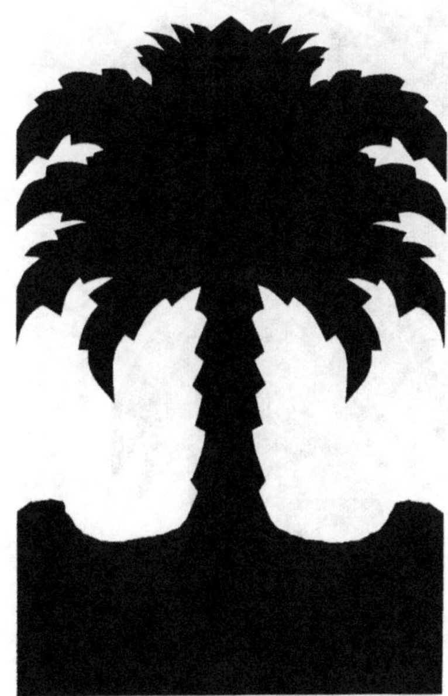

Sabal Palm

The sabal palm is the state tree of Florida. Some palms can grow over 70 feet high. They grow in warm places that have lots of sunshine. The leaves grow close to the top and fan out. There are many of varieties of palm trees.

Berock's Guide to Landscape, 68
The Trees of Florida, 13, 14, 130, 132
www.PalmTreesInfo.com

★ Easy.
✂ Double or Multi-image.
✂ Follow directions on page 8 or 9.
✂ Tape the pattern in place or make a light pencil tracing.
☺ Use a large hole paper punch to make opening between trees, then insert your scissors to finish the cutting.

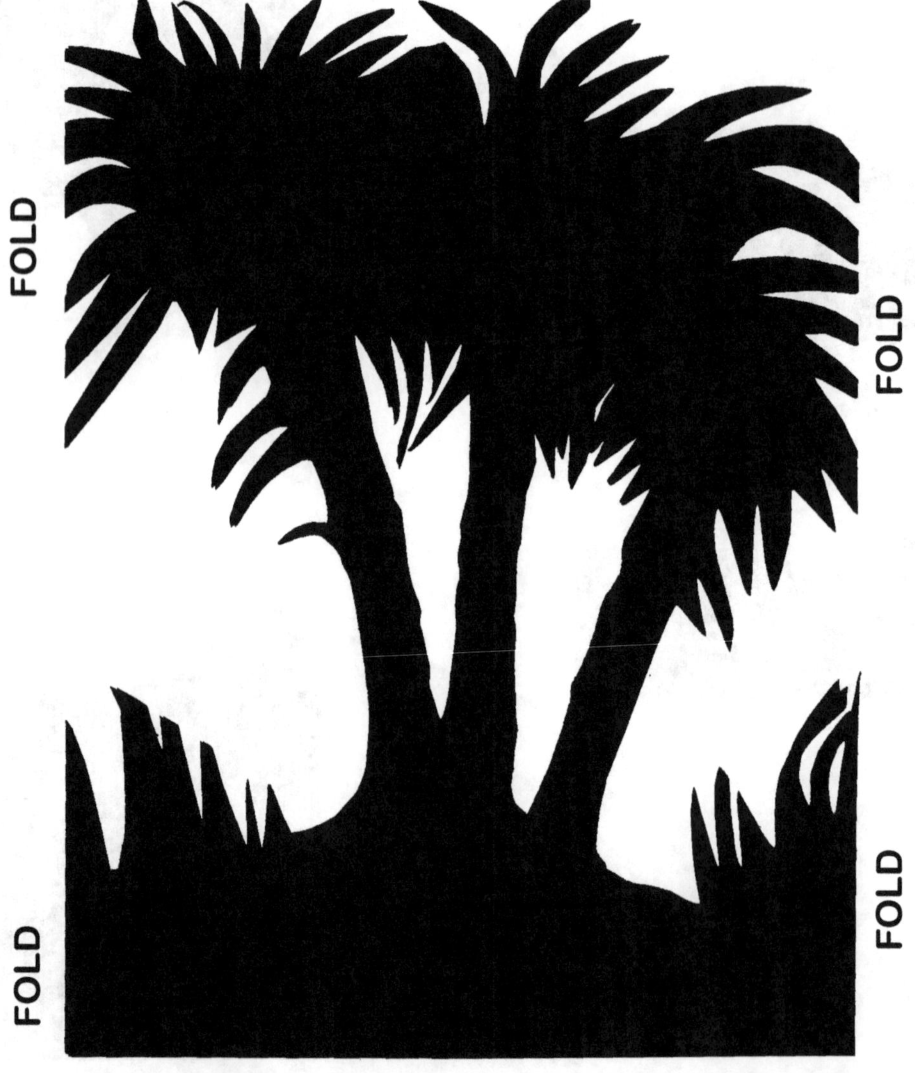

Saw Palmetto

The palm fronds are fan shaped and form a heavy ground cover throughout the south. They grow three to six feet high.

Berock's Guide to Landscape, 88
A Gardener's Guide to Florida Native Plants, 143, 152-153, 307
The Trees of Florida, 9, 131

- ★ Quick and easy.
- ✂ Single image or 3-Dimensional.
- ✂ Follow directions on page 6 or 7.
- ✂ Tape the pattern in place or make a light pencil tracing.

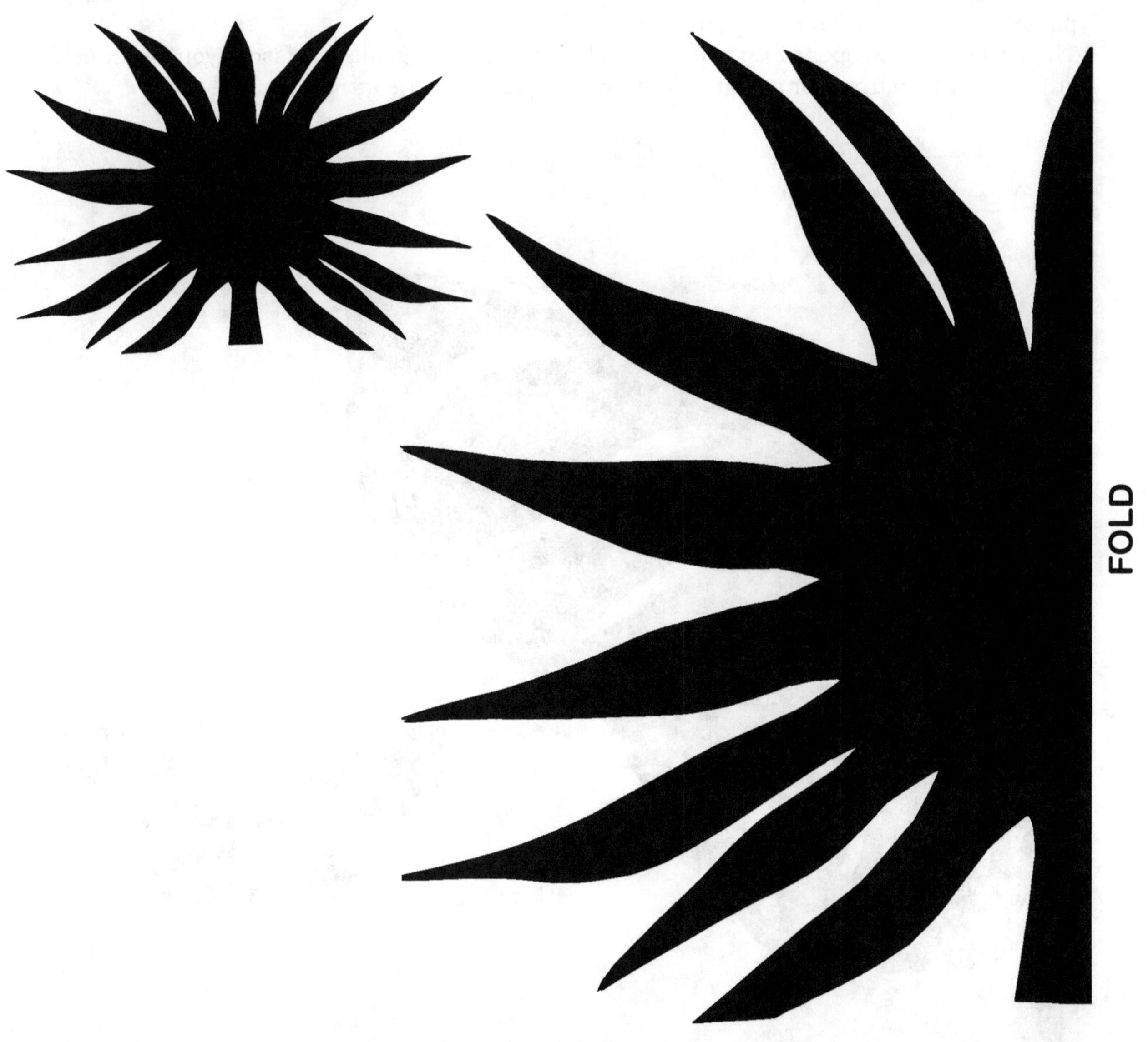

Zebra Longwing Butterfly

As the official state butterfly of Florida, the Zebra Longwing is seen mostly in the central and southern parts of the state. The long forewings are black with yellow stripes and markings. It feeds on the passion vine and flower. They live 5 to 6 months and are poisonous. The tongue or feeding tube is called a proboscis. Zebras nest together in groups, hanging from vines at night. There are 15,000 different kinds of butterflies in the world.

Butterflies of North America, 154
Florida's Fabulous Butterflies: Their Stories, 24, 25

- ★ Easy.
- ✂ Double or Multi-image.
- ✂ Follow directions on page 6 or 7.
- ✂ Tape the pattern in place or make a light pencil tracing.
- ✂ Use a small hole paper punch for the eye and wing design. You can also use a rectangular paper punch for the lower wing design.
- ✂ The stripes can be opened up with a punch and then using small scissors you can finish cutting out the stripes or cut-and-paste yellow paper for the stripes.

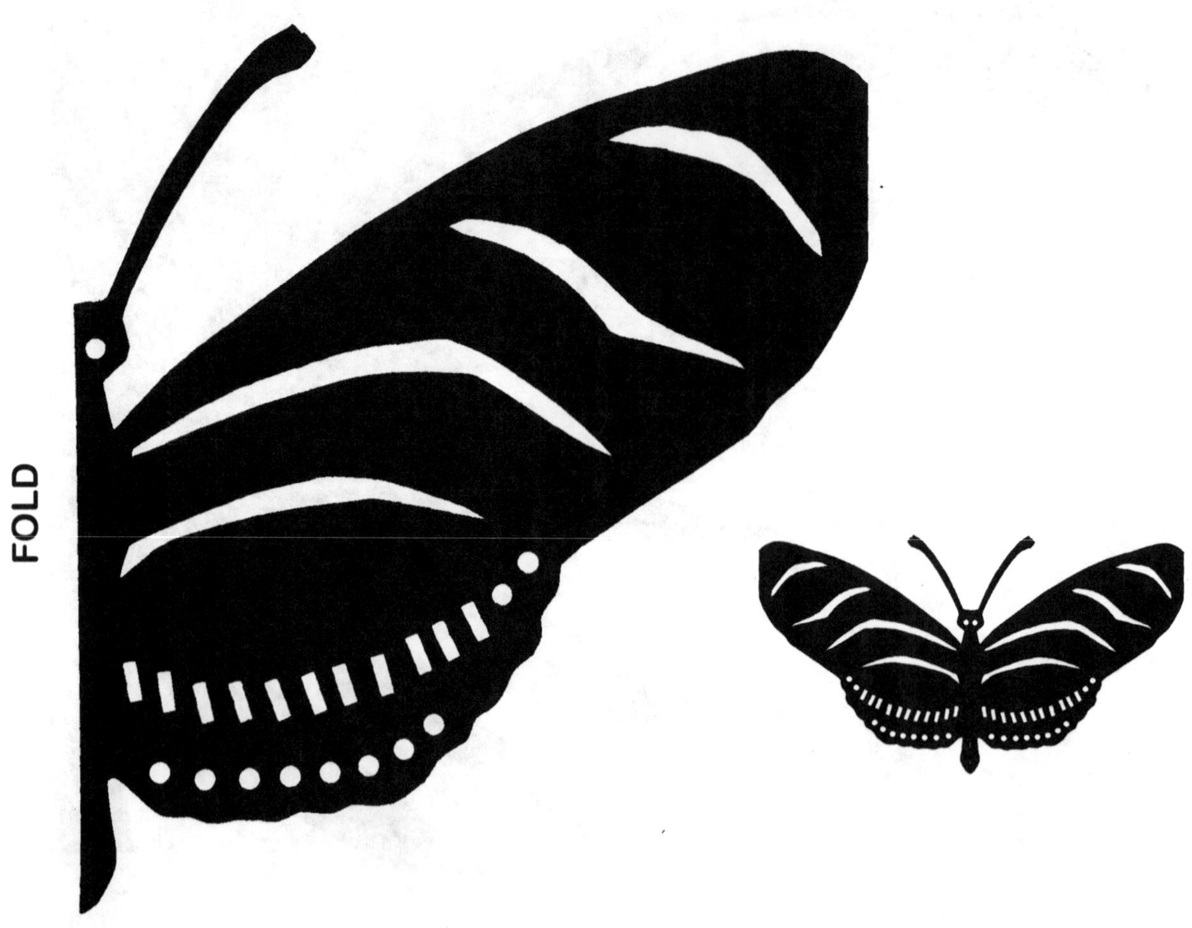

Anchor

An anchor is a heavy hook-like metal shape with arms that is dropped into the ocean by a chain to keep the ship or buoy from moving.

Eye Witness Books: Boats, 35, 43, 51

★ Quick and easy.
✂ Double or Multi-image.
✂ Follow directions on page 6 or 7.
✂ Tape the pattern in place or make a light pencil tracing.

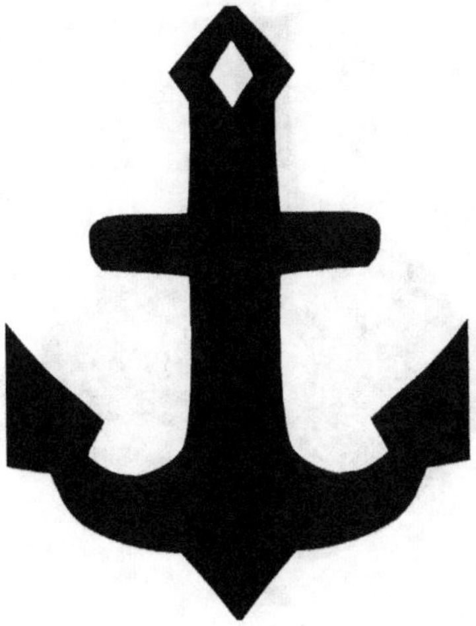

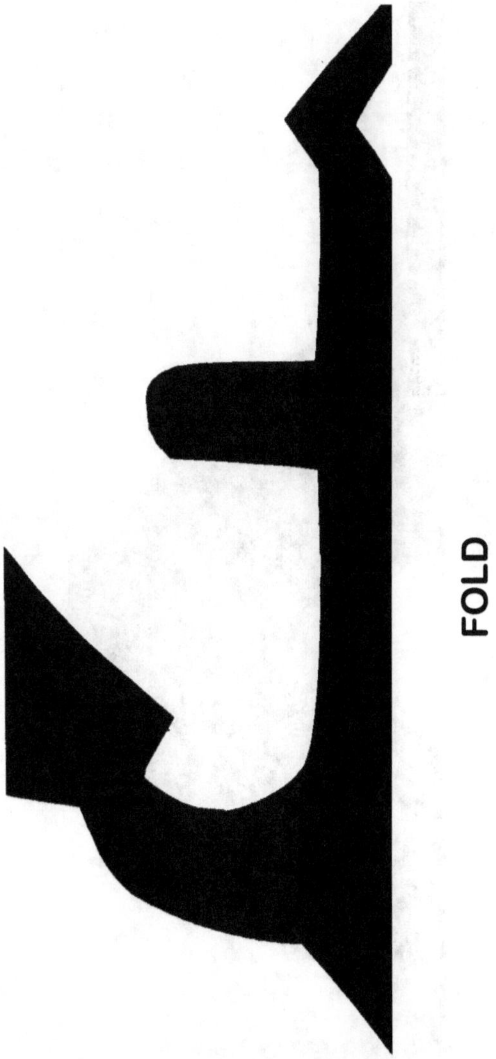

FOLD

Bathysphere

This old-fashioned device is a round hollow steel ball with small windows built for underwater exploration in the 1930s. An observer climbed in through the top and was lowered into the sea. It was not mobile as it hung straight down by steel cable and had to be pulled up with a winch.

Dive! My Adventures in the Deep Frontier, 60
Submersibles, 53-58, 61-62

- ★ Quick and easy.
- ✂ Double or Multi-image.
- ✂ Follow directions on page 6 or 7.
- ✂ Tape the pattern in place or make a light pencil tracing.

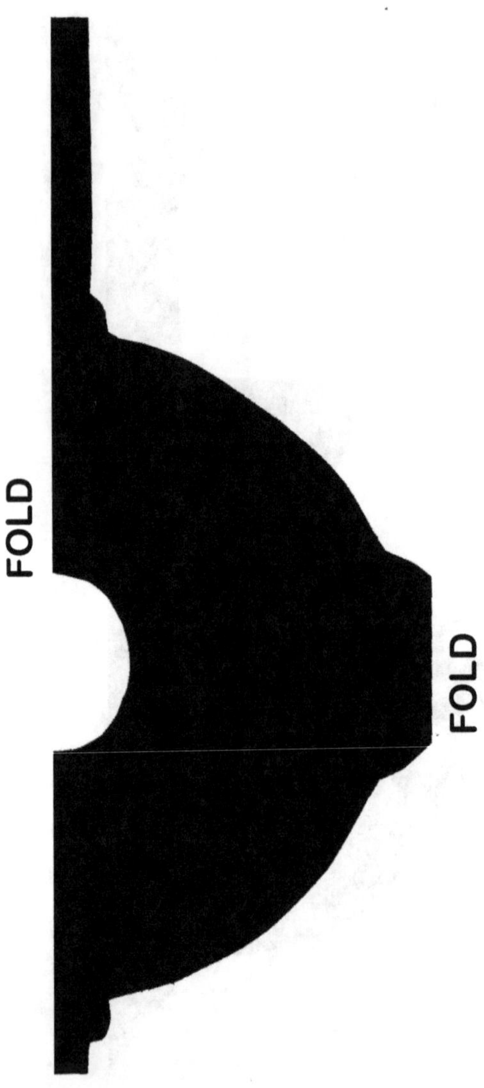

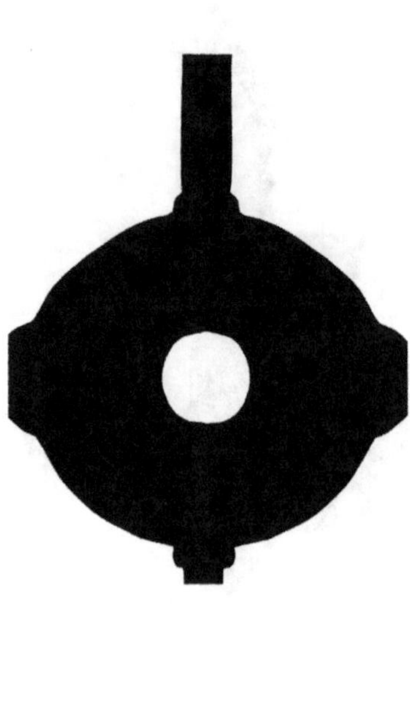

Buoy

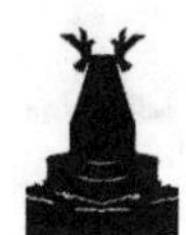

Buoys are large floating devices with markings that are held by an anchor in the water to mark a reef, channel or a direction for boats. Three types of buoys are: navigational, mooring, and fishing. They are like road signs for boats.

Boats, Ships, Submarines and Other Floating Machines, 37
www.nmm.ac.uk/.../sailsafe/buoys.html

- ★ Quick and easy.
- ✂ Double or Multi-image.
- ✂ Follow directions on page 6 or 7.
- ✂ Tape the pattern in place or make a light pencil tracing.

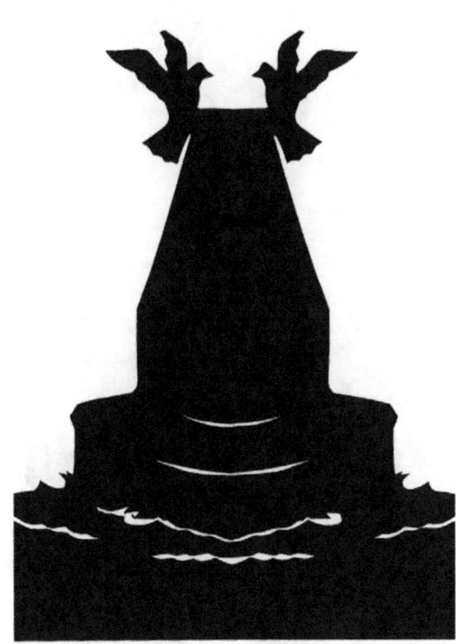

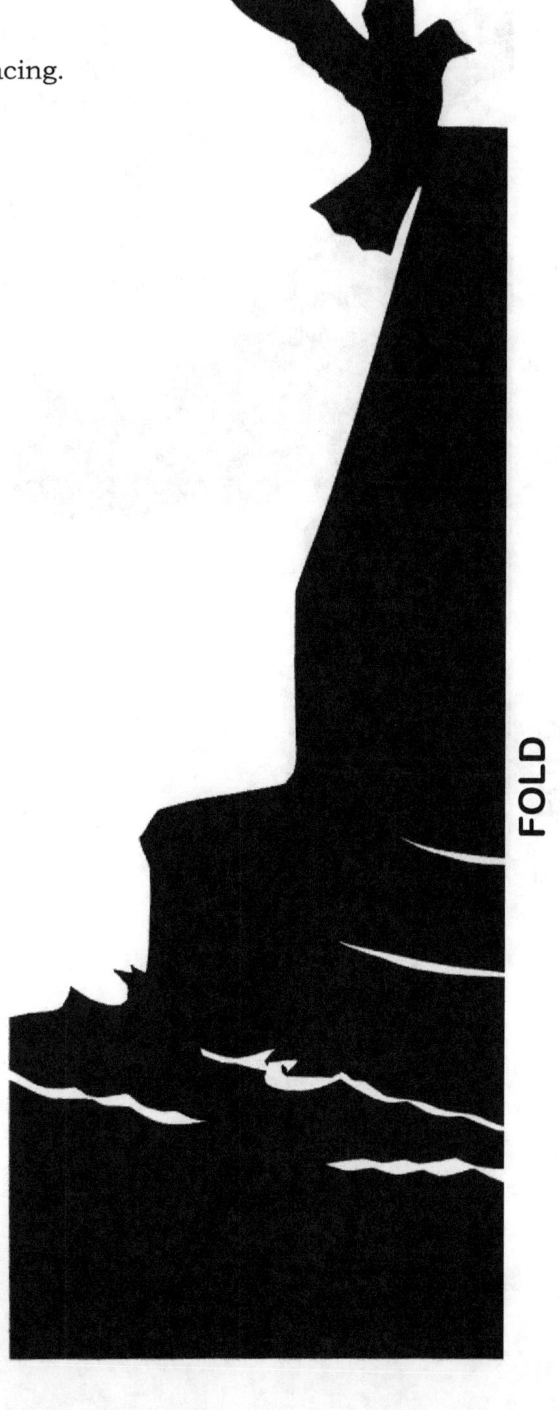

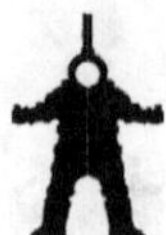

Deep Sea Diver (Jim Suit)

FOLD

FOLD

This diving suit is a waterproof one-piece garment made of canvas and rubber. It covers the wearer entirely except for the head and hands. Heavy rubber bands seal the suit at the wrists, leaving the hands free. The diver wears rubber gloves and leaded boots weighing about 40 pound and lead weights are fastened to the chest. A metal helmet with side and front windows covers the head and is attached to the diving suit. A non-collapsible pipe connects the helmet to an air supply on the ship and an attached lifeline can haul the diver to the surface.

Dive! My Adventures in the Deep Frontier, 45, 46, 49
Twenty Thousand Leagues Under the Sea by Jules Verne
Window on the Deep, 5, 7, 13, 15, 23

- ★ Quick and easy.
- ✂ Double or Multi-image.
- ✂ Follow directions on page 6 or 7.
- ✂ Tape the pattern in place or make a light pencil tracing.
- ☺ Make a mobile with fish swimming all around.

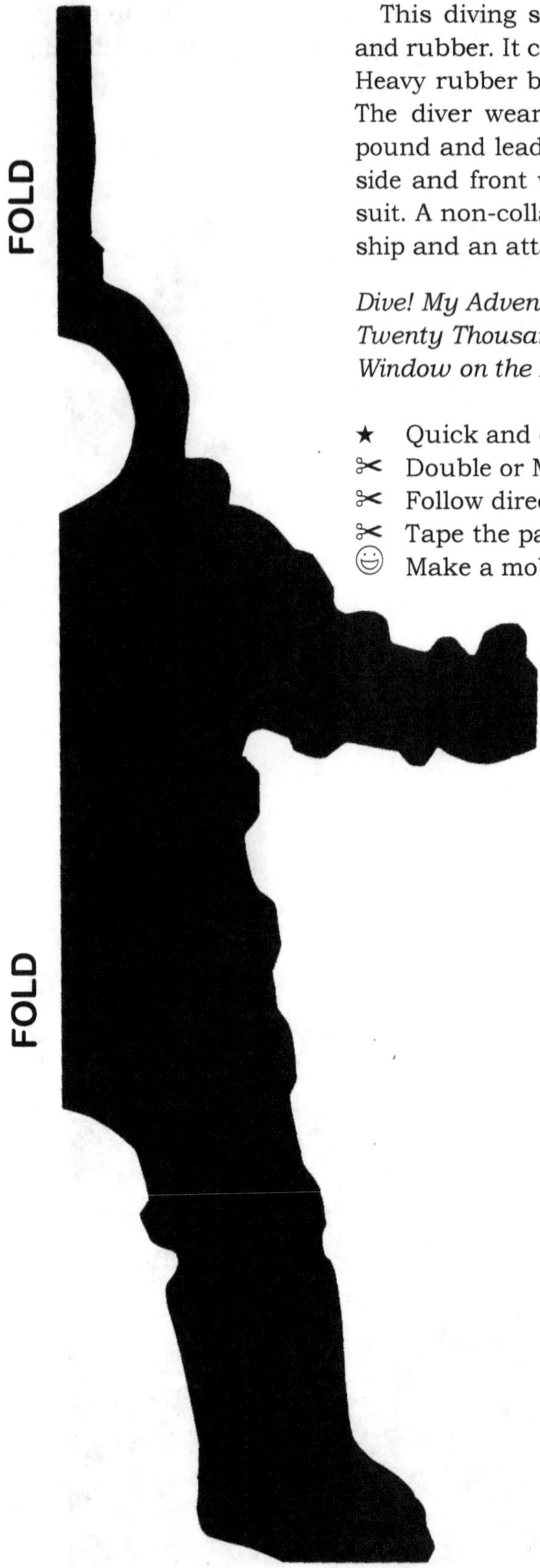

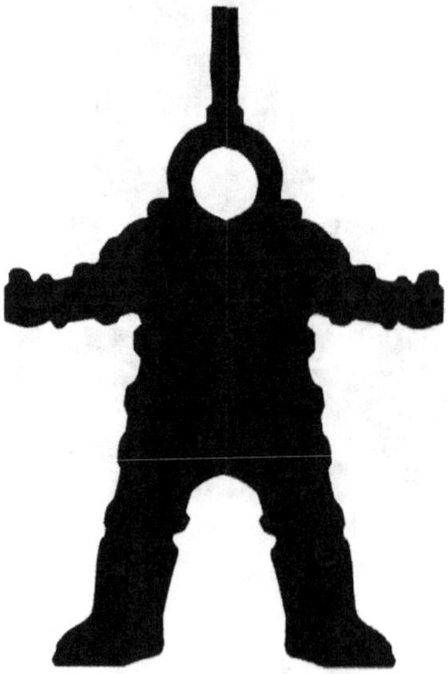

Kelp (Seaweed)

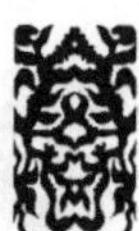

Seaweed is actually a form of algae and does not have true roots. These plants anchor to the rocks and are called holdfasts. They have long fanlike fronds that are home to many forms of marine life.

Eye Witness Books: Seashore, 18- 25
Wild Life and Plants of the World, 24, 25

- ⋆⋆⋆ Advanced.
- ✂ Double or Multi-image.
- ✂ Follow directions on page 6 or 7.
- ✂ Tape the pattern in place or make a light pencil tracing.
- ☺ Use a small hole paper punch to create seeds in the fronds.
- ☺ Create your own seaweed design. Use fish in the fronds.

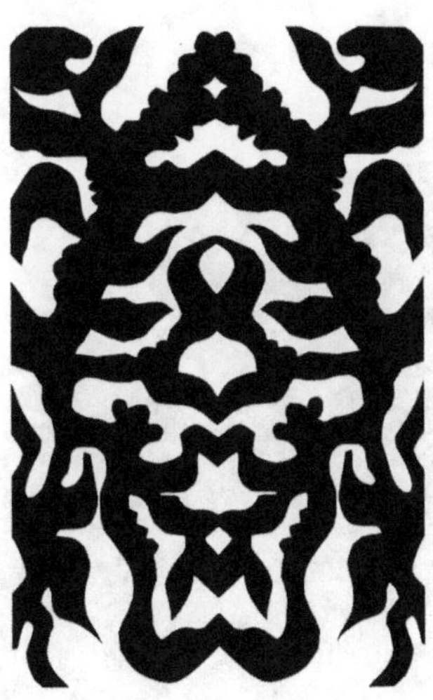

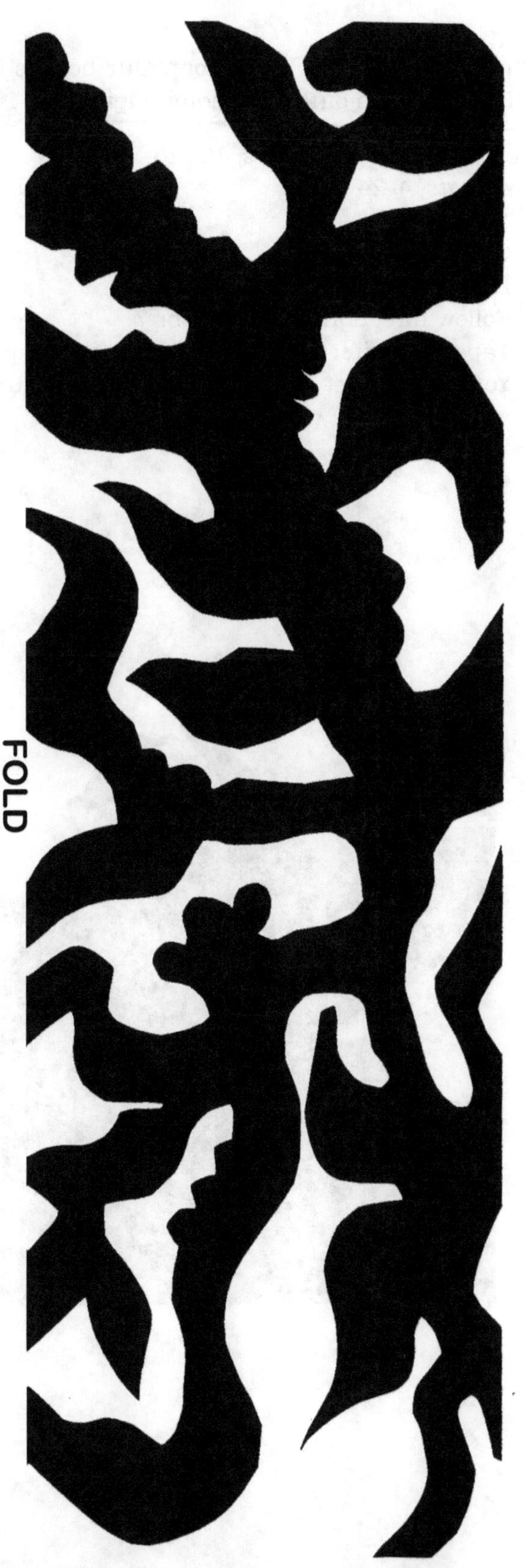

Powerboat

This powerboat is a speedboat. Our boat is a bow rider with an open bow in the front for extra seating. It has an outboard motor engine and is between 17' to 30' in length.

Essential Boating for Teens, 12, 26-32, 43
Powerboats, 4-24

★ Quick and easy.
✂ Double or Multi-image.
✂ Follow directions on page 6 or 7.
✂ Tape the pattern in place or make a light pencil tracing.
☺ You might want to use small scissors for the figure in the boat.

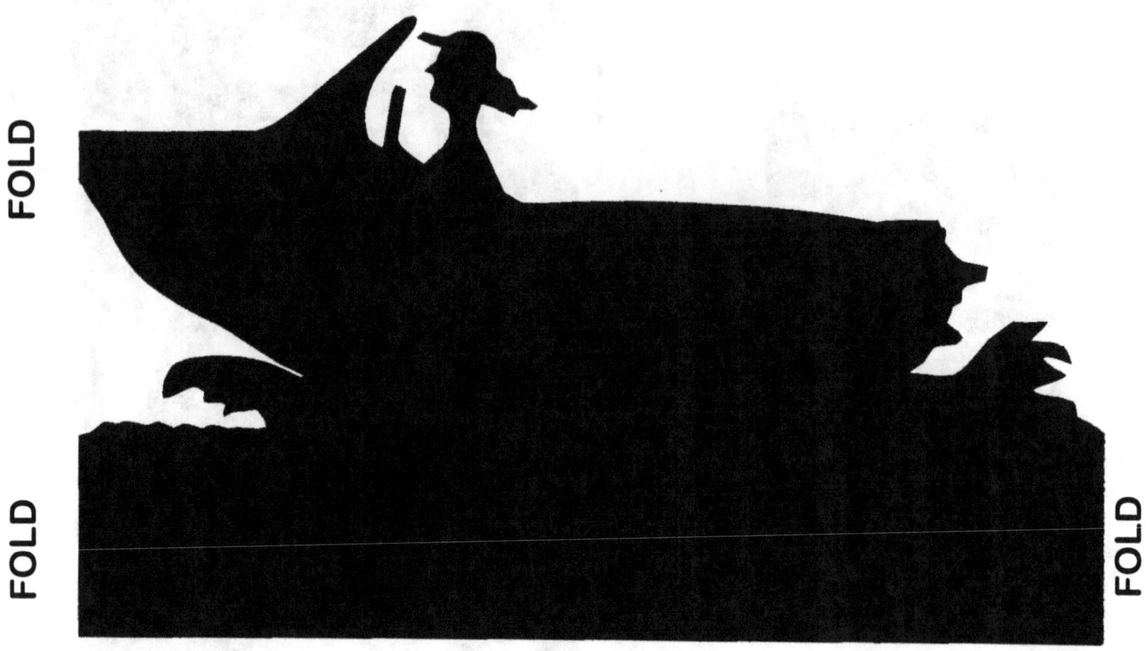

Sailboat

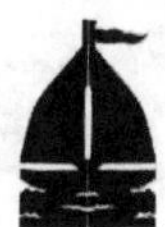

There are many types and sizes of sailboats classified by their sail and hull types. Our sailboat is a sloop with one mast and fore-and-aft sails.

Boats, Ships, Submarines and Other Floating Machines, 10, 11
Essential Boating for Teens, 12, 27, 34-41, 43
Eye Witness Books: Boats, 4, 14, 22, 23, 28, 29, 60-63

- ★ Quick and easy.
- ✂ Double or Multi-image.
- ✂ Follow directions on page 6 or 7.
- ✂ Tape the pattern in place or make a light pencil tracing.
- ✂ Cut off the extra flag.

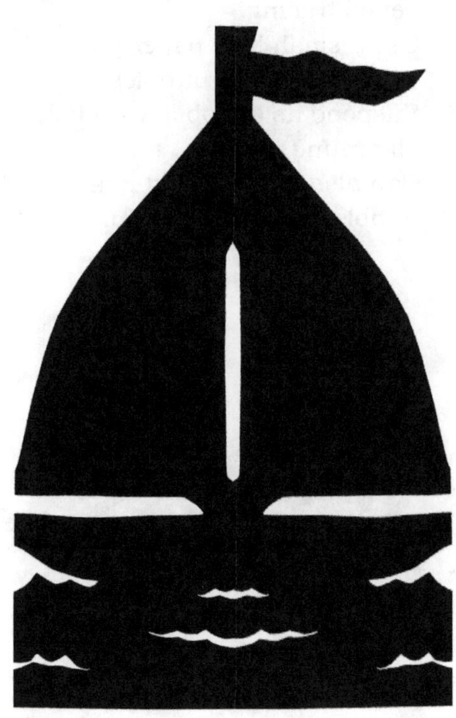

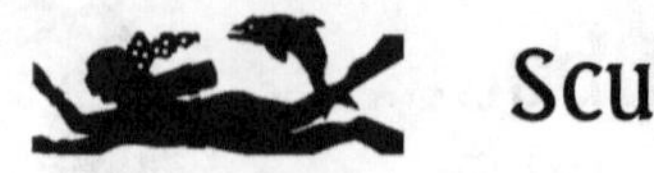

Scuba Diver

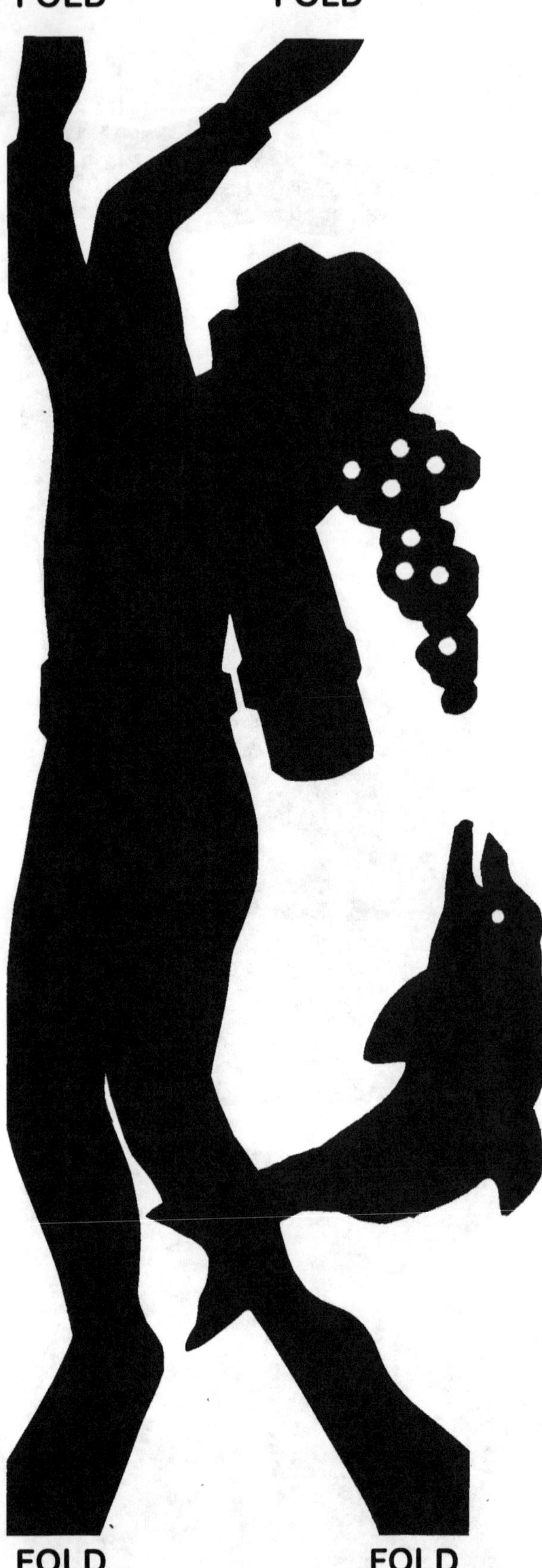

Scuba stands for: Self-Contained Underwater Breathing Apparatus. Invented by French explorer Jacques Cousteau, it is the air supply carried in a cylinder on a diver's back and is inhaled by a mouthpiece controlled by a regulator. A scuba diver wears a wet suit, face mask, foot flippers, a lead belt and a buoyancy compensator, like a life preserver. You need training to be a scuba diver.

Aquatic Life of the World 8, 490, 491
Dive! My Adventures in the Deep Frontier, 13, 27, 30-32
Window on the Deep, 8, 17, 21

- ★ Easy.
- ✂ Double or Multi-image.
- ✂ Follow directions on page 6 or 7.
- ✂ Tape the pattern in place or make a light pencil tracing.
- ✂ Use a small hole paper punch for the dolphin eye and bubbles.
- ☺ Suspend as a mobile with fish swimming all around.
- ☺ Can also be a top fold image at the bubbles and the dolphin.

Seaplane 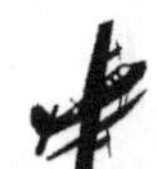

This airplane may be described as pontoon, amphibious, hydroplane, or seaplane. It has pontoons (like water skis) under the wings with which to glide in and land on the water.

Eye Witness Books: The Visual Dictionary of Flight, 18, 19
Wings Over Water: A Chronicle of The Flying Boats and Amphibians of the Twentieth Century, 1-128

★★ Intermediate.
✂ Double or Multi-image.
✂ Follow directions on page 6 or 7.
✂ Tape the pattern in place or make a light pencil tracing.
✂ Use a large hole paper punch for the windows and pilots window. Now use your small scissors to complete the cut and other delicate cutting areas.

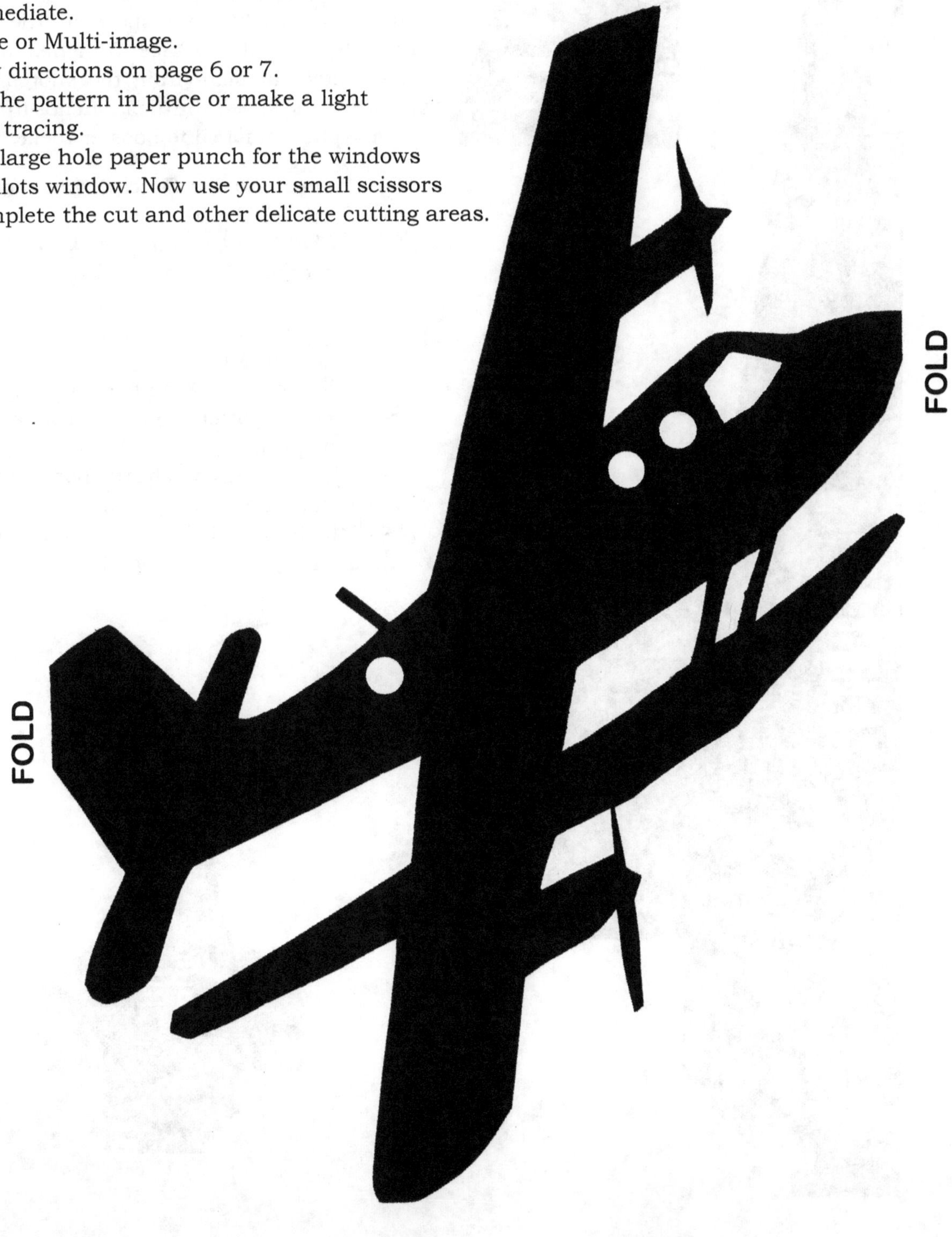

FOLD

FOLD

Space Shuttle

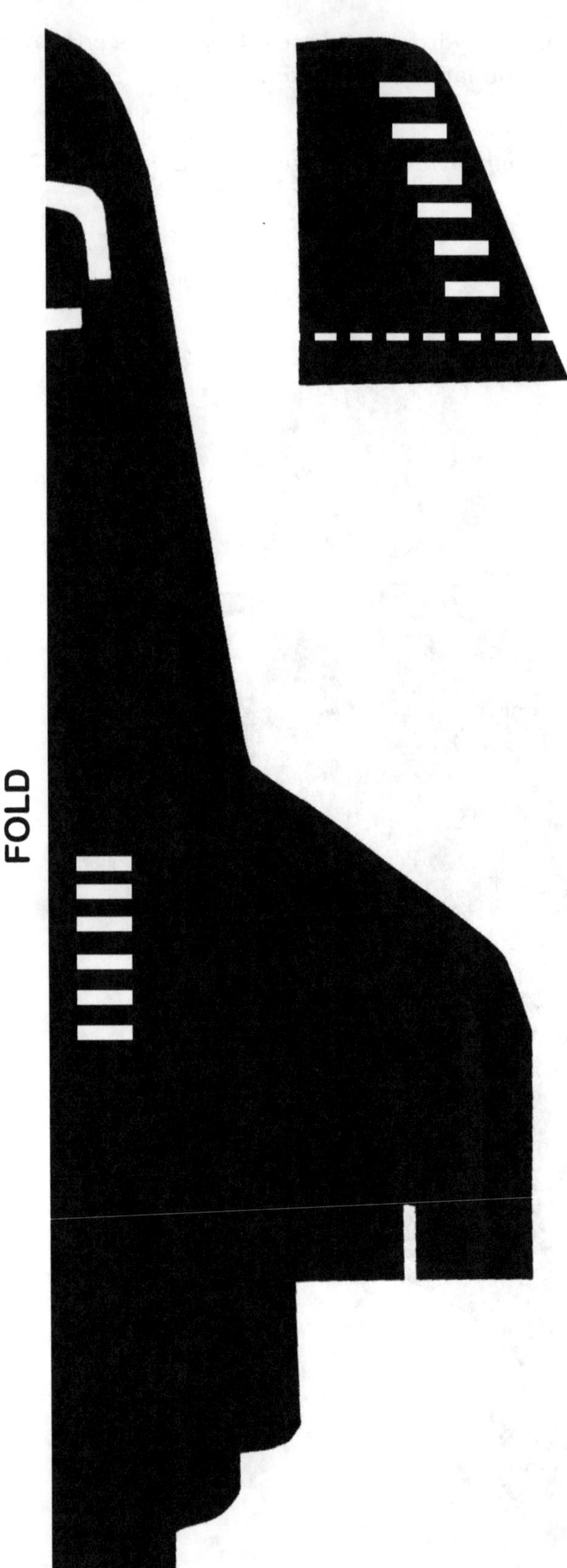

When landing the shuttle flies like an airplane, similar to a glider. Four shuttles were built (Columbia, Discovery, Atlantis, Challenger). Launching the space shuttle means a lifting of 4.5 million pounds. Space exploration is a vast frontier. The shuttle moves at 17,000 miles per hour. The height of the space shuttle is 149 feet 6 inches and it is 28 feet 5 inches in diameter. A spectacular sight from the shores of central Florida, the space shuttle launches from earth to atmospher attached to booster rockets.

Eye Witness Books: Space Exploration, 13, 16, 17, 24, 30, 35, 37
Space Shuttle: A Quantum Leap, 37-53
www.spaceshuttle.com

★ Quick and easy.
✂ Double or Multi-image.
✂ Follow directions on page 6 or 7.
✂ Tape the pattern in place or make a light pencil tracing.
✂ Add markings on shuttle body and tail with a rectangle paper punch.
✂ Attach the tail section by folding to the left on the dotted line and gluing it in place.

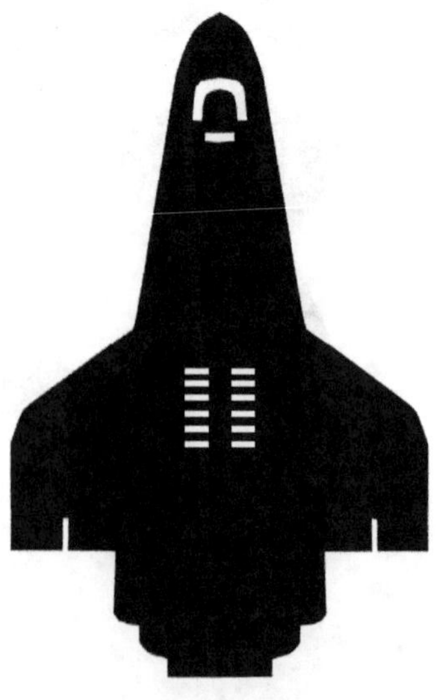

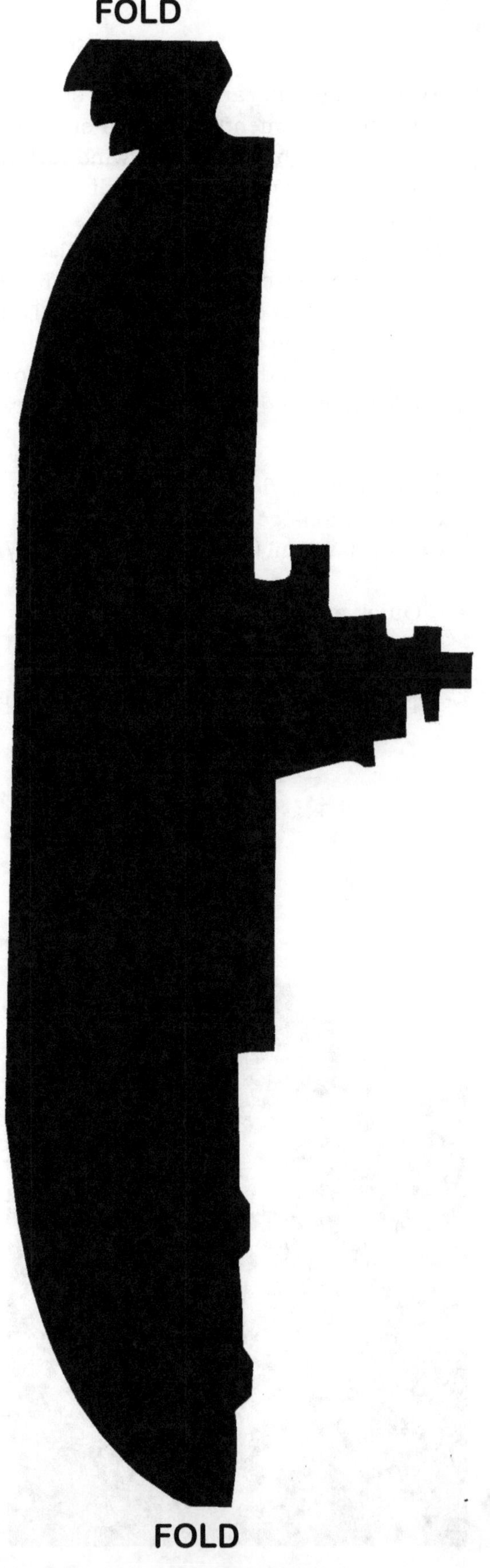

This kind of vessel is navigated under the water, submerges to depths in the ocean and has many types and classifications used by the government.

Boats, Ships, Submarines and Other Floating Machines, 32, 33
The Picture World of Submarines
Window on the Deep, 5-7, 14, 23,-24, 31-34

★ Quick and easy.
✂ Double or Multi-image.
✂ Follow directions on page 6 or 7.
✂ Tape the pattern in place or make a light pencil tracing.

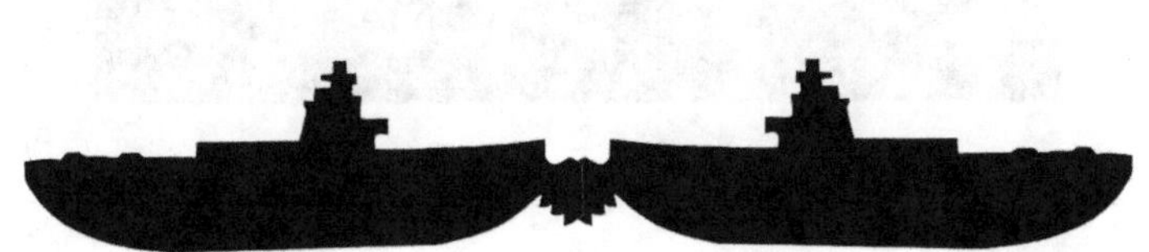

Waves

Everything from earthquakes to ship wakes creates waves. An ocean wave is the undulation (rising and falling movement) of the sea surface and is usually caused by winds. Waves are "born" (generated) in the fetch area (where wind and water interact) and travel across the sea until their "death" (collapse) as breakers on some distant shore. You might call this the life cycle of a wave. The wind and the water are its parents.

The highest part of the wave is called the "crest." The lowest part of the wave is called the "trough." Waves can be described by their height, wavelength, and wave period. The wave-height is the vertical distance from the crest to the trough. The wavelength is the horizontal distance between the crest of one wave and the crest of the next wave.

The wave period is the time it takes for two successive (one after the other) waves to pass a fixed point. Wave period is used to classify waves.

Waves: From Surfing to Tsunami by Drew Kampion and Jeff Peterson
www.ndbc.noaa.gov/educate/educate
www.onr.navy.mil/Focus/ocean/motion/waves1.htm

★ Quick and easy.
✂ Double or Multi-image.
✂ Follow directions on page 6 or 7.
✂ Tape the pattern in place or make a light pencil tracing.

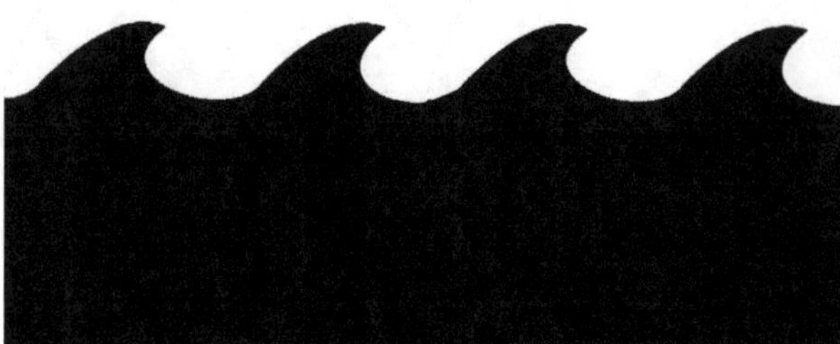

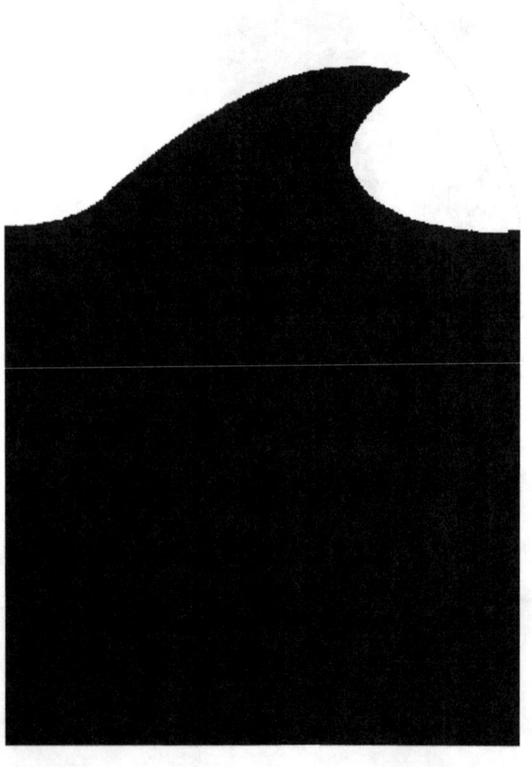

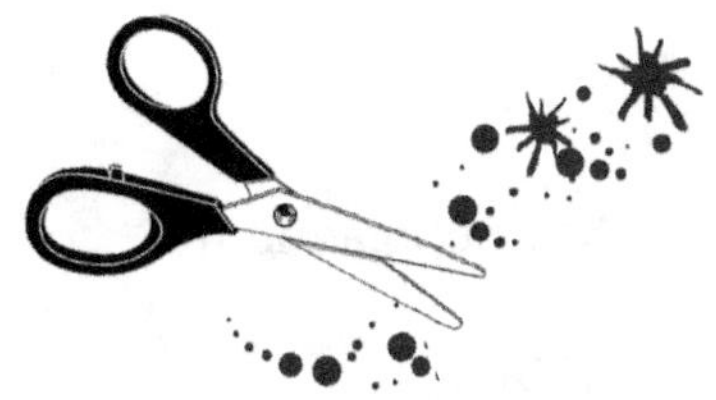

Bibliography

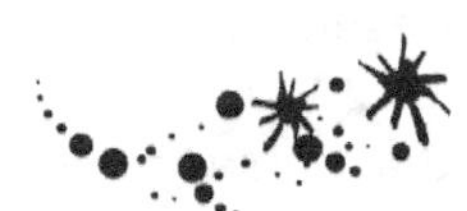

LIGHTHOUSES

Bansemer, Roger. *Bansemer's Book of Florida Lighthouses.* Sarasota, FL: Pineapple Press, 1999.

De Wire, Elinor. *Guardians of the Lights: Stories of the U.S. Lighthouse Keepers.* Sarasota, FL: Pineapple Press, 1995.

De Wire, Elinor. *Guide to Florida Lighthouses.* Sarasota, FL: Pineapple Press, 1987.

De Wire, Elinor. *The Lighthouse Activity Book.* Gales Ferry, CT: Sentinel Publications, 1995.

Gibbs, James. *Lighthouses of the Pacific.* West Chester PA: Shiffer Publishing Co., 1986.

Holland, Francis Ross Jr. *Great American Lighthouses.* Washington D.C.: Preservation Press, 1989.

Jones, Ray. *The Lighthouse Encyclopedia: The Definitive Reference.* Guilford, CT: The Globe Pequot Press, 2004.

Roberts, Bruce and Ray Jones. *Southern Lighthouses.* Guilford, CT: The Globe Pequot Press, 1989

Taylor, Tom. *Florida Lighthouse Trail.* Sarasota, FL: Pineapple Press, 2001.

www.uscg.mil/history/WEBLIGHTHOUSES/lighthouse_curriculum.html

BIRDS

Alsop III, Fred J. *Smithsonian Handbooks of Birds of Florida.* New York, NY: DK Publishing, Inc., 2002.

Bansemer, Roger and Bill Renc. *At Water's Edge: The Birds of Florida.* Dallas, TX: Taylor Publishing Company, 1993.

Brown, Mary Barrett. *Wings Along the Waterway.* New York, NY: Orchard Books, 1992.

Flieg, Michael G. and Allan Sander. *Birds of Southern Florida: Including the Everglades, the Keys, Sanibel and Captiva Islands.* London: New Holland Publishers (UK) Ltd., 2001.

Harris, Tim. *Vultures.* Danbury, Connecticut: Grolier, Scholastic Library Publishing, 2004.

Jones, Jemima Parry. *Eagles and Birds of Prey.* New York, NY: Alfred A Knopf, Inc.,1997.

Mackenzie, John P. S., *Birds of the World: Seabirds.* Toronto, Ontario, Canada: Key Porter Books Limited, 1987.

Pranty, Bill, Kurt Radamaker and Gregory Kennedy. *Birds of Florida.* Auburn, WA: Lone Pine Publishing, 2006.

Williams, Winston. *Florida's Fabulous Birds: Their Stories.* Tampa, FL: World-Wide Printing, 1985.

www.myfwc.com/critters/sandhillcrane.asp-9k

www.pelicanpete.com

FISH, MOLLUSKS AND CRUSTEACEANS

Abbot, Tucker R. *Seashells of the World.* Racine, Wisconsin: Golden Press, Western Publishing Company, Inc., 1985.

Andrews, Jean. *A Fieldguide to Shells of the Florida Coast.* Houston, TX: Gulf Publishing Company, 1994.

Aquatic Life of the World. Tarrytown, NY: Marshall Cavendish Corporation, 2001.

Blumberg, Rhoda. *Sharks.* New York, NY: Franklin Watts, Inc., 1976.

Cassie, Brian. *National Audubon Society: First Field Guide Shells.* New York, NY: Scholastic Inc. 2000.

Clark, Margaret Goff. *The Vanishing Manatee.* Dutton, NY: Cobblehill Books, 1990.

Dunn, John and Jonathan Alderfer. *National Geographic: Field Guide to the Birds of North America.* Washington D.C.: National Geographic, 2006.

Gilpin, Daniel. *Animal Kingdom Classification: Snails, Shellfish and Other Mollusks.* Minneapolis, MN: David West Children's Books, 2006.

Kurtz, Kevin. *A Day at the Salt Marsh.* Mt. Pleasant, South Carolina: Sylvan Dell, 2007.

Lundblad, Kristina and Bobbie Kalman. *Animals Called Fish.* New York, NY: Crabtree Publishing Company, 2005.

Parker, Steve. *Eye Witness Books: Seashore.* New York, NY: DK Publishing, 2004.

Parker, Steve. *Eye Witness Books: Fish.* New York, NY: DK Publishing, 2004.

Robins, Richard C., G. Carleton Ray, John Douglass and Rudolf Freund. *Atlantic Coast Fishes: A Field Guide.* New York, NY: Houghton Mifflin Company, 1986.

Sill, Cathryn and John. *About Crustaceans.* Atlanta, Georgia: Peachtree Publishers, 2004.

Stone, Lynn M. *Animals Without Bones: Lobster.* Vero Beach, Florida: Rourke Publications, Inc., 1996.

Stone, Lynn M. *Science Under the Sea.* Vero Beach, Florida: Rourke Publications, Inc., 2003.

Taylor, Leighton. *Creeps From the Deep.* San Francisco, CA: Chronicle Books, 1997.

Toftand, Kim Michelle and Allan Sheather. *Neptune's Nursery.* Watertown, MA: Charlesbridge Publishers, 2000.

Wildlife and Plants of the World. Vol. 1. Tarrytown, NY: Marshall Cavendish Corporation, 1999.

Woodward, John Danbury. *Eels.* Connecticut: Grolier, Scholastic Library Publishing, 2004.

www.flmn.ufl.edu/fish

www.sylvandellpublishing.com

MARINE MAMMALS

Aquatic Life of the World. Tarrytown, NY: Marshall Cavendish Corporation, 2001.

Clark, Margaret Goff. *The Vanishing Manatee.* Dutton, NY: Cobblehill Books, 1990.

Cox, Vic. *Whales and Dolphins.* New York, NY: Crown Publishers, Inc., 1989.

Eye Witness Dictionaries: The Visual Dictionary of Animals. New York: Dorling Kindersley, Inc., 1991.

Landau, Elaine. *Ocean Mammals.* New York, NY: Children's Press, Grolier Publishing, 1996.

Parker, Steve. *Eye Witness Books: Seashore.* New York, NY: DK Publishing, 2004.

www.sylvandellpublishing.com

SEASIDE MAMMALS

Blassingame, Wyatt. *The Strange Armadillo.* New York, NY: Dodd, Mead & Company, 1983.

Brock, Juliet Clutton and Don E. Wilson. *Mammals.* New York, NY: Dorling Kindersley, Smithsonian Institute, 2002.

Clark, Margaret Goff. *The Threatened Florida Black Bear.* Dutton, NY: Cobblehill Books, 1995.

Eye Witness Dictionaries: The Visual Dictionary of Animals. New York: Dorling Kindersley, Inc., 1991.

Hare, Dr. Tony. *Animal Fact File: Head-to-Tail Profiles of More Than 90 Mammals.* New York, NY: Checkmark Books, 1999.

Stuart, Dee. *The Astonishing Armadillo.* Minneapolis, Minnesota: Carolrhoda Books, Inc., 1993.

Souza, D. M. *It's a Mouse.* Minneapolis, Minnesota: Carolrhoda Books, Inc., Lerner Publishers, 1998.

www.flheritage.com/facts/

www.myfwc.com/panther/

REPTILES

Halliday, Tim and Kraig Adler. *Firefly Encyclopedia of Reptiles and Amphibians.* Buffalo, NY: Firefly Books (U.S.) Inc., 2002.

Rathmell, Donna. *Carolina's Story: Sea Turtles Get Sick Too!* Mt. Pleasant, South Carolina: Sylvan Dell Publishing, 2005.

Ruiz, Andres Llamas. *Reptiles and Amphibians: Birth and Growth.* New York, NY: Sterling Publishing Company, Inc., 1994.

www.seaturtles.org

www.sylvandellpublishing.com

OVER, UNDER AND BY THE SEA

Aquatic Life of the World. Tarrytown, NY: Marshall Cavendish Corporation, 2001.

Art, Henry W. *A Garden of Wildflowers.* Pownal, Vermont: Storey Communications Inc., 1986.

Brock, Jim P. and Kenn Kaufman. *Butterflies of North America.* New York, NY: Houghton Miffin Company, Hillstar Editions, 2003.

Conley, Andrea. *Window on the Deep.* New York, NY: Franklin Watts, 1991.

Earle, Sylvia A. *Dive! My Adventure in the Deep Frontier.* New York: Scholastic Incorporated, National Geographic Society, 1999.

Emmel, Thomas C. and Brian Kenney. *Florida's Fabulous Butterflies: Their Stories.* Tampa, Florida: World Publications, 1997.

Eye Witness Books: The Visual Dictionary of Flight. New York, NY: Dorling Kindersley, Inc., 1992.

Graham, Ian. *Boats, Ships, Submarines and Other Floating Machines.* New York, NY: Kingfisher Books, 1993.

Hanly, Gil and Jaqueline Walker. *The Subtropical Garden.* Portland, Oregon: Timber Press, 1996.

Hehner, Barbara. *First on the Moon.* New York, NY: Hyperion Books for Children, 1999.

Imes, Rick. *Wildflowers.* London, England: Quarto Publishing, 1992.

Jenkins, Virginia Scott. *Bananas: An American History.* Washington D.C.: Smithsonian Institution Press, 2000.

Koeppel, Dan. *Banana.* New York, NY: Hudson Street Press, Penguin Group, 2007.

Laszlo, Pierre. *Citrus: A History.* Chicago, IL: University of Chicago Press, 2007.

Lincoln, Margarette. *Amazing Boats.* New York, NY: A. A. Knopf, Random House, 1992.

Meerow, Alan W. *Betrock's Guide to Landscape.* Hollywood, FL: Betrock Information Systems, 2001.

Morris, Allen and Joan Perry Morrris. *The Florida Handbook.* Tallahassee, FL: Peninsular Publishing Company, 31st Biennial Edition, 2007.

Nelson, Gil. *The Trees of Florida.* Sarasota, Florida: Pineapple Press, 1994.

O'Brien, Patrick. *The Great Ships.* New York, NY: Walker Publishing Company, 2001.
Oliver, David. *Wings Over Water: A Chronicle of the Flying Boats and Amphibians of the Twentieth Century,* NJ, Chartwell Books, Inc., 1999.
Osoro, Rufino. *A Gardener's Guide to Florida Native Plants.* Gainesville, Florida: University of Florida, 2001.
Peterson, Jeff and Drew Kampion, *Waves: From Surfing to Tsunami.* Layton, Utah: Gibbs Smith, 2005.
Stephen, R. J. *The Picture World of Submarines.* New York, NY: Franklin Watts, 1990.
Stott, Carole. *Eye Witness Books: Space Exploration.* London, England: Alfred A Knopf with Dorling Kindersley, 1997.
Torres, George. *Space Shuttle: A Quantum Leap.* Novato, CA: Presidio Press, 1990
Inc, 1992.
Thompson, Luke. *Essential Boating for Teens.* Danbury, Connecticut: Children's Press, Grolier Publishing, 2000.
Understanding Science and Nature: Plants. Alexandria, VA: Time Life Education, 1993.
VanMeter, V.B. 1985. *Florida's Wood Storks.* Florida Power and Light Co. Corporate Communications, Miami, FL.
Wake, Susan. *Citrus Fruits.* Hove, East Sussex, England: Wayland Publishers Ltd., 1989.
Weiss, Harvey. *Submersibles.* New York, NY: Thomas Y. Crowell, 1990.
Werther, Scott P. *Powerboats.* New York, NY: Rosen Publishing Group, Inc., 2000.
Wild Life and Plants of the World. Tarrytown, NY: Marshall Cavendish Corporation, 1999.
http://edis.ifas.ufl.edu/UW065
www.spaceshuttle.com
www.nmm.ac.uk/.../sailsafe/buoys.html
www.PalmTreesInfo.com
www.sylvandellpublishing.com

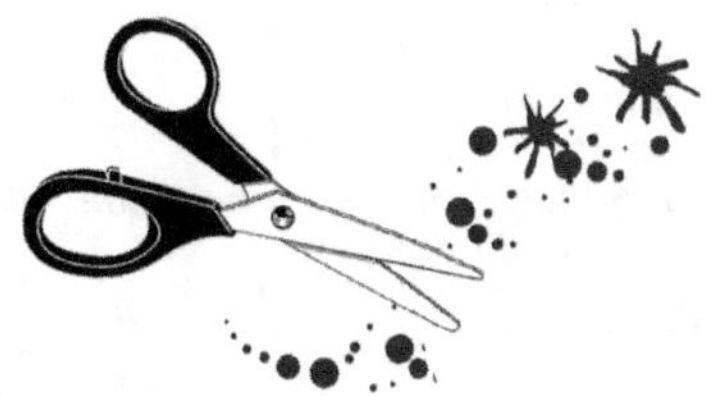

Index

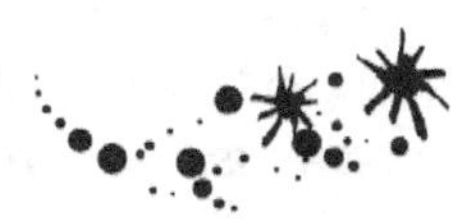

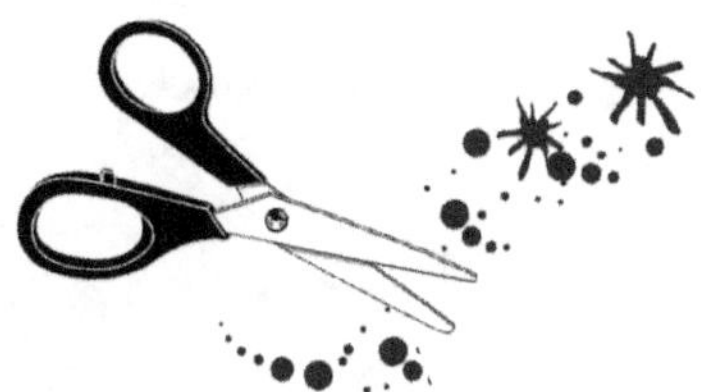

About the Author

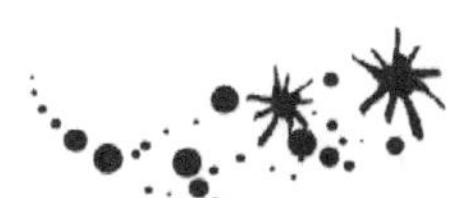

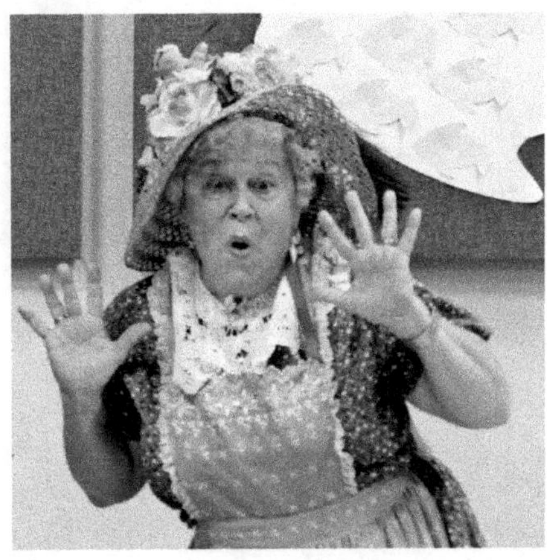

Linda S. Day (a.k.a. Grandma) has been entertaining folks with her magic scissors for more years than she would like to say. Besides being a whiz with her scissors, she is the award winning author of *Grandma's Magic Scissors,* a ForeWord Magazine Finalist, an honorable mention with the Independent Publisher's of America and a President's Book Award for Young Adult Non-Fiction from the Florida Publishers Association, *There's a Frog on a Log in the Bog, Frogazoom!* and a talented illustrator of dozens of books. Linda is a member of StoryMasters,™ a professional storytelling group that travels across the country. She is an Early Childhood Educator and has been a regional, state and district instructor in puppetry, arts and crafts, CDA accreditation, and Family History. She belongs to the National Storytelling Network, StoryCentral, the Florida Storytelling Association, the Central Florida Storytellers, the Guild of American Papercutters, and the Florida Publishers Association. When not illustrating or telling stories, she spends time with her eight children, twenty-three grandchildren and five great-grandchildren.

To book Grandma to speak at your conference, event or school, please write to her at

Grandma@daytodayenterprises.com
http://www.MyMagicScissors.com

www.ingramcontent.com/pod-product-compliance
Lightning Source LLC
LaVergne TN
LVHW080321110826
845155LV00026B/177

* 9 7 8 1 8 9 0 9 0 5 6 9 9 *